MW00630088

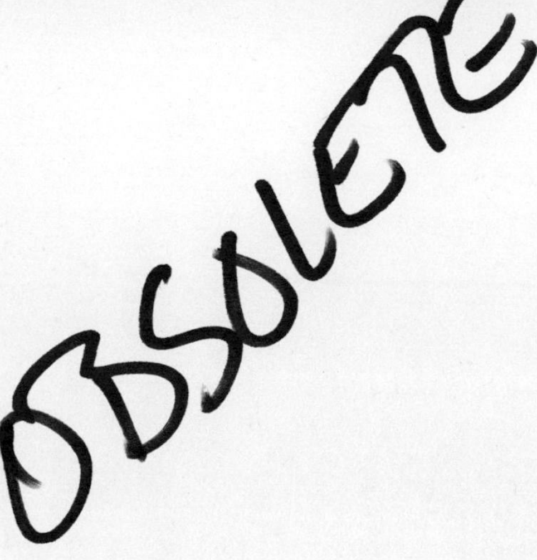
OBSOLETE

Western Man and the Modern World: V

Africa, Latin America, and The East

About the Series:

Western Man and the Modern World is a series of 5 separate books, each covering one aspect or period of World History.

A *Teaching Resource Book* accompanies the texts with a large selection of readings and exercises.

A *Sound-filmstrip* series is also available.
The texts are:

I *Origins of Western Civilization*
II *Rivalry, Reason, and Revolution*
III *Industrialism, Imperialism, and War*
IV *The Western World Today*
V *Africa, Latin America, and The East*

About the Author:

Leonard James, the author of the 5 texts, received his B.A. and Diploma in Education from the University of Bristol, England. As Frances Riggs Fellow he received his M.A. in History and Political Science from the University of Michigan. He was Chairman of the Social Studies Committee of the Secondary Education Board and President of New England History Teachers' Association; Chairman of Department of History, Cecil F. B. Bancroft Foundation, and also on the Independence Foundation at Phillips Academy, Andover, Mass. He is the author of *Following the Frontier: American Transportation in the Nineteenth Century*, (Harcourt Brace) for young readers, and of *The Supreme Court in American Life*, and *American Foreign Policy* (Scott Foresman).

The ***Athena Coin*** was found at Herakleia, a city near Pergamum, and dates back to about 400 B.C. Athena was recognized by the Ancient Greeks as the presiding divinity of states and cities, of the arts and industries: in short as the goddess of the intellectual side of human life. *Pergamenon* was also the Greek word for parchment.

Western Man
and
the Modern World: V

Africa, Latin America, and The East

by **Leonard F. James**

Content Editor	Jean P. KixMiller, *New Trier Township High School*
Project Co-ordinator	John R. L. Dent, *Pergamon Press Inc.*
Maps	David Cox & Jill Thompson, *Pergamon Cartographic Dept.*
Picture Research	Sandi Hughes-Jones and John Dent
Typography	Carl F. Zahn

Pergamon Press Inc. New York Oxford Toronto Sydney Braunschweig

To my wife
Maja
for her cheerful encouragement

Pergamon Press Inc.
Maxwell House, Fairview Park, Elmsford, N.Y. 10523

Pergamon Press, Ltd.
Headington Hill Hall, Oxford

Pergamon of Canada, Ltd.
207 Queen's Quay West, Toronto 117, Ontario

Pergamon Press (Aust.) Pty. Ltd.
Rushcutters Bay, Sydney, N.S.W.

Vieweg & Sohn GmbH
Burgplatz 1, Braunschweig

Library of Congress Cataloging in Publication Data

James, Leonard Frank.
Africa, Latin America, and the East.

(His Western man and the modern world, #5)
SUMMARY: One in a five volume series on the history of Western civilization, this volume traces the history of Latin America, Africa, Asia, and the Middle East from early times to their role in the modern world.
1. Africa--History. 2. Latin America--History. 3. Near East--History. 4. Asia--History. [1. Africa --History. 2. Latin America--History. 3. Near East --History. 4. Asia--History] I. Title.
CV245.J34 vol. 5 [D21] 910′.02′1812s [909′.09′811]
ISBN 0-08-017206-7 72-10952
ISBN 0-08-017207-5 (pbk)

First Printing March 1973

Second Printing February 1974

Printed in the United States of America

Contents

Maps and Diagrams

Maps

Diagrams

Art in Color

Introduction

The non-Western nations of the world contain more people and more square miles of land than do the Western nations. Now Western nations are becoming aware of the emerging nations of Africa, of the complexities of modern Latin America, of the massive problems of India, of the economic influence of Japan, and the vast expanse and huge population of China

This volume outlines the past history of each of the main areas of the non-Western world in such a way that an understanding of the issues of each major nation is possible. That such an understanding is essential is clear from the special attention being paid to China in international diplomacy and to Japan in international economics in the 1970's.

Events in the 20th century in the Middle East and the Far East have effected Western nations deeply. This volume puts into perspective the troubles of Arab-Israeli conflict, the India-Pakistan crises, and the upheaval in Southeast Asia caused by the long war in Vietnam.

Acknowledgments

The author's thanks go to Barbara McDonnell, Director of the Oliver Wendell Holmes Library, Phillips Academy, for her professional assistance. Thanks are also due Jean KixMiller, teacher of history in Winnetka, for her editorial comments and suggestions; to John Dent, co-ordinator of the project, who in addition to producing the filmstrips to complement the text, kept a tight rein on all in the enterprise, made many a valuable suggestion, and gathered up the many loose ends of getting a book to press; and to Sara Lofving, copy editor.

L.F.J.

1

Africa: The Challenge of Independence

The Land and the People
Historical Kingdoms of Africa
North Africa: Nationalism and Independence
French Sub-Sahara Africa
Independence for British Colonies
The Republic of South Africa
Problems for Britain and Portugal
Independence for Belgian and Spanish Colonies
Problems of New African Nations
Other New African Nations

World War II accelerated the demand of Black Africa for independence. The defeat in Asia of white administrators by Japan, and the winning of independence by Indonesia and other Asian people stimulated the agitation for independence in Black Africa. In 1956 Liberia was the only independent country in Black Africa. Between 1956 and 1968 independence was gained by thirty-three African nations. Each of these new nations, generally inexperienced in self-government, has an equal voice with the great powers in the United Nations. As a bloc they are capable of exercising much influence in international politics.

With independence they have inherited the problems of insufficient capital for industrial development and the higher standard of living that their people expect. Several of them have already experienced the problem that young nations may not be able to afford the criticism and distraction of opposition parties. Future violence may be precipitated by the racist policies of the Republic of South Africa, Rhodesia, and Portuguese Angola and Mozambique.

Major powers, particularly the Soviet Union and the People's Republic of China, see a great opportunity to extend their influence among the emerging nations of Africa, although these nations may be too jealous of their newly-won independence to allow any outside nation to jeopardize it.

Terms

1. Australopithecus
2. Lingua franca
3. Kikuyu
4. Uhuru
5. Mau Mau
6. *Colon*
7. National Liberation Front, FLN
8. Provisional Government of the Algerian Republic, GPRA
9. Secret Army Organization, OAS
10. Great Trek
11. Boer War
12. Apartheid
13. Verligtheid
14. Afrikaner
15. African
16. Afrikaans
17. Coloreds
18. Ibos
19. *Indigena*
20. *Assimilado*

People

21. L. S. B. Leakey
22. W. E. B. DuBois
23. Kwame Nkrumah
24. Hausas
25. Yorubas
26. Ibos
27. Alhagi Balewa
28. General Ironsi
29. Colonel Ojukwu
30. General Gowon
31. Julius Nyerere
32. Jomo Kenyatta
33. Patrice Lumumba
34. Joseph Kasavubu
35. Moise Tshombe
36. General Mobutu
37. Cecil Rhodes
38. Hendrik Verwoerd
39. Kaiser Matanzina
40. Ian Smith
41. Idi Amin

Places

42. Cape Bizerte
43. Cape of Good Hope
44. Cape Guardafui
45. Dakar
46. Ténéré
47. Songhai
48. Kilwa
49. Benin
50. Tunisia
51. Morocco
52. Algeria
53. Libya
54. Ghana
55. Nigeria
56. Biafra
57. Kenya
58. Tanzania
59. Zanzibar
60. Republic of South Africa
61. Rhodesia
62. Uganda
63. Zambia
64. Malawi
65. Zaïre (Belgian Congo)
66. Guinea
67. Angola
68. Mozambique
69. The Gambia

Events

7th Century A.D.	Kingdom of Ghana
13th Century A.D.	Kingdom of Mali or Melle
	Kingdom of Songhai
1772	Abolition of slavery in Great Britain
1792	Sierra Leone established by Great Britain as home for destitute freed slaves
1830	Algeria acquired by France
1881	Tunisia acquired by France
1880 on	Scramble for colonies in Africa by European Nations
1951	Libya independent
1956	Tunisia, Morocco, Sudan independent
	Ghana independent
1957	Guinea independent
1962	Algeria independent
1965	Unilateral Declaration of Independence made by Rhodesia
1971	Zaïre

1. The Land and the People

A Multitude of Nations

A brief study of Africa today must put that vast continent into proper focus in the world of the 1970's. The French sociologist Raymond Aron has called today the Age of Universal History, because events that occur in one part of the world affect every other part, and because the problems of one area are of increasing concern to all. A famine in India, a revolt in the Congo, the occupation of one country by another's troops can be of great concern to many more nations than the ones immediately involved. The continent of Africa can no longer be regarded as it has been in the past as "darkest Africa," unknown to most of the world except as colonial possessions of European powers. In 1945 there were only four independent nations on the vast continent of Africa, and only Liberia was a black one. The other three nations were Ethiopia, Egypt, and the Union of South Africa. By the end of 1959 three former colonies south of the Sahara Desert had become the independent nations of the Sudan, Ghana, and Guinea. In 1960 seventeen more African colonial areas became independent, and by December 1970 thirteen more had won their independence. In a little over one decade 33 new names had been added to the list of independent nations*.

Of all the continents, Africa contains the largest number of nations, one third of the total in the world. Each of these, from tiny Gambia with only 350,000 people, to Nigeria with 56,000,000, has an equal voice and vote in the United Nations. As a bloc, the black African nations can greatly influence international affairs. Separately, and even collectively, they may have little physical power, but violence or merely unrest in any one of them can become of great concern to the other powers.

*In 1960: Cameroon, Central African Republic, Chad, Congo Republic (formerly French), Republic of the Congo (formerly Belgian), Dahomey, Gabon, Ivory Coast, Malagasy, Mali, Mauritania, Niger, Nigeria, Senegal, Somali, Togo, Upper Volta. In 1961 Sierra Leone and Tanganyika; in 1962 Rwanda, Burundi, Uganda; in 1963 Kenya; in 1964 Malawi and Zambia; in 1965 The Gambia; and by the end of 1968 Botswana, Lesotho, Swaziland, and Equatorial Guinea.

Common Misconceptions about Africa

One of the most common misconceptions about Africa is that man appeared there much later than in other continents. The most recent archaeological discoveries now put Africa as the birthplace of the human race. The great apes, who were man's ancestors and collateral relatives, roamed the continent about 25 to 30 million years ago. Parts of the skeletons of an erect primate were recently discovered near Lake Victoria in Kenya. The archaeologist L. S. B. Leakey, who worked for years in Kenya and in Tanganyika, now part of Tanzania, discovered in the Olduvai Gorge in Tanganyika a large number of fossils of the apelike Australopithecus (southern apes) about 2,000,000 years old. Because a number of chipped tools were found with the fossils, this erect primate is labeled *homo faber*, man the toolmaker.

Another misconception about Africa south of the Sahara, sub-Sahara Africa, is that until the white man came to Africa in the late fifteenth century, Africa was completely uncivilized. Long before the birth of Christ Africa had traded with the Mediterranean and the Near East, and its contacts with China go back at least one thousand years. Travelers from Europe in the ninth century and later were amazed to see the size and the wealth of Timbuktu, one of the very old trading depots on the southern edge of the Sahara Desert.

A misconception with the most serious consequences today, especially for the United States, was the centuries-old attitude of regarding all people in sub-Sahara Africa as savage, and making the word "black" a term of degradation. Explorers spoke of "darkest" Africa, perhaps to give the impression of great danger; missionaries regarded the natives as "heathens"; and slave traders deliberately created the idea that blacks were inferior, because that might give some veneer of justification to the despicable slave trade in human beings.

A further misconception has been that the African natives were incapable of ruling themselves, and that the white man performed a service in the 19th century by taking over and running the natives in a paternalistic way. The Africans had their own forms of government, worked out over centuries of experience, to suit special conditions. The white man assumed that his ways were better and more civilized, superimposed them on the natives, and for generations deprived the Africans of the experience of governing themselves.

The Land and its People

In size Africa is 11,500,000 square miles, or three times the land area of the United States. It is 5,000 miles north and south from Cape Bizerte in Tunisia to the Cape of Good Hope in South Africa, 4,500 miles across the "bulge" from east to west from Cape Guardafui in Somalia to Dakar in Senegal, and 2,000 miles across the narrower southern region. It contains one tenth of the world's population and covers one fifth of the land surface of the earth.

Africa is a vast plateau averaging 2,000 feet above sea level, with narrow coastal plains, and very few natural harbors and sheltered anchorages for ships. Its rivers fall rapidly from the plateau down to the sea, and are open to ocean-going vessels for only 40 or 50 miles. Waterfalls and rapids have been by-passed by railroads, however, and stretches of the Congo are navigable for more than a thousand miles. But this necessitates the expense of repeated unloading and loading of cargoes.

The land south of the Sahara is largely savannah or grasslands that are scorched for half the year, and soaked with tropical rains at other times; some area is steppe land with wiry grass and thorny trees; and rain-soaked jungle lies in the region along the Congo River.

Nature has served Africa rather poorly because much of the land is low in fertility and is unsuitable for modern deep-plowing with mechanical equipment. Africa has cash crops such as the cocoa bean, cotton, and peanuts for the world market, but much of her production is limited to subsistence farming, inefficient in method and productive of enough for local consumption only. Africa is rich in several very essential minerals, however, producing uranium, much of the world's antimony and manganese, 50 percent of the world's gold, 75 percent of the world's cobalt, and over 90 percent of the world's industrial diamonds. These resources need great investments of capital, and much of this money can come only from outside the continent. One of Africa's greatest potential assets is its hydro-electric power; estimates by experts state that one dam properly located on the Congo River could produce as much electricity as the nations of western Europe now use.

The population of Africa is estimated to be about 300,000,000, of whom the majority belong to the Negro or black race and live south of the Sahara, particularly in the equatorial region, where skin pigmentation is the result of climatic conditions. Farther south are Negroid, or Negro-like, groups whose color ranges from olive brown to black; these groups are collectively referred to as Bantu, which is actually a term referring to language rather than race.

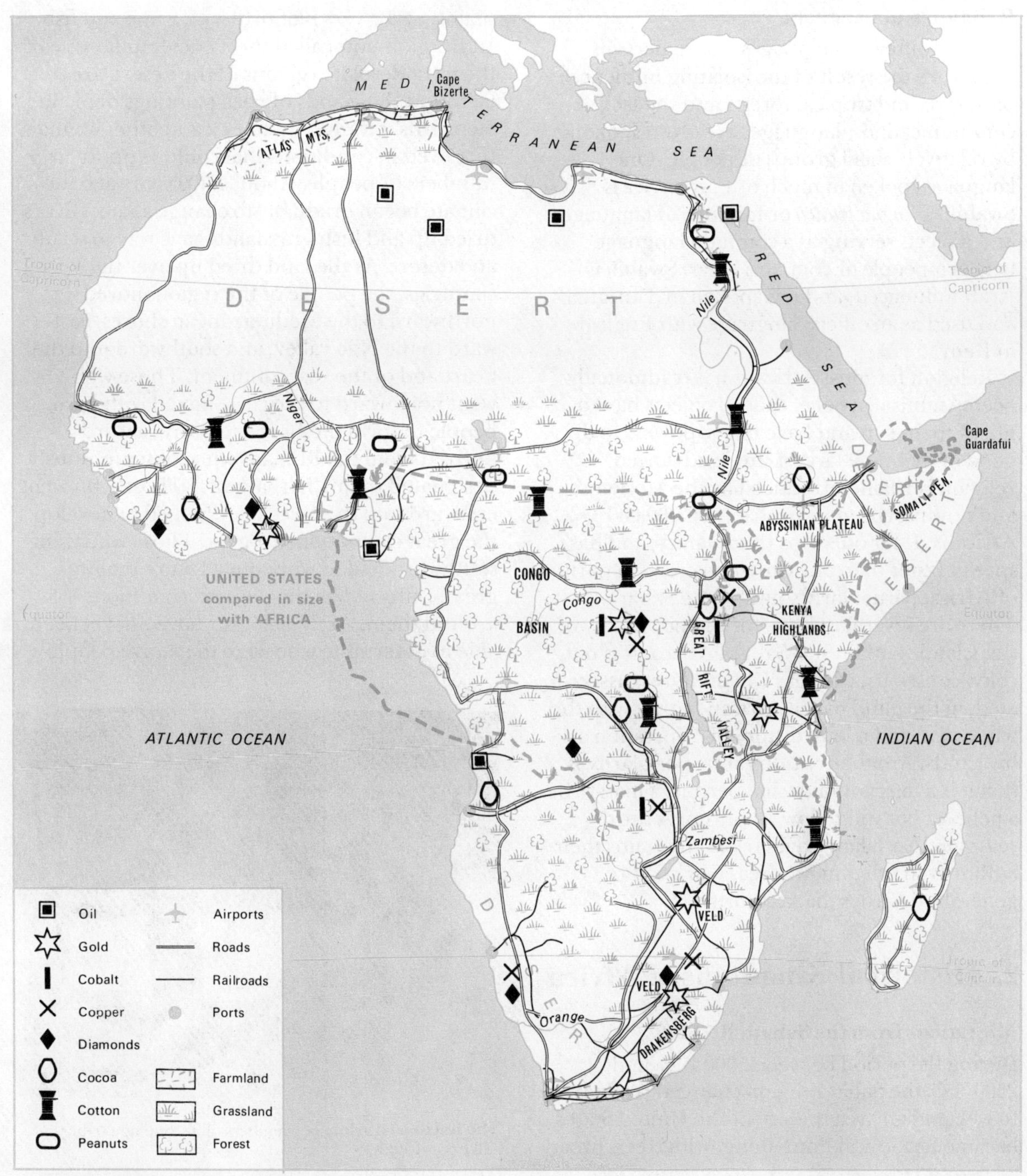

Africa. Land and resources.

Religion and Language

The 700 different languages and dialects in Africa are the result of the isolating influences of deserts and tropical forests and the lack of communications; languages are often spoken by relatively small groups of people. One language spoken in much of East Africa is Swahili, a *lingua franca* or mixture of languages and dialects serving as a common language between people of common ideas. Swahili is Arab-influenced, and it is spoken in Tanzania and used as an official language with English in Kenya.

Religion for most Africans has traditionally been Animism, a belief that all objects have a life of their own and have magic powers to do good or evil. The largest single advanced religion is Islam, introduced by the Moslems, and now practiced by probably 90,000,000 Africans. It far outstrips Christianity, and has spread faster than any Christian creed in parts of Africa, particularly south of the Sahara. There are several reasons for the popularity of the Islamic faith in sub-Sahara Africa. It is not color-conscious, whereas Christianity is associated, in the mind of the African native, with the white man and a long history of oppression at his hands. Another reason for its popularity is that it is a tolerant faith that permits a man to be a believer but still follow Animism. A third reason is that Islam leaves tribal chieftains their authority in religion, whereas Christianity generally destroys that authority.

2. Historical Kingdoms of Africa

Migrations from the Sahara Region

During the period between 5000 B.C. and 2500 B.C. the Sahara region changed from dry to wet, and an area the size of the United States became fertile and flourishing, with trees, broad plains, and rivers plentiful with game and fish. In a region now called the Ténéré, today one of the most desolate regions of the desert, are to be found thousands of rock paintings depicting elephants, giraffes, monkeys, and other animals that lived in conditions that could support large numbers of people. About 4,000 years ago the climate began gradually to change again. Rivers dried up and lush grasslands gave way to scrub and desert. As the land dried up over the centuries, the people of the region moved northward to the Mediterranean shores, eastward to the Nile valley, and southward into the heartland of the vast continent. Those who went northward to the coast mixed with local people to form the Berber culture, a word derived from the Romans who contemptuously designated them "barbarians." Those who went eastward into the Nile valley helped to develop the great civilization of Egypt. Those who went southward had to work out a future that was greatly affected by the physical conditions around them. Archaeologists have not yet been able to determine who were the native people

The Kalahari Bushmen. Members of a stone-age tribe that still exists today.

south of the Sahara, but they think that Bushmen and Pygmies were there from very early times. There is still a question whether the Negroes came in at a later date, or whether sub-Sahara Africa is the actual home of the Negroes, who today make up two thirds of the population.

Those who went southward had to overcome hostile conditions of climate and geography, and at the same time set up rules to govern themselves. Over the centuries small groups of people would split off from communities which had become too large to live off one region. These groups would go off into unused land and learn to support themselves. The habits of people who lived in river valleys differed markedly from those living in grasslands and in tropical forests, and consequently languages and dialects developed and were modified to suit each particular group. Until about 500 B.C. these people were nomads and lived in the Stone Age, always on the search for food. With the discovery of metals they were able to raise food and to hunt more easily, and support growing populations. By the 9th and 10th centuries people of several parts of Africa were as advanced in their ways of living as much of Europe. But in time the people of the sub-Sahara were relatively cut off from communication with the Mediterranean area while Europe advanced rapidly with Baltic and Atlantic trade closely linked to the Mediterranean by sea and land routes.

Early African Empires

As early as the 7th century A.D. a kingdom of Ghana, with its center some 500 miles northwest of modern Ghana, became the first of several African empires that owed their existence to their location. People south of the Sahara needed the salt that came from the north, and people in the north wanted the gold of Ghana, and the slaves and ivory of the region. Where the southern edge of the desert met the grassland, great cities grew as trading centers. Some grew and declined rapidly; others prospered and were famous for centuries. Ghana gradually collapsed as the desert took over, and then it declined rapidly after the Moors sacked its capital city. Ghana was replaced in the 13th century by the empire of Mali or Melle, which reached its peak during the 14th century. One of its chief towns was Timbuktu, which became world-famous for its Moslem university and its large and profitable book business. Another empire, which overlapped in time that of Mali, was Songhai which lasted approximately from 1350 to 1600 A.D., and was organized to protect its trade and commercial centers.

Moslem traders from the Mediterranean traveled along the shores of East Africa,

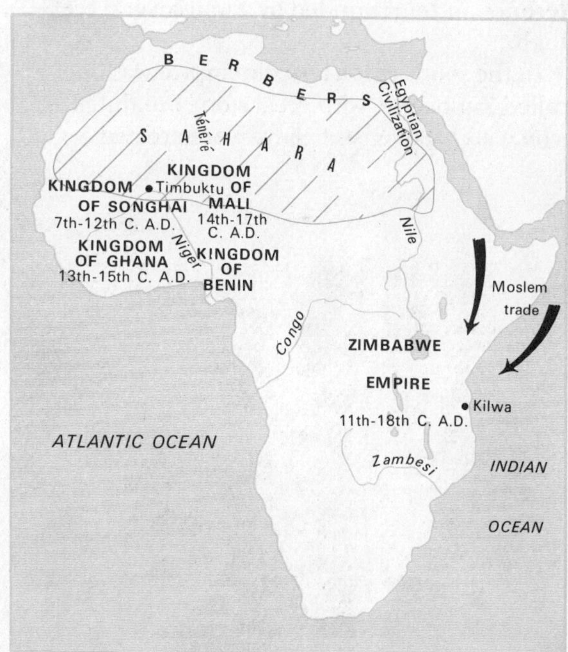

Early African Kingdoms

collected ivory from the region later known as Kenya and Tanganyika, and traded it along the coasts of Africa and Malaysia. By the 13th century the merchants of the island-city of Kilwa, off the east coast of Africa, exchanged their ivory, gold, and iron for porcelain and jewelry from China and India.

Another type of kingdom was the forest-empire of Benin, on the west coast in the region that is now Nigeria, discovered by the Portuguese in the 1470's. Visitors from Europe during the 16th and 17th centuries regarded Benin, the capital city, as comparable with European cities of the time. "The town seemeth very great," wrote one Dutch visitor in the early 17th century. "When you enter it you go into a great broad street, not paved, which seems to be seven or eight times broader than the Warmoes street in Amsterdam." Benin's streets were shaded by trees; it was six miles in circumference and surrounded by a wall several feet high.

In the south-east a historic empire was one called Zimbabwe, with great stone buildings which archaeologists believe were erected between the 11th and the 19th centuries; at one time this was almost a "gold rush" area for Africans from the east coast in search of gold. Zimbabwe was probably the heart and capital of a large African empire that had little contact with outside trading centers; it had declined before the great expansion of European colonialism in the 19th century.

Timbuktu. One of the ancient cities of Africa.

Slavery and its Effects

Slavery was probably always known to African people, but it was a system of slavery that used prisoners of war as a labor force. Even though slaves could be bought and sold as "wageless labor," they were working members of a community but on a lower social level because they were not kin-members of the group. Slaves used by the Europeans, however, were separate from the community.

It was the Portuguese who opened Africa to contact with the West, and their activities as slave-traders set a tone which led the world to regard the Africans as inferior people. The slave-traders, whatever their nationality, were not interested in Africa but in the New World and its insatiable demand for plantation and mine labor.

In 1501 the Spanish ruler issued a proclamation legalizing the importation of slaves into her New World colonies. In 1517 Charles I of Spain sold a concession to a courtier entitling him to ship 4,000 Negroes to the West Indian colonies. The courtier sold the concession to a syndicate of Genoese merchants, who bought their slaves from the slave-markets of Lisbon, where they had been brought by Portuguese slave-traders. This was the beginning of a lucrative business that lasted for more than three hundred years, at first monopolized by the Portuguese, and then challenged by the French, Dutch, English, and Americans.

One of the early sources of slaves for the New

World was the Niger River delta, and in this region new political groups formed to defend their new trade of slaves to the white man. Very few slaves were kidnapped by European slave-traders because the risk of losing business was too great. Competition for slaves was keen, and the African communities that supplied slaves to the white man became well able to look after themselves. The price paid for slaves was in "consumer" goods—muskets and gunpowder.

An African nation without them could be attacked and enslaved itself. An African tribe with them could prosper. From the beginning of the slave trade, African communities were in a constant state of warfare with one another, at increasing distances upriver and inland. Many communities suffered terribly, some even were destroyed, while others simply migrated deeper into the interior for safety. The profits to the slave-trader were enormous, frequently running to at least 100 percent and often higher. This vicious trade gave Africa nothing in return—no improved conditions of agriculture, no development of any of its natural resources, but only the constant drain on its people. How many slaves were taken from Africa during the three centuries from the early 16th century is impossible to determine. Conservative estimates indicate that 15 million were shipped into the New World, or more than 100,000 a year for 150 years; other estimates believe that 20 million is a minimum figure. These numbers do not take into account the millions who died in the dreadful quarters on slave ships. Perhaps as many more died as finally arrived. And even these incredible figures do not include the many more millions who died in raids in the interior of Africa and on the way to the coast.

The slave trade ended in the 19th century, partly because it was becoming less profitable, and partly because it came to be regarded as morally indefensible. Slavery was made illegal in England in 1772, and in 1833 throughout the British Empire. An interesting item is that Freetown in the British colony of Sierra Leone was established in 1792 as a home for destitute freed slaves.

Unfortunately for the African continent, a new wave of colonialism in the later 19th century brought another kind of subjugation to the African people. This occupation of Africa by European powers is usually designated as "New" imperialism rather than as colonialism, as the earlier settlement is called. Instead of traders and settlers from a mother country going out to organize trading stations or settle in what was almost unoccupied land, the 19th century movement included the annexation of native areas by foreigners who imposed their own government but did not give the natives any participation in it. Foreign development of industry was then introduced, using native labor, in contrast to the simple coastal trading of colonial days.

The slow rise of native nationalism, and the demand of the African people for independence, was based upon the belief that once the foreign rulers were removed, then the profits from industries and a better standard of living would go to the natives. The great problem that many of the newly-independent African nations face today is that they do not have the necessary large investments for the development of industries in their countries. Independence has brought freedom from foreign rule, but it has not yet been able to give the people a better standard of living. And the gap between the industrialized nations and the "developing" nations is growing wider rather than narrower as the Industrial Revolution picks up speed with developing technology.

3. North Africa: Nationalism and Independence

French Colonial Expansion

North Africa is the collective name usually given to the region north of the Sahara and stretching from the Atlantic Ocean eastward through the nation of Libya. It is sometimes called an island on land because it is shut off on three sides by the sea and on the fourth side by a mountain and desert barrier. Throughout history it has had no precise name, and today it consists of the independent nations of Morocco, Algeria, Tunisia, and Libya. To this land inhabited by "white Africans" the Greeks gave the name Libya, to distinguish it from Ethiopia, the land of black inhabitants. Later on much of the region became a Roman province, and was still later occupied by the Arab Moslems, who extended their control during the 8th century throughout North Africa and into Spain.

The first great change for nearly a thousand years was the French occupation of Algeria in the 1830's, the first step in the revival of a French colonial empire which had suffered the loss of Canada and India in the 18th century.

The conquest of Algeria began with a French expedition in 1830 and was not completed until forty years later. Much of the history of the French conquest of Algeria can be compared with the expansion of the American frontier westward against the Indians. European settlers moving in behind the French army were opposed by the natives who resisted the loss of their land; despite bitter fighting against the French the natives were finally subjugated by the 1870's after great loss of life. From that time until 1944 Algeria was kept in subjugation by the French, who punished as crimes such actions as criticism of the French government, failure to obtain official travel permits, and instruction in elementary education without official permission. As more French settlers moved in they took over control of Algeria from the Moslems until by the 1950's they were able to threaten to break away from France and govern the region for themselves.

Tunisia. Once French authority was established in Algeria, the kingdom of Tunisia, to the northeast, was threatened not only by France but also by other European powers. After the Franco-Prussian War of 1870 Chancellor Bismarck of the new German Empire encouraged France to expand her colonial empire by acquiring control over Tunisia. Bismarck probably expected such action to compensate France for her recent defeat in the war, and also perhaps to result in loss of some of her friends in Europe.

In 1881 the opportunity to extend French colonial control into Tunisia occurred when tribes from Tunisia raided across the border into Algeria. France occupied the country and established over it a protectorate which lasted for seventy-five years. Tunisia was treated quite differently from Algeria because public opinion by the 1880's expected colonial powers to act in a more civilized manner toward their colonies, and because Tunisia already had started to modernize through the abolition of slavery and Europeanization. Settlers from France and Italy came into Tunisia in increasing numbers, until by 1920 they made up nearly 10 percent of the population. Their attempt to win more power for themselves caused a reaction of Arab sentiment toward Tunisian nationalism.

Morocco. With the increase of French control in North Africa, it was to be expected that Morocco also would become the object of French expansion. The Sultan of Morocco was able to play one power off against the other and delay

French control until the 20th century. In the early 20th century Morocco was the center of two international crises in which Spain, France, and Germany were all trying to gain power in Morocco. Britain, who had strategic interests in Gibraltar across the narrow channel from Morocco, sided with France against Germany; Britain regarded Germany's activities in the Mediterranean with great distrust, and in 1912 she persuaded Germany to accept territory in Central Africa in return for giving France a free hand in Morocco. In 1912 the Sultan of Morocco, who had previously asked for French troops to put down tribal uprisings, signed the Treaty of Fez setting up a French protectorate over Morocco. For the next 20 years France tried to put an end to native resistance in Morocco.

Independence for North African Nations

Tunisia. The struggle for independence came first in Tunisia, largely because the Tunisians had been more exposed than Morocco or Algeria to liberal European influence. The first resistance came in 1911 as the result of growing tensions between Tunisians and the growing number of Europeans. The next wave of nationalism came as a result of World War I and the spread of principles of self-determination advocated by Woodrow Wilson. The nationalists formed the Liberal Constitutional Party, and were called Destourians from Dastur, the Arabic word for constitution.

This movement had little success, so a group of younger activists founded the New Destour Party which soon was led by a young lawyer named Habib Bourguiba. By 1938 disorders in Tunisia against French domination resulted in a state of siege and the arrest of Bourguiba. World War II temporarily halted resistance, but in 1946 the New Destour Party demanded full independence. In 1947 administrative reforms gave Tunisians a greater say in the administration of their country, but when the Tunisians were denied demands for a Tunisian parliament elected by Tunisians, they started a guerrilla resistance which by 1954 was tying down some 70,000 French troops. At the same time, resistance broke out in Morocco, just when France was suffering a series of bitter reversals in Indo-China. United Nations sympathy for Moroccans and Tunisians further embarrassed France, and in June 1955 she gave autonomy, or internal self-rule to Tunisia, as preparation for full independence in 1956. On March 2, 1956 Tunisia was recognized as a fully independent monarchy.

Within a month elections were held for a Constituent Assembly to write a new constitution. Habib Bourguiba was elected presiding officer and then Prime Minister of Tunisia. On July 25, 1957 the Assembly voted unanimously to abolish the monarchy, and proclaimed Tunisia a republic. In November 1959 new elections were held, and Bourguiba was elected as President.

Morocco. Morocco was the second of the three areas to receive independence. Agitation for self-government in the late 1930's was interrupted by the war and by much tighter French control. The Atlantic Charter and the meeting of Prime Minister Churchill and President Roosevelt at Casablanca in 1943 excited the Moroccans, especially since it was reported that Roosevelt told the Sultan that America was interested in Morocco's hopes for freedom. An Independence Party, the Istiqlal, published a manifesto in January 1944, calling for negotiations on independence. The French leaders took increasingly restrictive measures against rising political agitation, and in 1953 they deposed the Sultan "for his own safety," exiled him to Madagascar, and replaced him with a ruler they could manipulate. As resistance became violent, the European settlers thoroughly opposed to Moroccan independence attacked the Moslem quarters of Casablanca and killed scores of Moroccans. The French government, realizing that events had gone too far, brought Sultan Muhammed ben Youssef back from exile as Muhammed V, and commenced negotiations for independence. On March 2, 1956 the French Protectorate ended, and Morocco became a fully independent monarchy.

Algeria. After the French took over in Algeria in the early 1870's, very little was heard from Algeria because native political parties ceased to exist. Algeria's heavy contributions of manpower to France in World War I were rewarded after the war with limited participation in local governments, but distinctly as rewards for the past, and not as promise of more rights in the future. Between the 1920's and the liberation of northern Algeria from Vichy France in November 1942 by the Anglo-American forces, there was little real demand for Algerian independence because the Algerians did not have much feeling of being a nation of people with common interests.

The first actual incident which precipitated Algeria into bitter opposition to French rule occurred during the V-E Day celebrations in May 1945. Algerians celebrated with a nationalist flag of green and white, and demanded the release of an imprisoned nationalist leader. The police fired on the crowd, general riots immediately broke out throughout Algeria and resulted in the death of more than 100 Europeans and as many wounded. In retaliation the French used artillery and planes against the Algerians, killing a number somewhere between the official French figure of 1,500 and the nationalist figure of 45,000.

The French then made gestures toward self-government, offering voting rights in which eight Moslem votes would count no more than one European. From 1948, when rigged elections were held, to 1954, when revolution broke out in full flood, very little happened on the surface in Algeria. But underneath, military preparations were being readied by the Algerians. At midnight on October 31, 1954 the National Liberation Front (*Front de libération nationale, FLN*) issued a proclamation calling on Algerians to fight for their freedom. By 1958 the FLN had 60,000 trained men armed with automatic weapons, pinning down 500,000 French troops. No quarter was given on either side. The French treated the FLN as rebels to be executed when captured. The European settlers, or *colons*, backed up the French army fully.

Independent Tunisia and Morocco permitted Algerians to be trained on their soil, world public opinion strongly criticized the French, and the United States was in turn criticized by the French people for not giving France wholehearted support and by the Algerians for continuing to supply military equipment to the French.

The French army, which had already suffered humiliating professional defeats in France in 1940 and in Indo-China in 1954, now found itself fighting a vicious guerrilla war in Algeria. Backed up by the *colons*, the French military leadership in Algeria convinced itself that if only the Paris government would give it a free hand, it could win the war. Civilian leaders in Algeria seized control of the government there and called on the army to take over. Army officers and civilian leaders formed Committees of Public Safety to replace the authorities from Paris, while other army units seized the French island of Corsica and threatened a parachute invasion of Paris. The government in Paris, afraid that civil war was imminent, called upon General de Gaulle to come out of retirement and form a government. He agreed to do so on the condition that he would be given a free hand to change the French constitution. This was the end of the Fourth Republic of France, and the beginning of the Fifth Republic.

The army leaders in Algeria accepted de Gaulle's leadership, but the *colons* were less than enthusiastic, because they were uncertain of de Gaulle's intentions for Algeria.

The FLN proclaimed itself the Provisional Government of the Algerian Republic (*Gouvernement provisoire de la république algérienne, GPRA*) and was almost immediately recognized as the government of Algeria by the other Arab countries, the Communist nations in Asia, and by African nations as they became independent from 1957 on. The GPRA acted as an independent government by sending representatives to internationalist gatherings and to friendly nations. In December 1958 the United Nations, by a vote of 35 to 18, passed a resolution "recognizing the right of the Algerian people to independence and recommending negotiations between the two interested parties," the French government and the GPRA.

In September 1959 President de Gaulle refused to negotiate with the GPRA, saying that "the future of Algeria rests with Algerians, not as thrust upon them by machinegun and knife, but according to the wishes which they will freely express through universal suffrage." He then offered the Algerians three alternatives to choose from: (1) separation from France, with the probability that Algeria would be divided up to provide settlements for Europeans, (2) integration with the rights and benefits of French citizenship for Algerians, (3) internal self-government guaranteeing the rights of Europeans, Arabs, and other groups. De Gaulle promised Algeria a referendum on these choices at the end of four years, but insisted that peace must precede the referendum.

In January 1960 a week-long strike and a sit-in by Europeans who barricaded themselves in a part of Algiers was met with sympathy by the French army. For the next year de Gaulle attempted to remove from Algeria the officers whom he believed to be unreliable, but with only limited success. In April 1961 four French generals in Algeria, expecting the support of Legionnaires and parachutists, seized control of Algiers, Oran, and Constantine, but they did not get the airforce support necessary for a possible invasion of France. Because of the failure of this attempted *coup*, die-hard army officers joined civilian extremists in organizing the underground Secret Army Organization (*Organization de l'armée secrète, OAS*), which began a systematic reign of terror against Algerians and Europeans who sympathized with Algerian independence. In Paris more than 30 bombs were exploded in one week against homes of prominent French supporters of independence; in Oran and Algiers the OAS indiscriminately shot down in cold blood Moslem servants, workers, and children; government buildings, schools, hospitals, and law courts were blown up by the OAS in their bitter and senseless rage.

Its leader, General Raoul Salan, defended the actions of the OAS by claiming that since the French government was not carrying out their duty of safeguarding French soil, including Algeria, then the OAS had that duty. "Consequently, I, General Raoul Salan, commander-in-chief, decide the mobilization of all Algerians to oppose the combined action of the *de facto* power (the de Gaulle government) and the (Algerian) rebellion to save Algeria for the Fatherland."

So tense did the situation become that in February 1962 de Gaulle summoned military and naval leaders together, talked with each separately, and gave orders for military action against the OAS. In March all civilian airflights over France were banned, with the exception of regularly-scheduled commercial airlines, and all military personnel were confined to their bases at night.

The OAS who declared "there will be no quarter given or taken," stepped up the pace of indiscriminate attack upon civilians, and even warned that any Europeans who attempted to leave Algeria without OAS permission would be considered traitors and shot. Frenchman was now fighting Frenchman in a bitter war as the French army went into action against the OAS.

Finally, on July 3, 1962, President de Gaulle proclaimed Algeria an independent nation. On that date the French empire ceased as it had begun, in violence and bitterness. The new nation was in a state of economic collapse. Nearly 1,000,000 Moslems had been killed in seven years of guerrilla warfare, another 2,000,000 had been uprooted as displaced persons or refugees, and 800,000 Europeans had fled the country and abandoned several million acres of productive farmland.

Algeria suffered from two handicaps when it became independent. Its people had been allowed no say in government under the French, and its leaders came to power totally inexperienced. Furthermore, independence led immediately to a scramble for power by rival candidates ambitious for leadership.

More than ten years after independence, Algeria was still in the process of reconstruction. President Boumédienne has brought some order and stability, but political parties are still apt to be conspiratorial rather than a means of free expression of opinions. Boumédienne, as political head of state and also as leader of the religious community, has the problem of transforming his people into a nation that can play a role in modern international affairs.

Libya. Libya was for centuries part of the Turkish empire, but because it was so poor it was of no interest to the colonial powers of the 19th century. In 1912 Italy, anxious to extend its empire, took over as a colony this large 680,000 square-mile area, mostly desert, and its poverty-stricken population of around 1,000,000 people. During World War II Italy was allied to Germany, and suffered the loss of Libya when the Allies drove the German and Italian troops out of North Africa. The liberators had no use for it themselves, so in 1951 the United Nations announced its independence as a monarchy under King Idris I. In 1965 Libya joined the United Nations. In 1969 King Idris was overthrown by the army, and a republic proclaimed.

The discovery of oil in this desert land transformed Libya from a country with one of the lowest living-standards to an oil-rich country, the seventh largest oil producer in the world. Politically oriented toward Egypt, it is not renewing the British and American military bases which once were Libya's main source of income, and in 1972 formed an alliance with Egypt.

4. French Sub-Sahara Africa

The French referred to their colonies as "overseas territories," not as colonies. The term refers back to a decree of 1792, during the French Revolution, which abolished slavery and declared that "All men, without distinction of color, domiciled in French colonies, are French citizens." Although France had no possessions in Africa at this time, the principle was supposedly extended to the African territories which the French acquired in the 19th century.

Each of France's "overseas territories" elected members to the government in Paris, but in actual practice French colonial rule was authoritarian, and colonial Africans were subjects rather than citizens. The disaster that happened

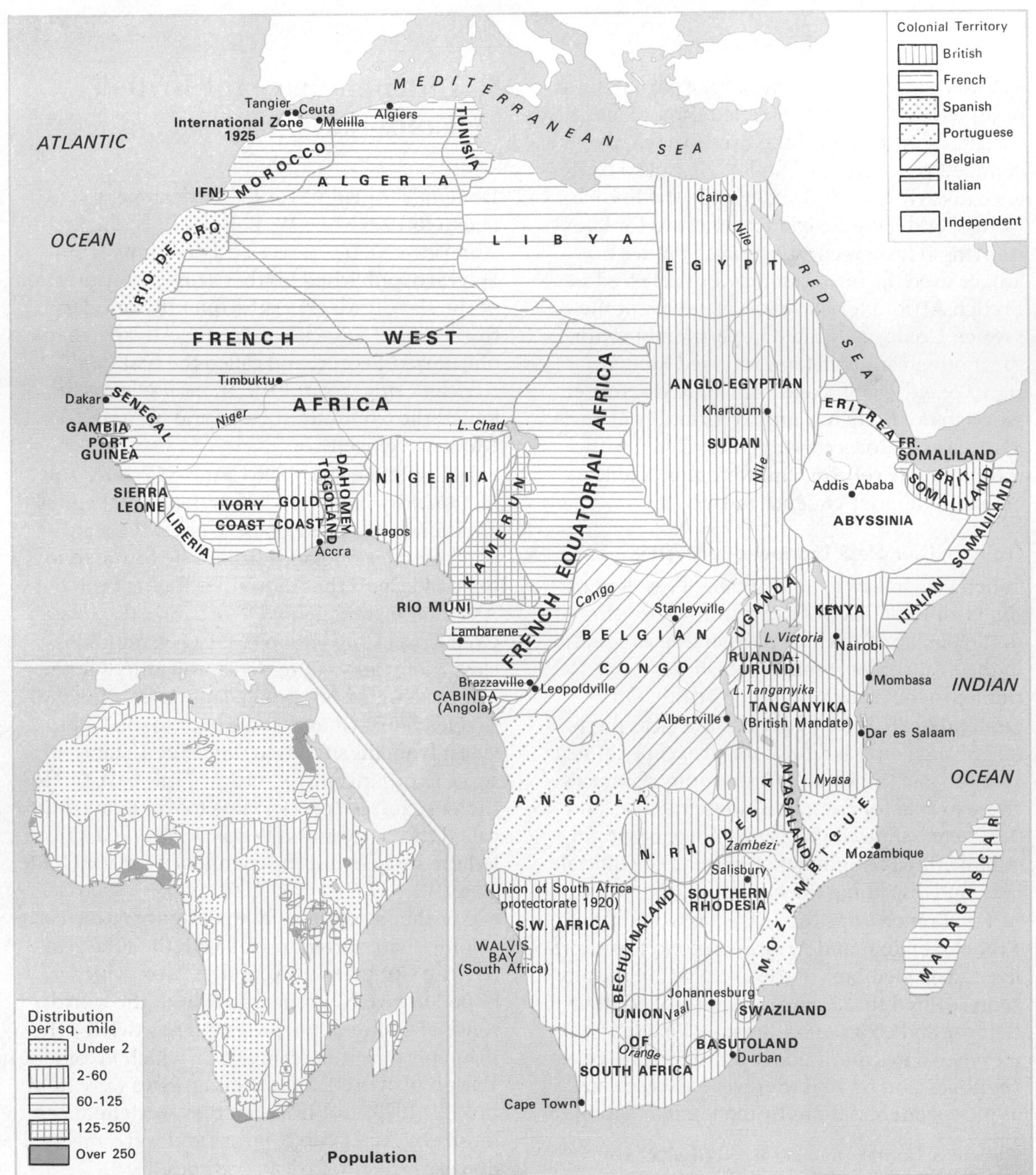

Africa, 1925–1945. Colonial territory. The inset map shows modern population distribution.

to France in 1940, when the larger part of it was occupied by German forces, led General de Gaulle, as the leader of the Free French, to change French colonial policy. He held a conference in early 1944 in Brazzaville in the French Congo, and there he laid foundations for later reforms. The new constitution of France no longer used the term colonies, but referred to French African territories as members of the French Union, associated in partnership with the mother country. They received limited rights of citizenship, and very limited representation in the French National Assembly in Paris. Tunisia and Morocco were not satisfied with this moderate reform, and were finally able to obtain their independence in 1956.

Guinea: Complete Independence, 1958

When General de Gaulle became President of the Fifth Republic of France in 1958, he offered to the people of Africa a partnership as equals in the French Community, which was quite similar to the British Commonwealth. On September 28, 1958, all French overseas territories voted on this offer, and all except Guinea voted to join the French Community. Guinea chose to vote for complete independence, and the French showed their annoyance by ripping out all official telephones, removing the official files, and disarming the native police.

The French hope that Africans would be Frenchmen first and Africans second was short-lived. The members of the French Community soon realized that France still controlled their defense and economic affairs. In 1960 fourteen member-states declared their independence as republics, and by 1961 they were all recognized as independent nations by the United Nations.*

*Cameroon; Central African Republic; Chad; Congo Republic (Brazzaville); Dahomey; Gabon; Ivory Coast; Malagasy; Mali; Mauritania; Niger; Senegal; Togo; Upper Volta.

5. Independence for British Colonies

Demands for rights for the African people began in 1896 when W. E. B. DuBois, the first American Negro to receive a doctorate from Harvard, published his thesis on the suppression of the slave trade. He subsequently founded the National Association for the Advancement of Colored People, and called the first Pan-African Congress in 1919. In his last years he joined the Communist Party and became a Ghanaian citizen.

In that same year 1896 Casely-Hayford, son of a wealthy merchant father, became the first African on the Gold Coast to enter the legal profession in England. In 1897 he founded in the Gold Coast the Aborigines Rights Protective Association, and helped to organize the United Gold Coast Convention (UGCC), a middle-class group advocating self-government in the colony. Kwame Nkrumah, later to become the first leader of Ghana, came back to the Gold Coast from his studies in the United States to serve as organizing secretary of the UGCC. He then organized his own mass movement group called the Convention People's Party (CPP) and led the struggle for independence for the Gold Coast.

Another attempt at independence for African colonies had started in 1919 with the First Pan-African Congress convened in Paris, which hoped to give Negroes throughout the world a sense of common purpose, and to work for the principle of self-determination which President Wilson proposed. Similar congresses were held in 1921, 1923, and 1927, but they were financed mostly by American Negroes and were able to do very little for African Negroes.

Two factors which gave great impetus to the demand for African independence were World

War II and the winning of independence by nations in Asia. The principles of the Atlantic Charter of 1941, accepted by all nations which fought against the Axis powers, contained the significant statement, "they respect the right of all peoples to choose the form of government under which they will live." In 1947 Great Britain gave independence to India and Pakistan, and the next year extended it to Burma and Ceylon. The former Dutch colony of the Netherlands East Indies proclaimed its own independence, and although it was denied by the Dutch, this action inspired other colonial people to demand similar rights.

Ghana and Nigeria: British West Africa

Ghana. Ghana was born in March 1957, the first black African colony of a white nation to become independent. Formerly known as the British colony of the Gold Coast, it took its name from the ancient state of Ghana, the old "gold and salt" empire. Kwame Nkrumah must be credited with winning his nation's independence. With his years of study at Lincoln University in Pennsylvania and later at the University of Pennsylvania as a background for political life, he used the Convention People's Party of the Gold Coast as the means to bring pressure upon the British government by starting a campaign of civil disobedience and strikes against British colonial administration. Endowed with great personal appeal, he gained increasing public support while a prisoner in a British gaol. So popular was his cause throughout the Gold Coast that the British decided to train colonial subjects in various colonies for self-rule.

Nkrumah became Ghana's first Prime Minister, and gradually he established himself as an autocratic leader to the extent that Ghana was sometimes referred to as Nkrumah's Land.

Kwame Nkrumah. A postage stamp.

He jailed political opponents, named streets and squares after himself, and over-zealously tried to transform Ghana into a modern industrial nation. He exhausted the nation's resources, incurred a substantial foreign debt, and wasted money on prestige items that were economically non-productive, such as an airline for Ghana, and expensive hotels. In 1961 while Nkrumah was in China on his own personal peace mission, the military group in Ghana declared Nkrumah deposed. Despite his deposition, the date March 6, 1957 is a red-letter day in the subsequent history of Africa, because Ghana's independence was actually a nationalist revolution that inspired other African colonies to demand or take independence. By the end of 1970 there were 32 more new African nations south of the Sahara.

Nigeria. When the Federation of Nigeria received its independence in 1960 it was hailed as a nation which could prove not only that Africans could rule themselves but also that different tribal groups could live together and become one nation. Its population of 56,000,000 was the largest of all the colonial areas, and its city of Ibadan was the world's most populous all-Negro city.

Named for the Niger, or Black, River, the new nation was a federation of three main tribes, each jealous of the others and fearful that any one would attempt to dominate the other two. As a colony its geographical boundary had nothing to do with tribal boundaries; consequently the new nation, now free from external administrative control, was in danger of disintegration unless tribal differences could be reconciled.

There are three distinct tribal and political regions. The northern region of flat savannah land is largely agricultural, with a population of about 32,000,000, of the Hausa and Fulani tribes, most of whom are Moslems living in a semi-feudal political system. The western region of some 10,000,000 people is the urbanized section of Nigeria, inhabited by the Yoruba tribe. The eastern region is the home of nearly 14,000,000 Ibos who, because they were willing to spend nearly half their public funds on education, became the most educated people of Nigeria, and filled important government positions and skilled occupations throughout Nigeria. They were regarded as arrogant by the other tribes, who envied the Ibos their skills and abilities, and resented Ibo pride in personal achievement.

Independence came to Nigeria in 1960, but it stood upon the shaky foundation of the three sections dominated by the Northern People's Congress or Party, which won the largest number of votes in the election. Its leader was Alhagi Balewa, a Hausa, who became Prime Minister of a Hausa-dominated government which soon faced the problems of corruption, inflation, strikes, and general discontent which exploded in 1966 in the assassination of Balewa by Ibo army officers.

A few months later the northern Hausas retaliated by killing General Ironsi, the Ibo Prime Minister of the Federation of Nigeria, and scores of Ibo army officers. In September, Hausa Moslem mobs savagely slaughtered more than 30,000 Ibos and maimed thousands more in the northern region, until by the end of the year more than one and a quarter million Ibos had fled in panic across the Niger River to their homeland in the eastern region.

In the following months Colonel Odumegwu Ojukwu, leader of the Ibos, demanded self-government for his eastern region, but was opposed by General Yakubo Gowon, a northerner and the Federation's ruler. In May 1967,

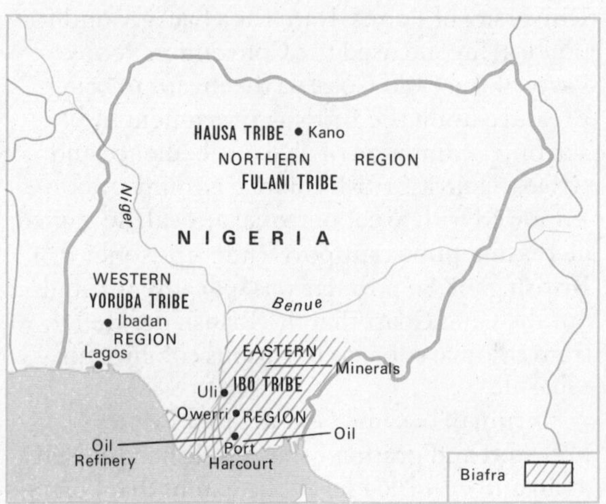

Nigerian Civil War, 1967–1970

Ojukwu, now a general, was obliged by his 300-man assembly to insist upon complete independence for the eastern region as the independent nation of Biafra.

The civil war which followed raised several significant issues for the people of Africa. The ordinary African saw the issue as one of tribal survival versus the threat of inter-tribal warfare. Tanzania's leader, Julius Nyerere, criticized the government of Nigeria for its military campaign against the Ibos, "You cannot kill thousands of people and keep killing more in the name of unity." On the other hand, leaders of states in which there are tribal groups feared Biafra's example as a serious threat to the stability of their own nations. Nigeria's leader, General Gowon, expressed their fears when he warned, "Who knows what African country will be the next victim?"

The war continued for more than two and a half years, with Biafra suffering increasing losses of land and people. In early January 1970, Nigerian federal troops claimed to have sliced secessionist Biafra into three sections, and were mounting a determined offensive against the one remaining Biafran airstrip at Uli. Thousands of refugees fled from the bush and poured into Owerri, the provisional capital, and added to the already-serious food shortage.

As the pressure against the remaining Biafran forces mounted, U Thant, Secretary General of the United Nations, announced that Biafran secession was unacceptable to the United Nations. This virtually prevented any further assistance to Biafra, and on January 11, 1970 its leader, General Ojukwu, announced over Radio Biafra that he was about to "travel out of Biafra to secure peace and security for my people." He left the country with his personal possessions, and his second-in-command, General Philip Effiong, saw no alternative but to surrender. When Biafra declared its independence in May 1967 it was a country of 30,000 square miles and a population of 14,000,000. In January 1970 it was barely a tenth that size, and its population was only 3,000,000. If the war continued, at least a half of the remaining population faced utter starvation.

On January 12, 1970, General Effiong surrendered Biafra to the Federal Nigerian government leader, General Gowon, who accepted the surrender and declared a general pardon "for all those misled into attempting to disintegrate the country." Biafra officially ceased to exist on January 15, 1970.

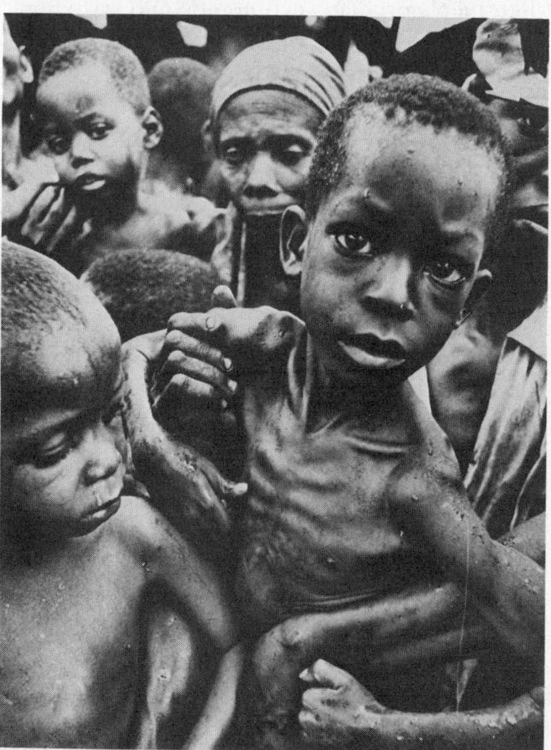

Biafran Children suffered terribly in the civil war. International Red Cross doctors were forced—by lack of food and supplies—to allow the sickest children to die so that they could save the stronger.

Immediately there were charges that Nigerians would deliberately starve Biafrans. Contradictory reports came from the League of Red Cross Societies and from an international group of newsmen who thought that the situation was more serious than the Red Cross stated. In late March 1970, the Red Cross was distributing 3,000 tons of food a week to the 3,000,000 people, but these were at best only subsistence rations. Nigeria appeared either to be preventing adequate supplies from reaching Biafrans or to be incompetently handling the crisis. The exiled Biafran leader General Ojukwu released a statement via the Biafran press office in Geneva that the Nigerian government would systematically destroy the elite of Biafra. "It is clear that Nigeria will not feed our people."

This attitude was a natural one after such a ruthless civil war, but three years later conditions were much better than had been anticipated in the wasteland that was Biafra in 1970. The Nigerian chief of state, General Yakubo Gowon not only forbade reprisals against the Ibos but deliberately re-integrated them into Nigerian life.

With its vast new wealth from oil, making it the eighth largest oil-producing country in the world, the government has re-imbursed many of the Ibos who lost their property.

Lagos, Nigeria. Woman on way to store passes Independence Fountain before Central Bank of Nigeria.

In 1972 Nigeria was producing oil worth about $1.5 billions, with a predictability of at least that much annually for the next thirty years. Nevertheless, Nigeria, which was once expected to be the showplace of Black Africa, has its serious problems, like many an emergent nation. Roads are primitive, poverty is abysmal, and the nation cannot provide the thousands of teachers needed for its planned educational system, and foreign business investment is discouraged because by law many businesses must be Nigerian owned.

Furthermore, the Ibos have not forgotten the misery they suffered at the hands of the other tribes. Their native ability, their skills, and their willingness to work are already alienating other tribes, who fear Ibo domination of the economy. However, time may provide this, the largest African nation, the opportunity to prove itself, and perhaps become a leader in Black Africa.

Kenya and Tanzania: British East Africa

In the nineteenth century the British were interested in controlling the territory between Egypt and the Cape of Good Hope in order to build a railroad from north to south and to deny this vast region to other imperialist nations. Britain did get control of the area, but the railroad has not yet materialized. The region of east-central Africa, unlike the "white man's graveyard" of West Africa, was suitable for settlement particularly in the region which became known as the White Highlands of Kenya. The British built a railroad from the East African sea-coast town of Mombasa to Lake Victoria in Uganda, and opened up the country to European settlement.

Kenya. The discontent which has in past years affected many African colonies burst into open civil conflict between natives and whites in Kenya, largely because 5,000,000 acres of the

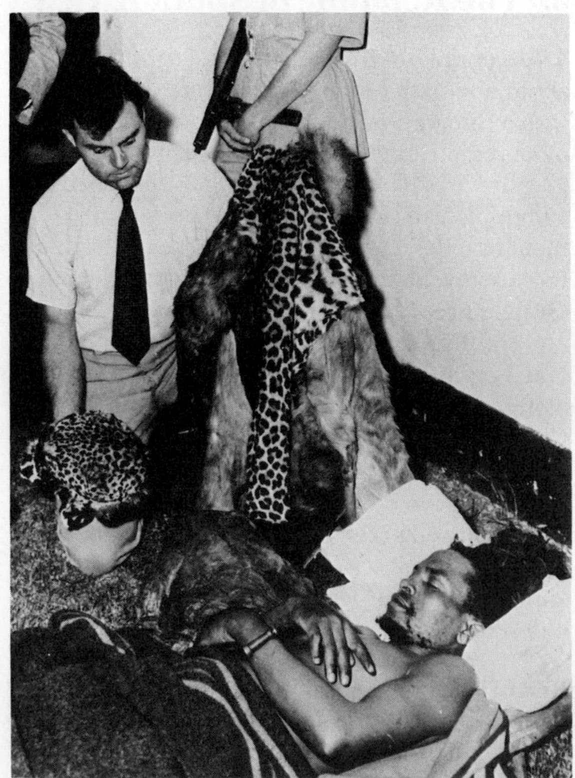

Mau Mau in Kenya. Dedan Kimathi, the last Mau Mau leader, after his capture. The Mau Mau used animal skins as disguises and practiced voodoo and other "witchcraft" in their terror campaigns.

fertile White Highlands were closed to native Africans. This area is the home of the Kikuyu of about one and a quarter million people who were bitterly resentful of being excluded from land which had traditionally been theirs. In 1953 the Kikuyu and other tribes organized a terrorist movement called Mau Mau, with its slogan of *Uhuru*, the Swahili word for freedom, with the objective of striking such terror into the white settlers that they would leave the country. One feature of the Mau Mau organization was an extremely solemn oath-taking ceremony forcing Africans into tribal action against the white man, under penalty of being expelled from the tribe. In two years of terrorist activities over 7,000 Mau Mau members, 500 security officers, and 1,300 civilians lost their lives. Of the total civilian deaths only about fifty were Europeans. The others were Africans who refused to collaborate fully with the Mau Mau. British authorities accused Jomo Kenyatta, a London-educated Kikuyu anthropological scholar, of being the leader of the Mau Mau, and they imprisoned him for several years.

The revolt was finally subdued, but the demand for independence spread so widely that in 1961 the British permitted elections in Kenya. Jomo Kenyatta's party won the majority of seats in the legislature, and he was released. After helping to train the Africans for self-government, Kenyatta won independence for Kenya in December 1963 and became its first Prime Minister and later its first President.

Kenyatta insisted upon a strong central government and a multi-racial society in which Europeans, Asiatics, Arabs, and Africans would live together as citizens of one nation. Kenya is now being closely watched as a possible model of a working multi-racial society in Africa.

Tanzania. Tanzania is a union of the two former British protectorates of Tanganyika and Zanzibar. Before World War I Tanganyika was the chief German colony of East Africa, but at the Versailles Conference in 1919 it was turned over to Great Britain as a mandate to be trained for self-government. Tanganyika became the pace-maker for East African independence under the leadership of Edinburgh-educated Julius Nyerere who in 1954 organized the Tanganyika African National Union. An advocate of an African, rather than a multi-racial nation, Nyerere won independence for Tanganyika in December 1961, and became its first President.

East African Presidents, 1970. Dr. Milton Obote of Uganda, Jomo Kenyatta of Kenya; and Julius Nyerere of Tanzania. (Dr. Obote was later deposed by General Idi Amin.)

Zanzibar, the other component of Tanzania, was a dependency of Britain until 1963, when it gained its independence under a government composed largely of a small Arab minority that had long dominated the island. In 1964 the African Moslems under Abeid Karume revolted against Arab domination and set up Karume as President. In April 1964 Tanganyika and Zanzibar, fearful of domination by the Communist bloc, united to form Tanzania with Nyerere as President and Karume as vice-president. (For brief descriptions of other former British Colonies and protectorates *see* p. 40.)

6. The Republic of South Africa

The Republic of South Africa is a country about one sixth the size of the United States, with a climate similar to that of the Mediterranean region and California. The landscape is greatly varied, but it can be simply described as a high plateau surrounded by a steep escarpment that descends rapidly to the sea. The main feature is veld, or grassy plain, which covers the Orange Free State and the Transvaal provinces, and continues into modern Rhodesia, Zambia, and Tanzania. The Republic has no harbors along its west coast, and only three ports from Cape Town up around the east coast, Port Elizabeth, East London, Durban.

The nation consists of the four provinces of the Transvaal in the north, the Orange Free State, the smallest province of Natal stretching along the Indian Ocean, and Cape Province, the oldest of the four.

Brief History

For more than 300 years there have been European settlers and their descendants in the Cape area. In 1652 the Dutch East India Company established at the Cape of Good Hope a watering and victualing station for their ships sailing to and from India. The company was not interested in encouraging colonization, and because labor was scarce the Dutch authorities permitted slavery, but they refused to open up the frontier for settlement. In 1794 the Netherlands was attacked by a French Revolutionary army, and the Dutch prince, William of Orange, fled to Britain to form a government-in-exile.

So strategic was the harbor of Table Bay in Cape Town that the British decided to prevent its use by the French navy. With the official consent of William of Orange, the British occupied Cape Town in 1795, withdrew in 1803, and when war broke out again between

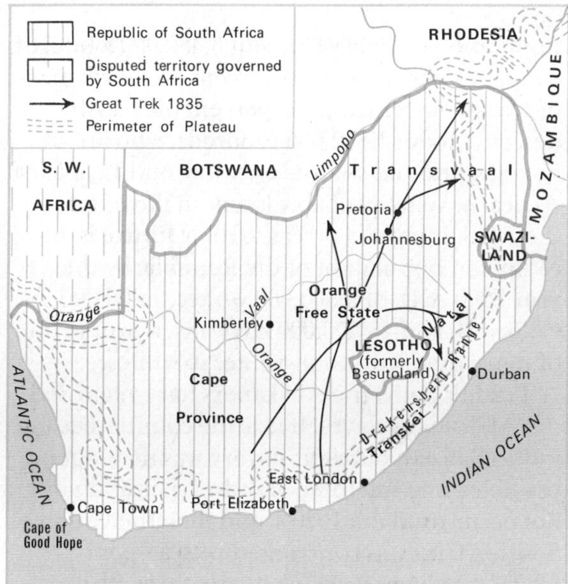

South Africa

Britain and France, re-occupied it in 1806.

In 1814 the Netherlands sold the Cape to the British, and the Dutch subjects who were there became citizens subject to British law. They became increasingly restive under British rule, however, and when Britain abolished slavery throughout her empire in 1833, the Dutch farmers, or Boers, decided to get away from British rule. Their Great Trek, or march, began in 1835 and continued until 1838 as other groups left the Cape to head northeast across the Orange and Vaal Rivers to found two independent republics, the Orange Free State and the Transvaal. They were attacked by African natives, who resented the intrusion of the white man and feared that they would lose their land and be enslaved. To the modern Afrikaners, as the present descendants of the Dutch call themselves, this settlement in a hostile country is a symbol of a heroic people who formed a nation in the face of great danger. Thus the foundation of the history of the Afrikaners has been their united front against what they still consider to be a black menace to their way of life. Just as the trekkers formed a *laager*, or circle of wagons, from which to beat off attack, so the Afrikaners of today insist they must present a united front against any danger which threatens them—or that they believe threatens them—from the African natives who outnumber them. The Great Trek is of importance because it explains much of today's thinking by Afrikaners and their policy of *apartheid* or separation of races.

The Boer War, 1899–1902

The principal figure in South African history during the later years of the 19th century was Cecil Rhodes, who went from England to Cape Town as a lad of 17, made a fortune in diamonds before he was 25, and went into politics in Africa. He became Prime Minister of Cape Colony, the area which the British had occupied since 1806, and set out to accomplish one ambition, to build a Cape to Cairo railroad, and another ambition, to create a federated nation of white people of all South Africa, by which Rhodes meant the area which today includes the Republic of South Africa, Rhodesia, Zambia, Malawi, and Tanzania.

When gold was discovered in the Dutch Republic of the Transvaal, a great tide of foreign miners, or "Uitlanders" as the Dutch called these outsiders, swept into the Transvaal. Because they paid high taxes but were not given representation, they called upon Rhodes to help them. Instead of biding his time, Rhodes unwisely saw in the situation the opportunity to persuade the two Dutch republics to form part of a great white South African nation. Rhodes encouraged rebellion inside the Transvaal, but partly because of poor timing by outside help organized by Rhodes, the scheme fell through.

The Boers declared war on Great Britain, and for three years they put up a stiff but ultimately hopeless resistance against the British.

Great Britain was lenient in its peace terms, and granted to the Transvaal and the Orange River Colony, formerly the Orange Free State, representative but not complete self-government. In 1910 the *Union of South Africa* was formed out of the two former Dutch republics, British Cape Colony, and British Natal. In 1931 the Union of South Africa became an independent nation but remained a member of the British Commonwealth, recognizing the British sovereign as its sovereign. South Africa continued to be a member of the Commonwealth until May 1961, when it proclaimed itself as the Republic of South Africa, an independent state without any formal relationship with Great Britain and the Commonwealth.

The Forces Shaping Apartheid

An essential factor to remember about the Republic of South Africa is that to the white inhabitants the Republic is their home. They are not administrators who can one day return to their homeland, for they have no homeland other than the one in which they live. They are descendants of Dutch and English settlers who have lived for generations in South Africa, and this is their land which they intend to defend against all-comers, especially against the Africans in their midst. The *Afrikaners,* descendants of the early Dutch settlers, speak their own language called *Afrikaans,* and they must be clearly distinguished from Africans, the collective name given to the natives, whom Afrikaners disparagingly refer to as *Bantus.*

The obviously distinguishing feature of the Republic of South Africa is its racial policy of *apartheid,* or separateness, which is the result of the great fear of the Afrikaners for the Africans who outnumber them by more than 3 to 1. The population of 1966 was about 3,480,000 white, of whom approximately 60 percent are Afrikaners of Dutch descent, and 40 percent of British descent, about 1,800,000 Coloreds, who are of mixed white and colored ancestry, and 12,465,000 Africans. What probably looms in the minds of the Afrikaners as a threat to their future is an estimated population of the Republic by the year 2000 A.D. of 6,500,000 whites, 7,000,000 Coloreds, and 28,500,000 Africans, a proportion of more than 5 to 1 non-whites to whites.

Traditionally, the Afrikaners have regarded the Africans as slaves, but as the country became industrialized, outright slavery was no longer possible. The full force of industrialization did not occur until the 1920's, and then the Union of South Africa was confronted with a "poor white" problem in which nearly three fifths of the Afrikaner population was close to the poverty level. As more farmers came into the towns they found many Africans holding semi-skilled and unskilled jobs. The government proceeded not only to classify jobs which only Afrikaners could hold but also to regulate higher pay scales for whites over blacks working at precisely the same jobs. In 1936 all blacks were denied the right to vote.

The experience of the early trekkers for survival convinced Afrikaners that uncompromising and rigidly enforced white supremacy or *baasskap,* literally "bosshood," was essential for survival. Today that attitude is stronger than ever, and is completely supported by the Dutch Reformed Churches which teach that God is the Great Divider, who established boundaries between people. They interpret this to mean not only complete separation of the races but also the corollary that compromise is impossible, and that discussion of the matter is useless.

The Afrikaners outnumbered the English descendants, formed their own Nationalist Party, won control of parliament in 1948 and set up a completely Afrikaner cabinet that opened a new chapter in the history of South Africa.

Apartheid in Action

The men most responsible for furthering the policy of apartheid are Dr. Hendrik Verwoerd who was Prime Minister from 1958 until his assassination in 1966, and Dr. John Vorster who succeeded him.

The policy of apartheid means "separateness," and apologists for the policy claim that whites and blacks are better off when they live in their own separate communities. But behind this simple concept lies a bitterly repressive system which denies to more than 14,000,000 people any rights whatever, and treats them not as human beings but as mere commodities. The laws and actions of the government expose apartheid for what it is.

In rural areas the African is no more than a serf because the law makes it a criminal offense for a farm worker to leave his employment without permission from his employer. In cities he must accept starvation wages without the right to bargain collectively or to strike. He must at all times carry a "pass book," without which he can hold no job, cannot move from one place to another, be in a town, or escape summary punishment. By the so-called Sabotage Act of 1962 a large number of minor offenses are punishable by death if committed to "further any political aim, including the bringing about of any social or economic change in the Republic."

Apartheid in Action. Natives must use separate transportation, restaurants, public rest rooms and even—as shown here—separate post offices.

Another Act, the "90-day law" of 1963, abolishes the right of *habeas corpus*, the right of a person to know what he is charged with in order to defend himself, and the right to a speedy trial. Any commissioned officer can arrest on the grounds of political *suspicion*, and without a warrant. Such an arrested person can be detained for 90 days for interrogation without the right to a lawyer. The 90-day periods can be repeated indefinitely, and a prisoner may be detained indefinitely even after serving his sentence.

Under the Suppression of Communism Act the Minister of Justice may arrest any person upon suspicion of his being a Communist; in practice this has included any person whose actions or ideas the government does not like. There is no appeal from such arbitrary arrest.

Another vicious form of arbitrary punishment is banishment. This is one of the most effective ways to prevent political opposition because it empowers the government "whenever it deems expedient in the general interest" to move any individual African or even an entire tribe from one place to another in South Africa. This has resulted in removal to a remote and desolate camp. From this action no appeal is possible, and no time limit is set on the period of banishment. Such a power over a person's life is one of the most inhuman that a government can exercise.

White persons who criticize apartheid, such as Alan Paton, author of *Cry, the Beloved Country* and *Too Late the Phalarope*, can be deprived of their passports and denied the right to travel. Another punishment for white citizens, is "house arrest," by which a person can be kept isolated in his home for an indefinite period and be deprived of the right to have visitors.

Because "separateness" is the eventual goal of the government, certain regions of South Africa have been set apart for the Bantu. Typical of these Bantustans, which are sometimes located on impoverished land which cannot support a people adequately, is the Transkei, about the size of Switzerland, in the southeastern region of the republic. This trial separate area is already proving incapable of supporting its population of 1,500,000 people. The government plans to set up seven more such reserves as "tribal homelands" for eight "national units" or tribes such as the Tsongos, Tswanus, Vendas, and Zulus. These Native Reserves are to have their own governments, flags, and other symbols of apparent self-government, but they are condemned by the Africans as little more than ghettos.

The Transkei Challenge

Dr. Hendrik Verwoerd was the father of self-rule for the Bantus; it was his Transkei Constitution Act of 1963 which set up the largest of these Bantustans. It was to be the testing-ground of "separate development," with the promise of future self-government and full independence. This same Act may prove embarrassing to the racist government of the Republic of South Africa, because the Transkei is now "talking back" and demanding more rights. Whites who remained in the area as civil servants to help in the administration are now becoming alarmed at the agitation for apartheid in reverse. Demands by Transkei Black leaders for more rights were underlined by the threat that Whites in the Transkei would be treated in exactly the same way as Blacks were treated in South Africa.

A further weapon in the hands of the Transkei Africans is the discovery in 1971 of vast deposits of titanium. The discoveries have also raised the embarrassing question that the South African government must answer. To whom do the deposits belong? To the Transkei, promised independence in due time? Or to South Africa? Paramount Chief Kaiser Matanzina and his brother George, Minister of Justice, have bluntly told South Africa to keep its hands off the deposits estimated to be worth $500,000,000, "Our interests supersede those of the South African government."

The deposits now being exploited by a European mining company are a challenge to the South African government. Once having set out a course of self-government for the Bantustans, it can scarcely reclaim the Transkei and argue that Bantustans belong to the Africans only until valuable metals are found there. The white government will probably have to open negotiations with the Transkei. This would be unpalatable for a government which has refused to recognize that the black man has any legal rights.

One of the most obvious paradoxes of apartheid is that the wealthy industrial economy of South Africa cannot do without African labor, and therefore that complete apartheid is impossible. Much of world opinion is opposed to the policy. The Security Council of the United Nations condemned it, and the Organization of African Unity has attempted, but without real success, to cut off trade relations with the republic.

Various proposals have been made to ameliorate the situation, but these proposals would eventually give the Africans more say in the whole country, and therefore they are strongly opposed by the Nationalist Government which insists upon strict racism and the denial to the Africans of any rights enjoyed by the whites. Unlike the United States, where the law provides for equal rights for all, the Republic of South Africa enacts legislation against any rights for the African.

For four years Prime Minister John Vorster publicly adopted a policy of *verligtheid*, "enlightenment," calling for gradual modification of apartheid. In July 1972 Vorster abruptly returned to uncompromising apartheid. Black chieftains of Bantustans demanded what "enlightenment" and the policy of Bantustans promised – the right of home rule in lands which have been set aside for the occupation and use by blacks only. Logically, the chieftains demanded the right to their own police, the right to conduct their own trade, and to manage all their own affairs without interference.

Vorster's leadership of the Nationalist Party was threatened when the party lost seats in by-elections. Diehards in the party, the *verkramptes*, criticized the "liberal" attitude; Vorster met the challenge with a return to strict apartheid, accusing opponents of that policy of *Boerehaat*, hatred for the Afrikaners, the backbone of the white supremacists.

Vorster met open criticism with force. Clubs and dogs were used against student protesters, and more churchmen are being arrested, prevented from preaching, placed under house arrest, or even deported.

Recent Apartheid Measures

Another phase of apartheid in action is the 1972 policy of forcing black workers in Johannesburg to leave the city at dusk and live in new barrack-like quarters described by Helen Suzman, Progressive Party member of South Africa's parliament, as an "Orwellian horror." So great has been recent demand for maids, cooks, gardeners, chauffeurs, and other domestic workers in Johannesburg that blacks outnumber whites two to one.

But the South African government did not want too many blacks on the streets at night. So it built hostels in the suburbs to provide accommodation for 60,000 workers, hostels strictly segregated according to sex, although most of the workers are married.

Out of a monthly wage of $30 to $50 a month, a black worker pays $8 for the incredible right to share one room with three other persons. The "barracks" have no elevators, no electrical outlets, no heating, and one small bathtub for every twenty persons. An Anglican bishop described the buildings as the work of "morally sick people." Protests influenced the city council to make two improvements, an open-air cinema, and a basketball court for the women. Under consideration is heating.

7. Problems for Britain and Portugal

Central African Federation

David Livingstone, famous African explorer and anti-slavery advocate, discovered for the white man the area around Lake Nyasa and the upper Zambesi River in the 1850's and 1860's. In 1889 Cecil Rhodes secured a charter for his British South African Company, and by it he was granted the right to explore and develop what later became the modern Rhodesias. The region called Nyasaland became a British protectorate, and the Southern and Northern Rhodesias remained possessions of the company until 1923. In that year Southern Rhodesia was given partial self-government, and Northern Rhodesia remained a British colony.

After World War II the Africans of Northern Rhodesia and Nyasaland began to agitate for independence, and when the vastly outnumbered whites asked for assistance, Britain suggested federation of the two Rhodesias and Nyasaland.

In 1953 Britain established the Central African Federation of the three areas, a region stretching 1,000 miles north and south, with a population of nearly 8,000,000 people consisting of some 250,000 whites and about 7,500,000 Africans, a ratio of about 30 to 1. Southern Rhodesia, with a 10 to 1 native superiority, had an economy based on mining, tobacco-growing, and ranching, and for the previous 30 years had been a white-dominated region. Northern Rhodesia, with a native population 30 times the size of the white, had been a primitive colony which in the 1920's produced large quantities of copper, and had by mid-century become the second largest copper-producing country in the world, providing the Central African Federation with some 65 percent of its revenues. Nyasaland was the smallest area but the most densely populated of the three with a 300 to 1 predominance of 2,700,000 Africans to 9,000 Europeans. The Federation looked like an ideal arrangement. Northern Rhodesia could supply the raw materials, Nyasaland the pool of labor, and Southern Rhodesia, with its 155,000 Europeans, could provide the government.

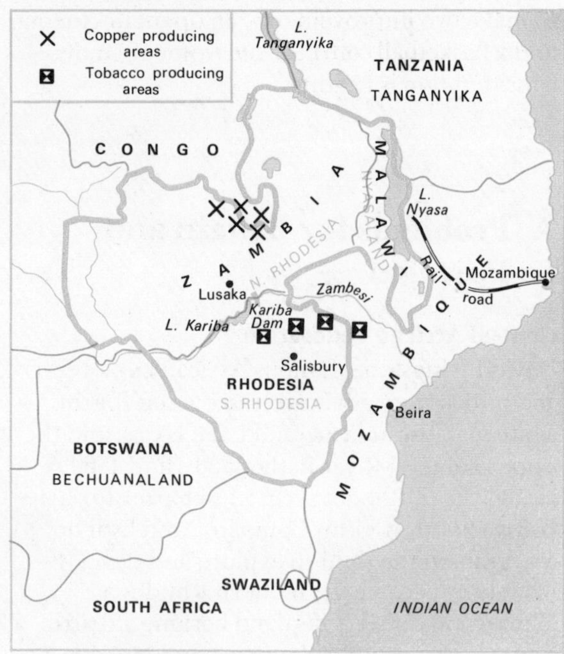

The Central African Federation. The map shows how this was split up into its present separate countries.

Malawi and Zambia

The Federation proved economically successful, but Africans resented white domination and arbitrary pay scales, and they continued to agitate for independence. In 1963 the British government permitted Nyasaland and Northern Rhodesia to become independent African nations under their native names of Malawi, Land of the Great Water, and Zambia, named after the Zambesi River.

Malawi is an agricultural nation, dependent upon crops that must compete in the world market, and land-locked except for a railroad that passes through the Portuguese colony of Mozambique. Because Portugal, the only remaining large colonial power in Africa, has dealt very harshly with agitation for African independence, Malawi has planned to build a railroad outlet to Tanzania, a neighboring African state. Upon obtaining independence, Malawi chose as its President, Dr. Kamuzu Banda, an American-trained physician. In recent years a situation very close to civil war has existed in Malawi because Banda has placed close restrictions upon his political opponents.

Zambia depends upon its valuable copper

mines along the Congo border; although the old British South Africa Company retains much of the country's mineral rights, a situation which President Kaunda has threatened to remedy by taking possession of the property for the nation. One of the world's largest hydroelectric developments is the Kariba Dam in Zambia; its construction became well-known because of "Operation Noah" which removed thousands of wild animals from the path of the rising waters.

Rhodesia

Southern Rhodesia, or simply Rhodesia, as it calls itself, was denied independence by the British government because its white minority refused to grant the black majority full participation in the government. In 1965 Prime Minister Ian Smith issued a "unilateral declaration of independence," popularly referred to as UDI, which declared Rhodesia to be independent. Great Britain, protested the action as illegal without the consent of the British government, attempted to apply pressure through economic sanctions or trade restrictions. Several African nations demanded that Britain remove the "white supremacy" government; the United Nations voted economic sanctions, but the results were basically ineffectual.

Proposal for Rhodesian Independence

After seven years of unsuccessful negotiations designed to bring Rhodesia back under British control, the Conservative government in Great Britain attempted to work out an agreement that hopefully would resolve the problem. In November 1971, Rhodesian Prime Minister Ian Smith and British Foreign Secretary Alec Douglas-Home agreed that in return for British recognition of Rhodesia's white-supremacist government, representing 250,000 whites, Rhodesia would gradually extend political power to the 5,000,000 blacks. The basic principles agreed upon were: (1) gradual but steady progress toward majority rule, (2) guarantees against any future changes restricting such progress, (3) Britain must be satisfied that the agreement was acceptable to all the people of Rhodesia.

A Commission headed by Lord Pearce was appointed by the British government to travel through Rhodesia explaining the program and getting reactions from the people. The Commission distributed 775,000 summaries of the independence proposal which, for some unexplained reason, the British Conservative government, the Labour Opposition, and most of Rhodesia's whites were confident the blacks would accept.

To the embarrassment of the British government and the great annoyance of the Rhodesian whites, the blacks rejected the proposal by a ratio of 99 to 1. Even if honestly applied, the agreement would have given the blacks a hope but not a guarantee of coming to political power in about seventy years. With extraordinary understatement, the Pearce Commission noted. "Someone has badly misjudged the Africans of this country."

Rhodesia's blacks are highly suspicious of the intentions of Ian Smith's government, and with good reason. In some parts of Rhodesia members of the African National Council, a political group opposed to the agreement, were detained until after the Commission had left.

More than 1,500 people were arrested in early 1972, and the Rhodesian government arrested and detained without trial four well-known critics of the Smith regime, the black African politician Josiah Chinamano and his wife, and the white Garfield Todd, former Rhodesian prime minister, and his daughter. After public protest, Todd and his daughter were later transferred from prison to house arrest. Other people have been detained to silence opposition, clear evidence that normal political procedures are not permitted in Rhodesia.

However, the significant consequences of the commission's referendum were not foreseen. Prior to this time African political parties were banned. The opportunity offered by the Pearce Commission to voice their opinions publicly has given the blacks of Rhodesia a political force that will almost certainly gain momentum. Already the African National Council, under black Bishop Abel Muzorewa, has become a nationwide black organization, the "one, sole voice and instrument of the African masses," according to Muzorewa.

Ian Smith's reaction was to move closer to apartheid. He told a group of local government officials that the country should seek separate economic development of white and black areas, clearly a plan to segregate the races.

The Africans now realize their political potential, and if the whites fail to resolve the problem through peaceful and acceptable evolution, violence can result. "It may take ten years," says Muzorewa, "but we will not stop until we reach our goal—freedom."

Olympic "Politics"

The Olympic Games of 1972 were threatened with dissension when twenty-one black states of the Organization for African Unity agreed to boycott the games if Rhodesia was allowed to enter contestants, even though some of them were black. Racist Rhodesia, whose declaration of independence is not recognized by the United Nations, was not invited by Mexico to the Olympic Games of 1968.

In 1971 the question of an invitation to Rhodesia was brought up before the International Olympic Committee, which came up with a curious solution. If Rhodesia, which in 1969 voted overwhelmingly to abandon their loyalty to the Queen of England, would temporarily adopt Britain's national anthem, "God Save the Queen," as its national anthem and would march under the old colonial flag, which includes the Union Jack, then it would be admitted to the Olympic Games.

Unexpectedly, Rhodesia accepted these extraordinary terms, and as many as 45 nations threatened to withdraw from the games. Pressure on the IOC forced it to back down and withdraw the invitation, to the great annoyance of Avery Brundage, its president.

Portuguese Angola and Mozambique

These two Portuguese possessions are 22 times the size of Portugal and are regarded by Portugal as "overseas territories" and an integral part of the Portuguese nation, not as colonies. Portugal therefore claims that what happens inside Angola and Mozambique is an "internal" matter, and is not a subject for public discussion or criticism by other nations.

Angola, or Portuguese West Africa, is more than 480,000 square miles in area, with a population of about 5,000,000, of whom only 300,000 are whites, a ratio of 17 to 1. Mozambique, or Portuguese East Africa, has an area of 298,000 square miles and a population of 6,870,000, including 130,000 whites, a ratio of more than 50 to 1.

Whatever the Portuguese government may claim, these territories are true colonies, run for the benefit of Portugal and not for the more than 11,000,000 Africans. Portugal claims that there is no color bar, and that natives or *indigenas* who reach a certain standard of education, speak Portuguese, own property, give up their native ways and live like Europeans, and are of use in administrative capacities, can become *assimilados*, or assimilated ones whose status is legally white. The number of Africans who have reached this favored status is very small; educational opportunities are very limited for the

Africans, and only a very few can possibly attain these standards. In 1958 there were fewer than 35,000 *assimilados* in Portuguese Africa, a ratio of 1 to every 350 *indigenas*.

Unlike some European former colonies, Portuguese Africa has not yet been developed or industrialized, partly because Portugal has little surplus capital to put into such projects, and partly because an industrialized Portuguese Africa would threaten Portugal itself, a basically agricultural nation with a rigid class system. Foreign investment and even branch offices of foreign businesses are deliberately discouraged in Portuguese Africa because criticism of Portuguese colonial methods is not welcomed.

Portugal benefits from her colonies through a very cheap, and frequently forced, labor system that she has imposed upon Africans for work on huge coffee and cotton plantations. As evidence of her "civilizing" mission, Portugal has insisted that for their own good the natives should be made to work. Once this principle was determined, then all active African males between 18 and 55 who are not actually at work can be presumed to be idle. An idle native is classified as a vagrant, and as such he can be put to work at whatever wages and job the authorities decide.

A vagrant's choices are to find a European employer, sign up with an agency to work in South Africa, or be drafted into some kind of public works organized by Portuguese administrators. This is no more than disguised forced labor, because natives who oppose the system can be classified as "undesirables" and condemned to work under the harsh conditions of the cocoa plantations of Sao Tomé, which are little more than penal islands.

In 1960 the United Nations requested information from Portugal on the condition of her overseas territories. Portugal rejected the motion on the grounds that there was nothing to report.

In 1961 the illusion created by Portugal that the people of her overseas territories were far more interested in becoming Portuguese citizens than in winning independence was abruptly shattered. Riots in Luanda, the capital of Angola, were followed by riots in other parts of the colony. In the terror that followed, hundreds of whites and thousands of natives were killed. In 1962 the General Assembly of the United Nations by a vote of 99 to 2 called on Portugal to "cease repressive measures against the people of Angola," and requested Portugal to initiate reforms that would lead to independence. But Portugal considers the colonies to be a "domestic" problem, of no concern to other nations.

Portugal's other colonial possessions are the Sao Tomé islands in the Gulf of Guinea, the Cape Verde Islands, 500 miles off the Atlantic coast and an important refueling station for ships and planes, and Portuguese Guinea squeezed in between Senegal and the Republic of Guinea. The position of this colony could very well encourage active assistance to its inhabitants by Senegal and Guinea.

Opposition to Apartheid

The two contradictory policies of African nationalism and white repression of Africans are probably headed for confrontation. Although the Republic of South Africa has been able to pursue successfully its policy of apartheid, there are forces working against white Southern Africa. Public opinion elsewhere is in general against apartheid because the trend of the past two decades is recognition of the principle of self-determination. Black African nations, although for the present busily occupied with internal problems, will probably give increasing assistance to the struggle for black freedom.

Despite superiority of military equipment enjoyed by White Africa, the pressures within these racist areas may become volcanic. Many statesmen of note, American and European, have warned of the danger. Secretaries of State John Foster Dulles and Dean Rusk, President John Kennedy, and three recent British prime ministers have expressed their fears of the world danger of a race war that could originate in Africa. Powerful nations may have to put increasing pressure upon the Republic of South Africa, Rhodesia, and Portugal.

U.N. Forces in the Belgian Congo, 1960

8. Independence for Belgian and Spanish Colonies

Republic of the Congo: Formerly the Belgian Congo

Unlike the British and French policies of limited native participation in colonial government, the Belgians denied any participation in government, not only to Africans but also to Belgians living in the Belgian Congo, once the personal possession of Leopold II of Belgium.

The Congo, which contains 15,000,000 people and an area of 900,000 square miles, 80 times the size of Belgium, is as large as Western Europe and is potentially enormously rich; it has the largest reserves in the world of uranium, and vast resources of copper, manganese, tin, and palm oil. Katanga Province in the southeast contains the greatest mineral resources of the country.

The Belgian government, with large commercial interests in the Congo, based their colonial policy on paternalism and a comparatively high standard of living for the Africans. Natives were given good vocational training and social welfare benefits, but no freedom to form trade unions, and no participation whatever in government. Congolese people were not allowed to visit Europe for fear they might gain an education and learn ideas of nationalism and independence. The Belgian governor-general had complete authority to administer the Congo, and he was responsible for his activities to the Belgian government only. Officially, no color distinction existed, but actually whites and blacks were segregated in towns, and certain types of employment were open only to whites.

In 1957 world copper prices dropped, and unemployment increased markedly in the Belgian Congo. In that same year the British colony of the Gold Coast became the independent nation of Ghana, and in the French Congo, General de Gaulle was offering to that neighbor political rights which would clearly lead to self-government.

The Belgians planned to give self-government to the Africans "ultimately," but set no date, and generally talked in terms of decades. In 1958 Patrice Lumumba, a native of the Belgian Congo, organized a native party called the *Mouvement National Congolais*, the Congolese Nationalist Movement, and met with Nkrumah of Ghana and with other African nationalists at the All-African People's Conference in Accra, Ghana. Another Congolese leader, Joseph Kasavubu, who demanded immediate independence, was arrested and exiled to Belgium. Riots broke out which so fired demands for independence throughout the Congo that the scared Belgian authorities announced new reforms leading to independence.

The Belgian government, now concerned only with perpetuating their commercial profits, virtually deserted their people in the Congo by giving the Congolese universal suffrage, releasing Kasavubu, and announcing June 30, 1960, as independence day for the Belgian Congo.

This complete abdication of any responsibility for training the Africans in self-government led to utter chaos. Belgian administrators, magistrates and professional people fled the country and left it without any Africans trained to take over this vast region. Since thc Africans had never been taught to think of themselves as responsible for their own future, they had not the vaguest conception of being a nation of people who must work together for a common objective. The country collapsed into tribal rivalries, and the only potential leaders in sight quarreled over what type of government should be set up. Lumumba wanted a single unified state, while Kasavubu preferred a federation of the several regions. In the meantime, Moise Tshombe set up a separate state of Katanga, the mining region which could provide two-thirds of the country's revenue. Not unexpectedly, he was backed up by the powerful and rich mining corporation, the Union Minière, which cared little about what happened to the Congo so long as its commercial interests were safeguarded.

Mutiny broke out in the Congolese armed forces, Tshombe was accused of murdering his prisoner Lumumba, the economy of the country collapsed, and thousands of Africans died from starvation. To bring some kind of order to the country, the United Nations sent in troops representing 15 nations, together with technical and economic aid. The United Nations was bitterly attacked by other African states for interfering in what they called a local problem, while the Soviet Union tried to extend the Cold War into Africa. For years various leaders and groups struggled for supremacy, and only recently did General Mobutu, with army support, take all power from an ineffectual parliament, and assume virtual dictatorial power in an attempt to give the Republic of the Congo some base for stability.

In the fall of 1971 the president changed the name of his country back to Zaïre, the name by which the Congo river was formerly known. Zaïre is a variant of the Bantu word *nzari*, meaning river. In the sixteenth and seventeenth centuries the powerful Kingdom of the Congo controlled both banks of the lower river and gave it the name Congo.

In the spring of 1972 President Joseph-Désiré Mobutu "unchristianized" his name to Mobutu Sese Seko, and forbade any priest, under the threat of imprisonment, to baptize a Zaïrois child with a Christian name.

Former Belgian Colonies: Rwanda and Burundi

Before World War I the land of Ruanda-Urundi belonged to Germany, but in 1919 was made a mandate of Belgium. The Watusi and the Bahutu are the two main tribes inhabiting the area, and the Bahutu, although more numerous, have traditionally been the servants of the tall, proud Watusi. Opinion about independence was divided, because while the Watusi looked toward independence, the Bahutu tribe preferred the protection of the Belgians until they could be assured of self-rule and the end of Watusi domination.

In February 1961 the Bahutu in Ruanda, the northern section, revolted against the Watusi.

On July 1, 1962, the Belgians divided the land into two nations and gave them independence as the Republic of Rwanda, and the Kingdom of Burundi. The change in both names was an attempt to forget colonial days. Unfortunately for the future of the two small nations, internal dissension has torn them both. The Bahutus of Rwanda massacred thousands of Watusi, with the result that some 150,000 Watusi fled to neighboring countries.

Tensions erupted into tragedy again in April 1972, when the Bahutus of about 3,000,000, or 85 percent of the total population, rebelled once again. In the countryside the Bahutus deliberately killed and disemboweled pregnant Watusi women. The estimates were that 10,000 Watusi were slaughtered.

Watusi revenge was merciless. Bahutus were rounded up and shot, bayoneted, or beaten to death, with deliberate elimination of educated Bahutus and even their young sons, who were dragged out of school to be massacred. The Burundi government admits to 80,000 deaths in the tribal conflict; United Nations reports estimate 200,000 killed, nearly one-sixth of the population.

Equatorial Guinea: Former Spanish Colony

In October 1968 two small pieces of territory just south of the bulge of West Africa became independent of Spanish rule. The island of Fernando Póo, popularly known as "Nanny Poo," and a thin slice of mainland territory called Río Muni, became the world's 133rd independent nation as the Republic of Equatorial Guinea. Whether its future will be peaceful is problematical. The 200,000 inhabitants of Río Muni are the illiterate and poverty-stricken Fang tribe, whereas the 15,000 Bubis of Fernando Póo enjoy the highest literacy rate in Black Africa, and a relatively high standard of living.

But with a Fang president the future of the minority Bubis looks rather bleak. Even before independence the Fang-dominated provisional government spent a year's budget in celebration of freedom. Why Spain gave freedom to this possession is not certain, but it has been suggested that she hoped to obtain Black Africa's support in her demands to get Gibraltar back from Britain.

9. Problems of New African Nations

Leaders of many Black African nations have faced and will face similar basic problems. In the days of colonial dependency, the right to be independent was necessarily the greatest issue to African people. African leaders who suffered imprisonment or other penalties at the hands of colonial administrators were heroes. But opposition to colonial rule may not necessarily qualify a man to be a constructive leader of a young nation which faces almost insoluble difficulties.

Nationhood and Tribal Loyalties

One of the common problems is the need to channel tribal loyalties into the building of a nation-state. To be successful in such a task, the new government must offer more than mere symbols of nationhood – a flag, a national anthem, and the other outward trappings of independence. It must offer a life that is better in every respect than tribal life, and ideas that rise above local tribal loyalties.

Education

Education can be an expensive investment for the future, but it is a necessary one for any nation that hopes to improve the condition of

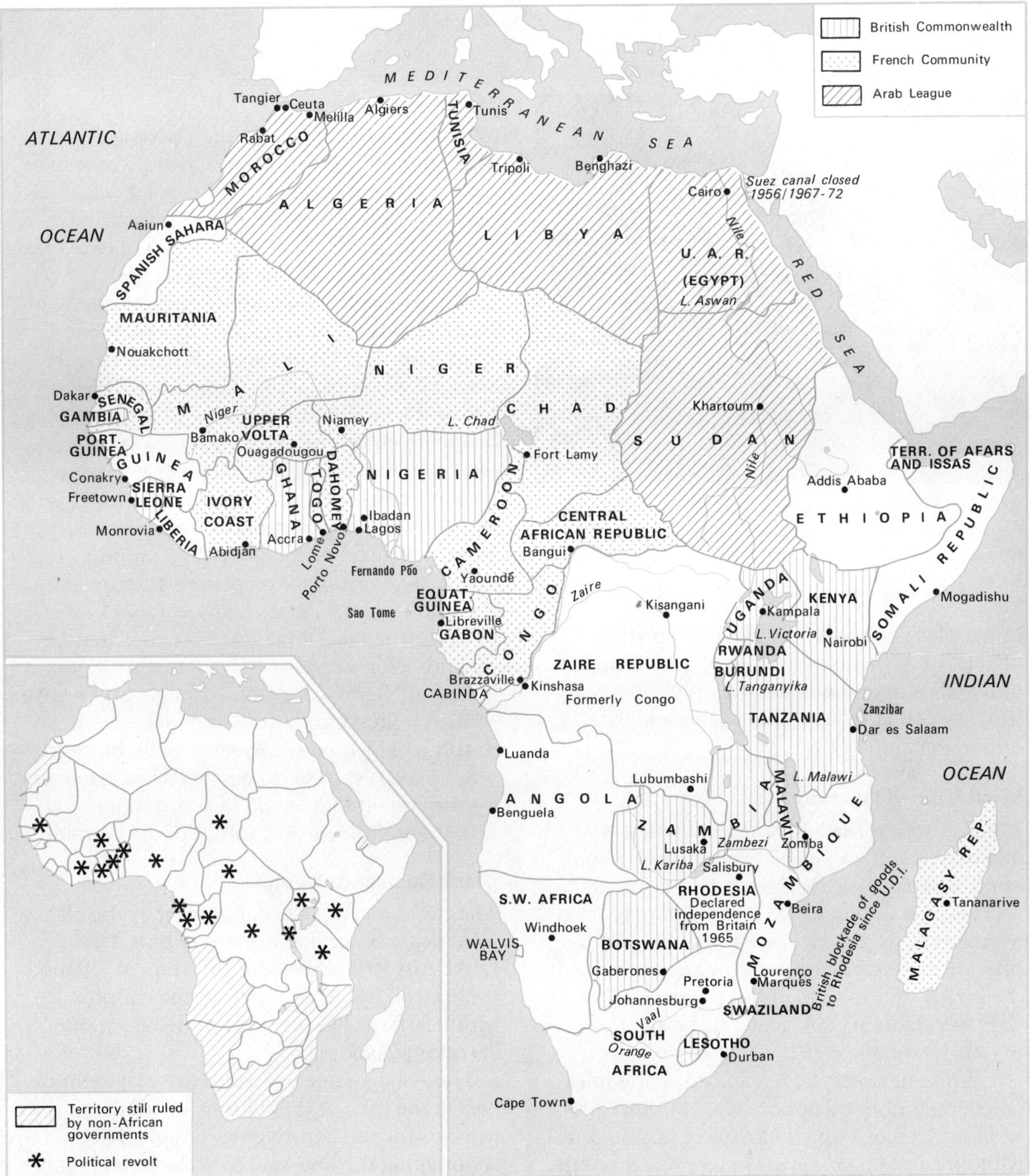
British Commonwealth
French Community
Arab League
MEDITERRANEAN SEA
ATLANTIC
OCEAN
INDIAN
OCEAN
RED SEA
Tangier
Ceuta
Melilla
Algiers
Tunis
Rabat
MOROCCO
TUNISIA
Tripoli
Benghazi
Cairo
Suez canal closed 1956/1967-72
ALGERIA
LIBYA
Aaiun
SPANISH SAHARA
U. A. R. (EGYPT)
L. Aswan
Nile
MAURITANIA
Nouakchott
MALI
NIGER
Dakar
SENEGAL
GAMBIA
PORT. GUINEA
Niger
UPPER VOLTA
Bamako
Ouagadougou
Niamey
L. Chad
CHAD
Khartoum
SUDAN
GUINEA
Conakry
SIERRA LEONE
Freetown
LIBERIA
Monrovia
IVORY COAST
Abidjan
GHANA
Accra
TOGO
Lome
DAHOMEY
Porto Novo
NIGERIA
Ibadan
Lagos
Fort Lamy
TERR. OF AFARS AND ISSAS
Addis Ababa
ETHIOPIA
SOMALI REPUBLIC
Mogadishu
CAMEROON
Yaounde
Fernando Poo
CENTRAL AFRICAN REPUBLIC
Bangui
EQUAT. GUINEA
Sao Tome
Libreville
GABON
CONGO
Zaire
Kisangani
UGANDA
Kampala
KENYA
L. Victoria
Nairobi
RWANDA
BURUNDI
L. Tanganyika
ZAIRE REPUBLIC
Formerly Congo
Brazzaville
Kinshasa
CABINDA
TANZANIA
Zanzibar
Dar es Salaam
Luanda
Lubumbashi
L. Malawi
ANGOLA
Benguela
ZAMBIA
Lusaka
Zambezi
L. Kariba
MALAWI
Zomba
MOZAMBIQUE
Salisbury
RHODESIA
Declared independence from Britain 1965
Beira
S.W. AFRICA
Windhoek
WALVIS BAY
BOTSWANA
Gaberones
Pretoria
Johannesburg
Lourenço Marques
SWAZILAND
British blockade of goods to Rhodesia since U.D.I.
MALAGASY REP.
Tananarive
Vaal
SOUTH AFRICA
Orange
LESOTHO
Durban
Cape Town
Territory still ruled by non-African governments
Political revolt

Africa, 1972

Africa and Democracy. A traveling team instructing natives of the Gold Coast in 1954 in the methods of voting.

its people. The hundreds of languages and dialects of Africa are a barrier to communication and co-operation, and they must give way to a very few languages that can be widely understood.

What Kind of Government?

Another widespread difficulty is a political one of government. Can inexperienced people effectively exercise the rights of democracy?

Can a new nation which is struggling to train technicians, find money, start new industries, provide more jobs, and feed the people, afford the luxury of opposing political parties? Can they risk changing governments before the new nation gets on its feet? It is easy to denounce African leaders who have silenced, sometimes jailed, their political opponents, but there may be basic decisions which have to be acted upon without constant criticism from political groups. The distinction between helpful and destructive criticism is sometimes a very difficult one to determine.

Mutinies and Revolts

When leaders fail to keep their promises—and frequently these can be too grandiose to be practicable—there may be internal dissatisfaction. In 1959, on the eve of Nigeria's independence, the Duke of Gloucester said to its leaders, "The future may not be easy. You have a heavy task before you." During the next decade 30 of Black Africa's nations gained independence, 15 in 1960, and 15 subsequently. That decade saw civil wars ravage the Congo and Nigeria, two of the largest and potentially richest African countries, and serious disturbances or military *coups* in more than 25 of them. Governments were overthrown in the Central African Republic, both the Congo republics, Dahomey, Ghana, Nigeria, and Upper Volta; mutinies and anti-government plots were attempted in Burundi, Chad, Gabon, Guinea, Ivory Coast, Kenya, Senegal, Tanganyika, Togo, Uganda and others. Four African leaders were assassinated in Nigeria, Togo, the Congo, and Kenya.

Such military takeovers were not necessarily simply a bid for power by army men, but sometimes were responses to demands by citizens for a government that would be more concerned with the well-being and future of the people.

Black Racism in Uganda

The racial intolerance denounced by the blacks of Africa is becoming evident in East Africa. In August 1972, President Idi Amin of Uganda ordered 55,000 Asians to leave the country within 90 days, because they were, he announced, "economic saboteurs."

The Asians came to East Africa in large numbers at the turn of the century as railroad workers for the British government. They set up shops along the line, and over the years became the merchants, traders, money lenders, and professional people of East Africa. In Uganda, up to August 1972, some 90 percent of the

Ugandan Asian Refugee. A young girl arriving in London with her two dolls—African and Western.

businesses were owned by Asians, whose economic success, general arrogance toward the natives, and their social and political aloofness earned them the enmity and envy of the blacks.

When Uganda gained its independence in 1962, the Asians were offered the choice of Ugandan citizenship or British passports. Many thousands chose the latter because British passports entitled them to live in England if they chose to do so at a later date.

In 1968 the Labour Government, responding to public discontent at increasing immigration from Jamaica and Asian Commonwealth nations, introduced the restrictive immigration policy which removed from the holder of a British passport the automatic right to enter and live in Britain. Instead, the British government issued "vouchers" to heads of families allowing them and their families to enter Britain. For 1972 the quota was set at 5,000 vouchers, with a future annual rate of 3,500. Uganda's action opened an issue which may have serious political consequences in England.

There are estimated to be 150,000 Asians in Uganda, Kenya, Tanzania, and other East African countries who were offered and accepted British passports when those colonies achieved independence. Kenya and Tanzania closed their doors against Asians expelled by Uganda. If the anti-Asian policy spreads, there may be expulsion also for some of the 140,000 Asians in Kenya, the 75,000 in Tanzania, the 10,000 in Malawi, and the 4,000 in Zambia.

Britain was immediately faced with what could become a serious crisis for any government which relaxes the immigration laws. There are already 1,500,000 Indians, Pakistanis, and Jamaicans in England, and they are generally resented in the towns where they live. Britain has nearly 1,000,000 unemployed, a housing shortage that has existed since the last war, overcrowded schools, and increasing costs for local welfare.

The Asians ordered to leave Uganda have had to sell their property in a hurry for what they could get; some arriving in England have reported that they were not allowed to take any money out of Uganda. The threat of a sudden influx into England of destitute people, without resources or jobs, dependent upon local or national welfare, and without homes has already raised public opposition to letting down the present immigration bars. The British government is caught between the moral obligation to honor the 1962 promise to admit holders of British passports, and the rising tide of public opposition.

President Amin followed his expulsion order with the threat to seize all foreign businesses in Uganda, including British, and decreed that all Asians expelled from Uganda must leave on a government-owned airline or by planes chartered from other lines, subject to the approval of the Uganda government.

The effects on Uganda may be more serious than the government realizes, because nearly all the lawyers, doctors, architects, hotel operators, and food distributors are Asians. Of the 25,000 Asians who are Uganda's citizens, many are leaving because they fear the anti-Asian mood which is spreading throughout East Africa.

Attempts at Regional Organization

Because several of the geographical frontiers have no relation to boundaries which are left over from colonial days tribal locations, some African nations have attempted either to unite or form regional federations and at the same time consider common economic and defense problems. Ghana and Guinea; the Senegal and Sudan republics; and the so-called Casablanca Group that included Algeria, Ghana, Guinea, and Mali, are examples which were attempted but proved unsuccessful.

One grouping has broader aims than others. The Organization of African Unity, OAU, includes in its objectives economic, educational, and defense co-operation, as well as liberation of African territories under white rule.

Need for Capital Investment

The most urgent, and probably the most difficult, problem is the need to raise the standard of living in nations that can acquire only very limited "savings," either in surplus goods to sell for money, or in labor that can be taken out of the fields and placed in more productive jobs to make goods to sell abroad. African nations must attract foreign investments and loans if they are to industrialize and raise the standard of living. But because they are only recently freed from colonial rule, they are afraid that foreign investors will influence their politics, and through economic influence try to run the African nations. This is what the Africans mean when they speak of neo, or new, colonialism.

Some leaders of African nations believe that they cannot afford completely free enterprise methods for their industries. They are in a hurry to develop their countries, and they believe that their governments must carefully plan and own industries, directly using socialist principles.

Although they have attained the independence to manage their own affairs, these young African nations will doubtless face difficult challenges ahead.

10. Other New African Nations

Former French Colonies

Republic of Cameroon. After World War I the German colony of Kamerun was divided into the mandates of British Cameroons and French Cameroun. In 1960 the French mandated area became independent, and after a plebiscite was held in British Cameroons in 1961, the northern part chose to be joined with Nigeria, and the southern part to Cameroun. The republic has a population of about 4,600,000.

Central African Republic. This is the new name for the former colony called Ubangi-Shari. Made independent in 1960, this nation of 1,300,000 was taken over by a military *coup* in late 1966.

Republic of Chad. This country, about the size of Alaska, is a completely rural nation, with a portion of its territory in the Sahara and Libyan Deserts. Its population is about 3,000,000.

Congo (Brazzaville) Republic. To distinguish this former French colony of the Congo from the Belgian Congo (which is now the Republic of the Congo), the name of its capital is frequently given. With a population of 840,000, it is chiefly agricultural, although an oil field is under development.

Republic of Dahomey. With a population of 2,000,000 people, this small country of only 32,000 square miles, is only 77 miles wide, with an economy based on palm oil, cotton, tobacco, and coffee. In 1965 the civilian government was overthrown by a military *coup.*

Republic of Gabon. A country of about 500,000 people, it is perhaps best known as the African home of Dr. Albert Schweitzer, who built a hospital at Lambaréné and worked there for more than 50 years until his death in 1965 at the age of 90. Its chief exports are forest products, and iron ore deposits, oil, gold, and manganese.

Republic of Ivory Coast. This republic of nearly 4,000,000 is economically stronger than most of France's former West African colonies. It has maintained close relationships with France through Félix Houphouët-Boigny, its first President, and has been favored with a considerable amount of French assistance. Its capital of Abidjan is one of the fastest-growing cities in Africa, and is known for its very handsome presidential palace which the French presented to the Ivory Coast. Its economy is essentially agricultural, with cotton, rice, cocoa, coffee, and lumber its chief products.

Malagasy Republic. Formerly known as Madagascar, this island, the fourth largest in the world, is roughly 250,000 square miles in size, with a population of over 6,000,000, who are a mixture of Africans, Arabs, Malayans, and Melanesians. In late 1958 the island's local assembly announced the existence of La République Malgache within the French Community. In July 1960 the republic announced its complete independence. Vanilla, pepper, and cloves are its main crops.

Republic of Mali. Originally called the French Sudan, then the Sudanese Republic, the nation of Mali, like Niger and the Upper Volta, is landlocked. Much of its land is desert, and its chief crop is peanuts. Only through arrangement with Senegal can Mali have access to salt-water ports. Twice the size of France, it has a population of over 4,000,000, of whom the majority are Moslems.

Several cities of the ancient empires of Mali and Songhai are located here, but are today of little importance. The fabled Timbuktu, once the terminus of great caravan routes across North Africa, is today only a small town of a few thousand people.

Two unsuccessful attempts at federation were made by Mali, one with Senegal, Dahomey, and others, to form the Mali Federation; the other was a proposal for federation with Ghana and Guinea to form the Union of African States. But unity among African nations has had no positive success so far.

Republic of Mauritania. Because Mauritania is largely within the Sahara Desert, the government has encouraged the people to make the sea an important means of their livelihood. Recent finds of copper veins may help to industrialize the economy of the people, who have been nomads and simple farmers.

Republic of Niger. Completely landlocked, the Republic of Niger hopes that the nations which are drained by the Niger River can control and develop its waters. The country has a population of 3,000,000, is 500,000 square miles in extent, and is dependent upon agricultural products.

Republic of Senegal. Senegal's population of about 3,500,000 are dependent upon cattle raising and upon its peanut crop, which is the largest in the world. Its large phosphate deposits, and its plans to develop the Senegal River valley may help to diversify the economy.

Republic of Togo. After World War I the German colony of Togoland was divided into two parts and given back as mandates under the League of Nations to Great Britain and France. In 1958 British Togoland determined by plebiscite to become part of the state of Ghana. In 1960 the French section of Togoland became the independent republic of Togo, with a population of fewer than 2,000,000 dependent on coffee, manioc, and cocoa.

Togo and Ghana have one cause of friction that could cause future trouble between them. Almost 500,000 of the Ewe tribe live in Ghana, and another 500,000 in Togo, a clear example of a geographical frontier that cuts across tribal loyalties.

Republic of Upper Volta. Named after the Volta River, this new republic is an agriculturally poor and landlocked nation of nearly 5,000,000 people dependent upon farming and grazing.

Other Former British Colonies

Republic of Sudan. The Sudan poses the problem of a white and black nation roughly divided between white Arabic Moslems in the north, and Negro Animists in the south. Great Britain moved into Egypt in 1882, and took over the Sudan, which then was officially ruled by both nations as the Anglo-Egyptian Sudan, although in fact it was ruled by Britain. Since independence in 1956 it has suffered continually from internal strife, largely because the northern Arabs treated the southern section of the country as a colony.

The Sudan is about one quarter the size of Europe, is mostly agricultural, and is highly dependent upon a cotton crop which competes on the world market. Like Egypt, the Sudan depends heavily upon the Nile River.

Seventeen years of fighting between the 4,000,000 Blacks of the south and the 11,000,000 Arabs of the north apparently ended in 1972 with the signing of a compromise agreement. The peace may be an uneasy one after so many years of bitterness and ruthless killing of blacks, but both sides have recognized that they must live together.

Republic of Somali. Before World War II the three nations Great Britain, France, and Italy held pieces of territory in what is called the Horn of Africa. After World War II Italian Somaliland was placed under United Nations control. In 1960 British Somalia was joined with former Italian Somaliland to form the independent republic of Somali. The people are dark-skinned non-Negro Moslems who claim for their nation *Somalia irredenta* or "unredeemed Somalia" which lies inside both Ethiopia and Kenya. Consequently, border disputes between Somali and the other two nations have continued since independence.

French Somaliland still remains under French rule as "overseas territory." Its one claim to notice is the port of Djibouti, which is connected to Addis Ababa, the capital of Ethiopia, by 400 miles of railroad.

Uganda. Uganda produces a large cotton crop, coffee, tea, peanuts, and tin. Its great lake area, part of Lake Victoria Nyanza, and lakes Kioga, Albert, and George, could provide hydroelectric power for Uganda and its neighbors. Its 7,000,000 people became independent from Great Britain in 1962, and have suffered the problems of struggles for power between rivals seeking leadership. (*See* p. 36.)

The Gambia. The Gambia is a narrow tongue of land, twenty miles at its widest point, stretching for two hundred miles along the Gambia River, on the western "bulge" of Africa. Its total population of 400,000 depends chiefly upon peanuts, which account for 95 percent of its exports. In 1965 it became a fully independent member of the Commonwealth, and in 1970 asserted its separate identity by proclaiming itself a republic named The Gambia.

Botswana, Lesotho, and Swaziland. These three countries became independent in the years after 1965. Botswana was formerly the British possession of Bechuanaland, lying between the Republic of South Africa and Rhodesia. Lesotho was the former British possession of Basutoland, which is completely surrounded by the Republic of South Africa. Swaziland, home of the Swazi people, retains the name it had as a British possession.

Botswana is the largest of the three, but can support only a limited population because much of it is part of the Kalahari Desert. Drought and unemployment obliged great numbers of its people to look for jobs in the Republic of South Africa, where they are denied the very rights they had won for themselves at home.

King Seretse Khama with his English wife. He was prime minister in 1965.

In 1957 Botswana, or Bechuanaland as it was then called, was much in the news. Its young King Seretse Khama, while still under British jurisdiction, visited England, fell in love with an English girl and married her. The British government, disturbed by the great outcry from the adjacent Republic of South Africa, kept the married couple in exile for seven years. The British were forced to allow Seretse Khama to return to Bechuanaland because its people would accept no other king. In 1960 Seretse gave up his throne, formed a political party, and won the election. When the colony of Bechuanaland became the independent nation of Botswana, its first Prime Minister was Seretse Khama.

Lesotho, meaning Lowlands, is the former British protectorate of Basutoland. Offered independence by the British in 1965, it preferred to postpone it until October 1966. Unfortunately, it immediately ran into difficulties. The 2,000 tribal chiefs owed allegiance to Paramount Chief Moshoeshoe, who became King Moshoeshoe as a constitutional monarch. However, he wanted more power than he received, and demanded control of the police, the army, and foreign affairs. Prime Minister Leabua Jonathan placed the King under "protective custody" in December 1966. Moshoeshoe was freed from house arrest in March 1968. Lesotho's pastoral population of 550,000 people depend entirely upon rainfall for their well-being.

Swaziland was the last of the British dependencies in Africa to receive its independence. In September 1968 it became a constitutional monarchy under King Sobhuza II, the second smallest sovereign state in Africa. About 90 percent of its people are of the Swazi tribe, and are now producing iron ore and asbestos in large amounts.

Name	Date of Independence	Form of Government	Former Name	Former Colonial Power
		Nations of Sub-Sahara Africa		
Botswana	1966	Republic	Bechuanaland	Great Britain
Burundi	1962	Kingdom	Ruanda-Urundi	Belgium
Cameroon	1962	Republic	French Cameroun	France
Central African Republic	1960	Republic	French Equatorial Africa	France
Chad	1960	Republic	French West Africa	France
Congo (Brazzaville) Republic	1960	Republic	French Congo	France
Dahomey	1960	Republic	Dahomey	France
Equatorial Guinea	1968	Republic	Fernando Póo and Río Muni	Spain
Gabon	1960	Republic	Gabon	France
The Gambia	1965	Republic	Gambia	Great Britain
Ghana	1957	Republic	Gold Coast	Great Britain
Guinea	1958	Republic	French Guinea	France
Ivory Coast	1960	Republic	French Ivory Coast	France
Kenya	1963	Republic	Kenya	Great Britain
Lesotho	1966	Kingdom	Basutoland	Great Britain
Malagasy	1963	Republic	Madagascar	France
Malawi	1964	Republic	Nyasaland	Great Britain
Mali	1960	Republic	French Sudan	France
Mauritania	1960	Republic	French West Africa	France
Niger	1960	Republic	Niger	France
Nigeria	1960	Republic	Nigeria	Great Britain
*Rhodesia	1965	Republic	Southern Rhodesia	Great Britain
Rwanda	1962	Republic	Ruanda-Urundi	Belgium
Senegal	1960	Republic	Senegal	France
Sierra Leone	1961	Republic	Sierra Leone	Great Britain
Somali Republic or Somalia	1960	Republic	British and Italian Somaliland	Great Britain and Italy
Sudan	1956	Republic	Anglo-Egyptian Sudan	Great Britain and Egypt

*Rhodesia illegally declared itself to be an independent nation in 1965 (*see* p. 29).

Name	Date of Independence	Form of Government	Former Name	Former Colonial Power
Swaziland	1968	Kingdom	Swaziland	Great Britain
Tanzania	1961	Republic	Tanganyika and Zanzibar	Great Britain
Togo	1960	Republic	Togoland	France
Uganda	1962	Republic	Uganda	Great Britain
Upper Volta	1960	Republic	French Sudan	France
Zaïre	1960	Republic	Belgian Congo, Republic of the Congo	Belgium
Zambia	1964	Republic	Northern Rhodesia	Great Britain
Liberia	1847	Republic	Settlement founded in 1822	
Republic of South Africa	1961	Republic	Union of South Africa	Member of Commonwealth of Nations
Nations of North Africa				
Algeria	1962	Republic	French Algeria	France
Egypt (United Arab Republic)	1956	Republic	Egypt (Monarchy)	
Ethiopia		Kingdom	Emperor Haile Selassie reputed to be 225th consecutive ruler.	
Libya	1951	Kingdom	Italian Libya	Italy
Morocco	1956	Kingdom	French and Spanish Morocco	France and Spain
Tunisia	1956	Republic	Tunisia	France

Review Questions

Section 1

1. Why can the continent of Africa, although limited in physical power, exercise influence in world affairs?
2. What have been some common misconceptions about Africa?
3. In what ways has geography hindered the development of Africa?
4. Why should Islam be more popular than Christianity in Africa?

Section 2

5. What was the effect of the migration of people who had once lived in the fertile Sahara period?
6. What evidences are there that early African kingdoms were civilized?
7. Were white men solely responsible for the slave trade in Africa?
8. On what basis can white men be criticized for the institution of slavery?
9. Was the "new imperialism" of the 19th century better or worse than the slave trade and slavery? Why?

Section 3

10. How did Tunisia and Morocco win independence?
11. How was the issue of independence for Algeria complicated by special French interests?
12. What did the trouble in Africa have to do with the establishing of the Fifth Republic in France?
13. Why was Algerian independence delayed for several years after the FLN declared itself to be the Provisional Government of the Algerian Republic?
14. Why did Algeria experience stormy years after its independence in 1962?

Sections 4 and 5

15. What was the French Community?
16. Why was Kwame Nkrumah an important personality in the issue of African independence?
17. What have been the causes of instability in Nigeria ever since its independence?
18. Why did other African nations seem to avoid interference in the Biafra-Nigeria controversy?

Section 6

19. Why has the Great Trek become symbolic to the Afrikaners today?
20. By what series of events did the two independent Boer Republics become members of the British Empire?
21. What is the purpose of apartheid, and how does it operate? Does it give the African natives "separate but equal" treatment?
22. Does the Republic of South Africa give to all white citizens all the rights of a democratic society?

Sections 7 and 8

23. Why did Britain form the Central African Federation? Why did the Federation dissolve ten years later?
24. What problems do Rhodesia, Mozambique, Angola, and the policy of apartheid present today?
25. Despite the fact that the Africans in the Belgian Congo had a relatively high standard of living under Belgian rule, they revolted. Why was this?

Sections 9 and 10

26. What problems are facing new African nations today? Give examples of African nations that have experienced some of these problems.

2

Latin America: The Growth of Nationalism

The independence of the former Spanish colonies of Central and South America was won by the people themselves. European threats to interfere in Latin America, perhaps to win the former colonies back for Spain, led the United States to declare its Monroe Doctrine of "hands off" the Western hemisphere. Subsequent intervention by European powers in Venezuela in the late 1800's resulted in the Roosevelt Corollary to the Doctrine which in effect made the United States the self-appointed policeman of Latin America. Intervention by the United States in their internal affairs caused resentment in Latin America, and led to the attempt of the United States to implement the "good neighbor" policy of President Franklin Roosevelt.

The attempt of the Soviet Union to arm Castro's Cuba with nuclear missiles obliged the United States to intervene, but with criticism from some Latin American countries suspicious of the intentions of their powerful neighbor.

Faced with the Dominican crisis of 1965, presumed to be a threatened Communist take-over in the Caribbean, the Johnson Administration sent in United States forces to intervene. The action seemed to be justified when the Organization of American States supplied a joint military force, the first such action in Latin American history.

The serious economic and social problems of Latin America were recognized in the initiation of the Alliance For Progress, an only-partially successful co-operative enterprise to resolve basic economic problems.

Terms

1. Savanna
2. Llano
3. Pampas
4. Mulatto
5. Mestizo
6. Creole
7. Peninsulares
8. Fazenda
9. Cabildo
10. Hacienda
11. Roosevelt Corollary
12. Clark Memorandum
13. Good Neighbor Policy
14. Act of Havana, 1940
15. Rio de Janeiro Conference, 1947
16. Bogota Conference, 1948
17. Organization of American States, OAS
18. Alliance For Progress
19. Favella

People

20. Toussaint L'Ouverture
21. Henri Christophe
22. Simón Bolívar
23. Francisco de Miranda
24. José de San Martín
25. José de Sucre
26. Juan Perón
27. Fulgencio Batista
28. Fidel Castro
29. Rafael Trujillo
30. Juan Bosch
31. Wessin y Wessin
32. Col. Imbert
33. Salvadore Allende

Places

34. Andes Mountains
35. Great Escarpment
36. Orinoco River
37. Magdalena River
38. Amazon River
39. La Plata River
40. Yucatan Peninsula
41. Hispaniola
42. St. Augustine
43. Venezuela
44. Chile
45. Viceroyalties of:
    Peru
    New Granada
    La Plata
    New Spain

Events

1504 Founding of Santo Domingo
1521 Conquest of Mexico by Cortes
1527 Conquest of Peru by Pizarro
1550 Viceroyalties of Peru, New Granada, La Plata, New Spain
1565 Permanent Settlement of St. Augustine
1810 Revolts in Spanish America
1824 Battle of Ayacucho: End of Spanish Empire in South America
1889 Republic of Brazil established
1904 Roosevelt Corollary
1930 Clark Memorandum
1947 Inter-American Treaty for Continental Defense
1948 Organization of American States
1959 Batista ousted by Castro
1961 Alliance For Progress
1962 Cuban Missile crisis
1964 Boycott of Cuba by OAS
1965 Intervention in Dominican Republic by the U.S.A. and OAS

1. The Land and the People

Geography: The Land

The modern twenty-four independent countries of Latin America occupy an area almost three times that of the United States, and reach nearly 6,000 miles from the Texas border to Cape Horn, and nearly 3,000 miles across from Ecuador to the coast of Brazil. This vast expanse of land contains some of the richest natural resources of the world, but their full development is hampered by the geography of the South American continent. The history of South America has been greatly influenced by geography because in the past the continent has been isolated from the rest of the world, and the regions of the continent have been separated from each other.

The west coast has the "backbone" of the Andes Mountains which run without break for 4,500 miles from Venezuela to the southern tip of Chile, and stretch east and west from 120 to 500 miles. Dozens of peaks rise above 16,000 feet and make communications from the west coast to the east very difficult. Mountain passes through the Andes are little more than simple means of communication, and there are not yet highways across the continent. The Andes, descending almost directly to the sea, leave the countries along the Pacific Ocean with only a narrow coastal strip which offers only a very few good harbors.

The Atlantic coast is better than the west but it is also affected by the "Great Escarpment" of a steep mountain range and plateau that runs southward for 1,700 miles, almost the total length of Brazil and descends sharply into the sea.

Important to social and economic development of South America are the vast plains which comprise about three-fifths of the land area of the continent, and the river system which includes some of the largest rivers in the world. Inland from the Atlantic coast are the great low-lying fertile areas, each served by great rivers. To the north are the tropical grasslands, the *savannas* of the Orinoco valley, and the *llanos*, plains, of Venezuela. South of these are the wet forests of Brazil that merge into the vast pampas region of southern Brazil and Argentina. These are the great treeless, grassy plains, stretching nearly 1,000 miles at the widest point, that start in Brazil's southern province of Rio Grande do Sul, and reach southward to Patagonia. This region is one of the greatest pasture areas in the world, producing great supplies of beef, mutton, wheat, corn, and cotton for Europe.

The rivers of South America are important because they have provided highways into the interior. In the north the Orinoco River drains the great plains for 1,700 miles but it has proved of little use because of its serious flooding in the rainy season. The Magdalena River has been Colombia's highway into the interior for 600 miles, carrying most of the nation's freight from the harbors of Cartagena and Barranquilla up river.

The largest river and river system in the world is the Amazon, 4,000 miles long, draining a river basin of 2,750,000 square miles, with 40,000 miles of navigable waters. Three thousand miles from the Atlantic the tributaries begin to meet, until the Amazon is eight miles wide before it has flowed more than a quarter of its length. The Amazon Basin comprises half of the territory of Brazil, Venezuela, Colombia, Ecuador, Peru, Bolivia, and Paraguay, but the rains are so heavy that they leach the soil and make it unproductive for agriculture.

To the south the La Plata River estuary and its great tributaries the Uruguay and the Paraná Rivers drain the basin which includes parts of Argentina, Uruguay, Paraguay, Bolivia, and Brazil.

South America. Physical and economic features.

The People

The people of Latin America are made up of three main groups, the Indians, the whites, and the Negroes. The Indians, descendants of the Mayan, Aztec, and Inca Civilizations, number roughly 30,000,000, about one-seventh of the total population, ranging from 12 percent in Mexico to less than 1 percent in Argentina, Chile, and other countries. The Indians have never accepted the white man's civilization, and despite more than four centuries of exposure to European customs and ideas they have deliberately refused to be assimilated. This is an extraordinary phenomenon in man's history.

The Negroes were brought in because the Spanish and Portuguese authorities were not only unable to enslave the Indians and use them on the plantations but treated them with such severity that they simply resisted passively and died off in great numbers. Madrid and Lisbon remedied this shortage by deciding to import slaves from Africa; they then found them to be better plantation workers, physically sturdier than the Indians and able to be assimilated. Today the largest concentrations of Negroes are in Haiti, where they are the vast majority of the population, and in the Dominican Republic, Brazil, Colombia, and Cuba. The children of intermarriage between Negroes and whites are *mulattos*, and of intermarriage between Negroes and Indians are *zambos*. Negroes have played important roles in Latin American politics, economics, and cultures.

The often-repeated legend that slavery was introduced to the Americas when a Dutch ship sold slaves to Virginia in 1619 is incorrect. The first slaves were taken from Africa to Cuba in 1512. By 1550 there were thousands in the West Indies and in the Portuguese colony of Brazil. The tragedy of slavery is that slave-traders deliberately labeled Africans as savages, as an excuse for their inhuman trade. This they by no means were, because in Africa they had formed their own complex societies to suit their needs and their natural surroundings. Several ancient African kingdoms were highly developed and wealthy (*see* Ch. 1). Negro slaves were brought into the New World simply as a convenient labor force, and because slave-trading was tolerated by civilized nations, the slave-trader was considered to be a businessman trading in goods. Not until the 19th century was European society to disapprove of this "peculiar institution," as it was sometimes conveniently called.

The Negro in Latin America was able to make a greater contribution than the Negro in North America because he had some rights, even though he was a slave. For centuries slavery had existed in Spain and Portugal, but there the slave had legal rights, he could buy his freedom and was not treated as a chattel or piece of property, as he was in North America. Although some slaves did win their freedom in North America, they were an anomaly or exception, and did not enjoy all the privileges and rights of the white man. The Negro brought to Latin America his various abilities and culture, especially in music and dancing and also his desire for freedom. In Brazil during the 17th century insurrectionary groups of Negro slaves organized their own Republic of Palmares, named after the great palm trees, and for more than sixty years some 20,000 Negroes ran their own government under a king, as an outstanding example of Negroes who, without encouragement or assistance, and in the face of great odds, could organize their own social order.

In the wars for independence in the early 19th century the Negroes contributed well-organized and well-disciplined troops who fought under Simón Bolívar and San Martín.

A well-known Negro was Toussaint L'Ouverture, who led a rebellion against the French in

Toussaint L'Ouverture

Haiti, where 500,000 Negroes were slaves, and helped it to win its independence in 1804. Henri Christophe, the uneducated slave, was a volunteer under Lafayette during the American Revolution, and after Haitian independence ruled the northern part of the island as Henri I.

In Brazil one of the greatest of Negro leaders was Jose de Patrocinio, the journalist and leader of the movement which brought about the abolition of slavery in Brazil in 1888.

The *mestizos*, children of European fathers and Indian women, have today taken over leadership, and play a dominant role in Latin America. They form a significant proportion of the population of Mexico, the nations of Central America, and those countries north of Brazil. In early colonial days these mixed marriages were legal, and the mestizos were people of ability and were admitted to the lesser offices in State and Church. They were a lower middle class group in general, composed of artisans, shopkeepers, and farm agents, and they became the majority of the population in towns and cities. Although by the end of the first century of colonial rule they suffered some social stigma, by 1800 mestizos were becoming an increasingly-important group and were ready to join the *creoles*, the descendants of Spanish people born in Latin America, and to fight for independence.

Europeans have played an important part in the development of Argentina, Brazil, Chile, Costa Rica, and Uruguay. The Spanish and Portuguese administrators and settlers were followed later by Italians, Germans, Portuguese, and smaller groups of other European stock. In more recent years Japanese have migrated to the South American continent. But Latin America has not attracted the number of Europeans it could easily absorb. The Spanish discouraged settlement of foreigners in their colonies, and conditions after the wars of independence did not attract settlers.

Several conditions discouraged people who could have helped to develop the continent: *the hacienda*, the self-contained agricultural community that resembled feudalism; the obvious instability of governments; the sharp social distinctions; and the lack of initiative in productive enterprises. European immigrants avoided Latin America just as they avoided the southern slave states because they could not compete with the Negro slave and the poor white in the South, or with Indian labor in South America.

2. Latin America Wins Independence

Conditions in Spanish America

Latin America is split into two parts—those countries whose people are descendants of the Spanish Colonies and those countries that developed out of the Portuguese Colonies. Today the language a country uses reflects this split (*see* Vol. I, Ch. 7 for an account of the development of the colonial empires).

By the end of the 18th century the approximately 15,000,000 people in Spanish America were sharply divided into racial and social groups. At the apex of the social scale were the *peninsulares*, those who came directly from Spain. They numbered about 300,000 and were the backbone of Spanish rule, and formed the ruling caste from which they almost completely excluded creoles who were Spaniards born in America. The peninsulares held all the offices in Church and State, in the universities and the army, and served as viceroys, captains-general, governors, judges, merchants, all of whom looked down upon colonial-born Spaniards.

Below them in the social scale were some 3,000,000 creoles, who owned the *haciendas*, or vast landed estates, and mines, and were the professional class of lawyers and doctors, and served in local political and judicial positions. They increasingly resented the discrimination shown by the peninsulares, and in time were to form the spearhead of action in the wars for independence.

Below them were 5,000,000 mestizos whose position by 1800 was that of belonging to neither the white nor the Indian society of which they were a mixture. The mestizo, an outcast in society, had been forced to live by his wits and to have no sense of loyalty to European rulers.

Below the mestizos were the 7,500,000 Indians who worked as servants, laborers, or lived apart in their own mountain and jungle communities. Although the system of forced labor for Indians had been abolished, many of them were obliged to seek work at pitifully low wages. The Indians still suffered the burden of hard labor because Negro slavery was less extensive in the Spanish colonies than in Brazil. It is estimated that of the 800,000 Negroes in Spanish America, one half of them were in Cuba and Puerto Rico. In fact, by the 18th century more than half the Negroes in Spanish America were free citizens.

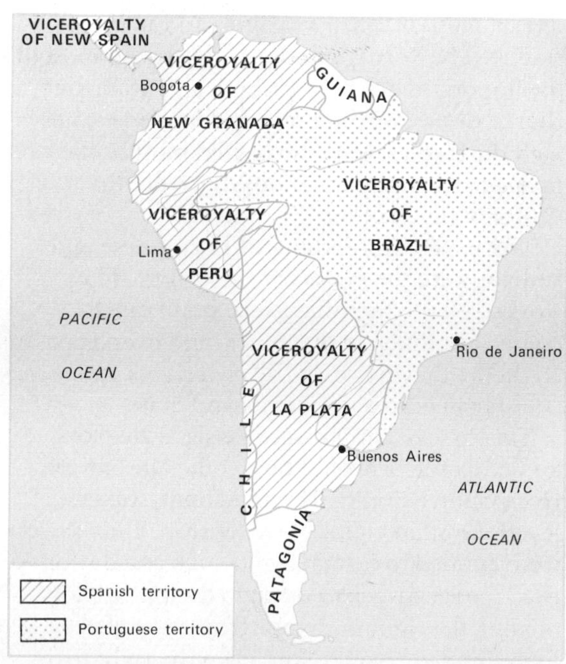

Colonial Latin America. *See* map on Central America.

Conditions in Portuguese America

The population of Brazil around 1800 was estimated to be 3,500,000, half of them Negroes. Although class distinctions were less pronounced than in Spanish America, the whites owned most of Brazil's wealth and ran the colony. The Portuguese-born controlled most of the important offices in Church and State, but shared ownership of mines and landed estates with the creoles, who also owned most of the *fazendas*, the vast plantations that were the center of much of the life of Brazil.

The mixed descendants of Portuguese and Indians were the *mamelucos* or *mestiças*. They worked on the fazendas, were small ranch-owners, foremen in the mines, and overseers. In theory they possessed all civil rights and could hold offices in Church and State.

Next in social order were ex-slave Negroes and mulattoes who, although officially barred from Church and civil employment, still enjoyed the other rights of citizenship. Even slaves were entitled to certain rights such as a day or two free each week to work on their own plots of land, the right to change from a cruel to a more humane master, and even the right to purchase their liberty.

Revolt in Spanish America

The grievances of creole, mestizo, and Indian against Spanish colonial rule, particularly against the draining away of profits from Latin America to pay for the extravagances of Madrid, were brought more sharply into focus by 18th century European ideas. Voltaire, Montesquieu, and Rousseau were read by colonists, and young creoles were particularly influenced by Rousseau's concept that governments should be based upon the consent of the governed. Young creoles also read the Declaration of Independence, heard about Franklin, Jefferson, and Paine, and learned about Lexington and Concord and the success of the American Revolutionists.

The French Revolution, following so closely upon the American Revolution, further excited the Spanish colonists, but the Reign of Terror dampened the enthusiasm of the creoles. They feared that if revolution should occur in Spanish America, the mestizos and the Indians might destroy the peninsulares and the creoles. So the creoles saw the Spanish monarch as a safeguard against the possible loss of their own position, and they became less revolutionary in outlook.

The catalyst that set off revolution in Latin America was Napoleon's policy in Europe. He decided to break his enemy England by closing the continent of Europe to British trade, and to carry out this plan he marched into Portugal and Spain in 1807. The British carried off the monarch of Portugal to safety, but Napoleon deposed the Spanish king and put his own brother Joseph upon the throne of Spain. In 1810 revolts broke out in various parts of Spanish America against Napoleon, and developed into the wars of independence that finally threw off European control.

The Campaigns of Simón Bolívar

In April 1810, the *cabildo*, the town council, of Caracas expelled the Spanish captain-general and appointed a junta, a committee, to rule in the name of the deposed Ferdinand VII. The movement was originally led by wealthy creoles who wished to gain power for themselves but did not want to break completely from Spain. But others, under the leadership of Simón Bolívar, demanded complete independence.

Bolívar, born into a wealthy landed family in Caracas, lost his parents while still a child, was brought up by a tutor who was a disciple of Rousseau, and in 1804, when he was 21 years old, came into his family fortune of several million dollars. He determined to free his people from foreign rule, and in 1810, as leader of the rebels of Caracas, joined with the sixty-year old creole Francisco de Miranda, who had visited the new United States and spent several years in London plotting the overthrow of Spanish rule in America.

South American Independence. *See* map of Central America.

In July 1811 Bolívar and Miranda called a congress which declared the large area of Venezuela to be free of Spanish control. As virtual dictator of Venezuela, Miranda suffered a crushing defeat by a patriot Spanish force, and was obliged to sign a humiliating capitulation. Indignant at the capitulation, Bolívar accused Miranda of treachery, and betrayed him to the Spaniards, who gave Bolívar safe conduct to the Dutch island of Curaçao, and sent Miranda as a prisoner to Madrid, where he died in 1816.

Bolívar soon left Curaçao, went to New Granada, now the modern nation of Colombia, organized resistance against Spain, returned to Venezuela where he defeated Spanish troops and was proclaimed Liberator in 1813 and dictator in 1814. But the overthrow of Napoleon in Europe and the restoration of Ferdinand VII to the throne of Spain drastically changed Bolívar's fortunes. Ferdinand was able to send 10,000 Spanish troops to support the royalists in Spanish America. The revolution in the North collapsed, and Bolívar left the mainland to find asylum in Jamaica.

San Martín: War for Independence in the South

While Bolívar was fighting in the North, José de San Martín was helping the cause of independence in the South. He helped the government of Buenos Aires to expel the Spanish troops, and then enlisted a force to attack across the Andes into Chile. The crossing of the Andes was an incredible task, because five mountain ranges had to be crossed, and the men had to manhandle their twelve cannons through the passes. Horses, cattle, and men died from exhaustion and the extreme cold, but San Martín's expedition overcame the tremendous odds, took the Spanish troops by surprise, and by 1818 had made Chile independent.

In 1820 San Martín went northward by sea, and after varying success finally declared Peru to be independent in July 1821, although the royalist troops had not been completely driven out of the Viceroyalty.

During the years of San Martín's successes, Bolívar returned from Jamaica to Venezuela, where he was made President, and then marched westward to liberate New Granada. At the city of Guayaquil the two leaders, Bolívar and San Martín, met in July 1822. San Martín requested Bolívar's aid to send an expedition into Peru, and even offered to serve under Bolívar; but Bolívar did not agree with San Martín's belief that Peru should be ruled by a European monarch. San Martín left the conference, and sailed for Europe, where he died in obscurity in Boulogne in 1850.

The final great battle of the war was fought

Simón Bolívar. The great inspiration of Latin American independence.

by Bolívar's lieutenant, José de Sucre, at Ayacucho, in upper Peru, in December 1824, a victory which was the end of Spain's empire in South America, although civil strife continued in each of the new states between rival contestants for power.

The Monroe Doctrine

Despite the defeat of the royalist forces it was by no means certain that the new republics would continue long to be free from foreign interference. In Europe the French king, Charles X, helped Ferdinand of Spain to defeat the constitutional limitations placed on the king, and to become an absolute monarch. There was also the danger that France and other members of the Quadruple Alliance would assist Spain to win back her colonies in South America.

Great Britain and the United States were opposed to foreign intervention in the Americas, and early in 1823 George Canning, the British Foreign Secretary, suggested to the United States ambassador in London that the two nations issue a joint declaration to discourage European intervention. But President Monroe and his advisors decided that the United States should act alone, and issued the Doctrine which announced that the United States would not interfere in European affairs, would not interfere with existing European colonies in the Western hemisphere, and would not permit further colonization, and would view as an unfriendly act any European intervention in the independent republics which the United States had recognized. This Monroe Doctrine was a clear warning to Europe to keep hands off the Western hemisphere.

The Collapse of Bolívar's Hopes for Unity

During his years of fighting for independence, Bolívar hoped that eventually he could set up a great united state of Gran Colombia, comprising New Granada, Venezuela, and the region of Ecuador. It was an impracticable scheme because not only did the three regions have nothing in common and express no desire to be joined, but they were separated by mountains and jungles, even though they were officially part of Spain's Viceroyalty of New Granada.

The great physical strain of years of fighting left Bolívar an ailing man and a vindictive and suspicious one who believed that he could trust nobody. On September 1828 he was saved from assassination only by the quick action of a faithful lieutenant. Disillusioned, he wrote "There is no good faith in America or among the nations of America." In May 1830, close to death from tuberculosis, he planned to go into exile in Europe. He got as far as Santa Marta on the Caribbean coast, and there heard of the collapse of Gran Colombia when Ecuador and Venezuela withdrew. "Those who have served the revolution," he wrote, "have ploughed the sea." On December 17, 1830 he died.

The Struggle for Independence in Mexico

The struggle in Mexico was much more difficult than in the other Viceroyalties because there the economic system was completely feudal, and the Indians saw little reason to fight against Spain for a "national independence" in which they would have no say. The revolution broke out in 1810 under the priest Father Hidalgo, who wanted not only to break with Spain but also to win the land back for the Indians. Father Hidalgo's forces were easily defeated and he himself was shot. Not until 1821 did the local creole leader Agustín de Iturbide unite whites and Indians in a successful revolution. Iturbide had himself elected Emperor Agustín I by his soldiers, but he was soon ousted by a republican rising which established the republic of the United States of Mexico in 1824.

Independence in Central America

Several revolutionary movements occurred in the captaincy-general of Guatemala, the modern Guatemala, San Salvador, Honduras, Nicaragua, and Costa Rica, between 1811 and 1814, but all were easily repressed by royalist troops. Then in 1821, influenced by events in Mexico, a junta convened in Guatemala City and declared in favor of independence. Emperor Agustín of Mexico attempted to coerce the territory into Mexico, but after his forced abdication in 1823, a general constituent assembly declared the several provinces to be the sovereign United Provinces of Central America. But regional differences, the ambitions of rival leaders, and other factors led to the break-up of this one republic into the five independent states of Guatemala, Salvador, Honduras, Nicaragua, and Costa Rica.

Revolution in Brazil

When Napoleon's forces occupied Portugal in 1807, King John VI was rescued by the British forces, and sailed to Brazil, where he set up a government in Rio de Janeiro. After the fall of Napoleon he returned to Portugal, and left his son Pedro to rule as his regent in Brazil. But Pedro joined the independence movement, proclaimed Brazil an independent nation in 1822 and ruled as Pedro I, Emperor of Brazil. In 1831 he was forced to abdicate in favor of his son Pedro II, who did much to assist the development of Brazil and encouraged European immigration. In 1889, while Pedro was in Europe, his regime was ousted and replaced with a republic.

Independence without Democracy

Before the colonial period ended there were eight Spanish colonies in the New World,* totaling nearly 7,000,000 square miles, but with a population of only 16,000,000. The single Viceroyalty of New Spain, from Mexico to California, had nearly half that total. Far-sighted leaders hoped that once Spain was driven out of Spanish America these colonial areas would join together to make up only a few nations. Simón Bolívar for a brief time had set up his La Gran Colombia, and other leaders had attempted to organize a confederation of Peru and Bolivia, and to keep the large Viceroyalty of La Plata as one new

---

*The Viceroyalties of New Spain (Mexico), New Granada, Peru, Rio de La Plata, and the Captaincies-General of Guatemala (Central America), Cuba, Venezuela, and Chile.

nation. But these efforts had failed because several of the important factors which brought success to the American Revolution and the creation of the United States were missing in Spanish America.

The North Americans had enjoyed over a hundred years of local self-government before Great Britain attempted to enforce its restrictions upon the thirteen colonies, whose people enjoyed a generally common heritage and culture. Although there were rich and poor in North America, there were no inferior or subjugated people, except for the Negro slaves.

In Latin America there was no experience whatever in self-government, and although the several revolutionary leaders fought for independence, they had no program to establish any kind of democracy. The creoles fought for rights for themselves, not for mestizos or Indians.

The republics that emerged in Latin America from the revolutionary wars for independence were republics only in the limited sense that the heads of government were elected, or selected, and were not hereditary monarchs. The only tangible achievement of the wars for independence was the removal of the Spanish monarch and the substitution of local dictators who maintained rigid social distinctions, continued the feudal system of landholding, and kept political power in their own hands.

Because the military played an important role in liberating the colonies from European control, it was destined to play a significant part in the future. Generally, the Army allied itself with the landed aristocracy and the Church hierarchy to dominate the rural areas. Not until the latter part of the 19th century did conditions change, and then because industrialization in the United States and Europe introduced new methods. Natural resources in Latin America were developed, and trade more than doubled, although the benefits were seldom enjoyed by the peasants and workers, whose numbers nearly tripled between 1875 and 1914 to 80,000,000.

World War I so disrupted Latin American export trade that many nations determined to industrialize more rapidly so as to avoid dependence upon foreign nations as markets for raw materials, and as a source of manufactured goods. This drive for industrialization resulted in the growth of such large cities as Mexico City, Buenos Aires, São Paulo, Santiago, and others which attracted large numbers of rural people.

In turn a middle class and an organized labor class emerged and played an increasingly important role in politics. The middle and working classes had several objectives in common. They wanted representative government, better schools and public service, assistance for increased industrialization, and in the rural areas the peasants demanded the break-up of landed estates and distribution of the land. Fascist and Communist organizations saw an opportunity to use these emerging forces of change. The Fascist groups tried before World War II to exercise leadership, and the Communists tried to do the same after the war, but until the emergence of Castro in Cuba, the Communists achieved only limited success.

3. Factors which Hinder Development

The Village

Some of the problems of Latin America today are common to several of the republics, although in varying degrees. The problems are to a large extent the inheritance of conditions that existed before the wars for independence and continued afterwards. Many of the republics share the problems of poverty, economic backwardness, illiteracy, political corruption, and the "revolution of rising expectations," which is the demand from poverty-stricken people for better conditions, from people who are beginning to realize that they have the power to secure more rights and better standards of living.

Until World War I the majority of people in the Andean countries, in Central America and Mexico lived either in small villages or on the hacienda. Much of Latin America consists of a comparatively few large cities, many small towns, and hundreds of thousands of villages.

A Bolivian Indian holds samples of fish caught in Lake Titicaca. (Thor Heyerdahl employed a group of these Indians to help build *Ra*, the historic replica of the raft believed to have once sailed from North Africa to the Caribbean.)

The small towns are usually composed of one hundred to two hundred families, and are self-contained communities with few contacts with the outside. The village may range from the communal Indian village to communities where land is individually owned, but it is almost always a community with its own local traditions and a government in which every male takes part and which runs its own civic affairs of roads, public works, the school and the Church. Many a village is so self-contained that "outsiders" would neither wish to live there nor be allowed to. They would have neither house nor land, neither family nor friends. This isolation leads to localism in politics and to the development of *caciquismo* or local bossism that looks after and protects its own people.

Regionalism

The one factor that held together the Latin American colonies was the king, the symbol of all authority. Once this symbol of authority was removed, there was no one person, no single authority to take his place. The Latin American republics had no Continental Congress as in the United States, to give direction to the revolution and to obtain funds, there was no one leader respected by all, no such document as the Declaration of Independence to bind the several parts into a nation, and there was certainly nothing to resemble the Constitutional Convention in Philadelphia to weld the former colonies into one nation.

The creoles and the military took over and quarreled among themselves, because in due time the mestizos became soldiers and minor officers and demanded a say in governing their countries. The Indians gained nothing, because

The Atacama Desert, Chile. This arid landscape depicts much of the continent's problems. Much of the land is poor; communications are bad – this is the Great Pan-American Highway – yet this desert contains deposits of copper and nitrate that require vast capital to extract.

they no longer had even the protection of the king, who had previously enforced certain of their rights, and to some extent prevented their exploitation.

The Hacienda

The *hacienda*, or the *fazenda*, as it is called in Brazil, is not only a large agricultural estate of the owner, the *hacendado*, but is also a completely self-contained community that governs the daily life of its people, literally from birth to death. The hacienda grows as much as it can to supply its own needs, and buys as little as possible from the outside. It produces its own food, its cloth, its furniture, its farm tools, raises its own cattle and horses, and makes the equipment for them. The hacienda is not a financial investment or a business in the ordinary sense, but a way of life. To the *peons*, the peasants, the hacienda is their home and their livelihood. They work a day or two a week for the hacendado, who gives them the use of a plot of land, provides seeds and the use of animals, but pays no money wages. Anything the peon needs he can buy at the "company store," not paid for in cash but charged off in extra labor or kept on the books as a debt which obliges the peon to remain on the hacienda because he can never pay it off.

The hacienda contributes almost nothing to the national economy or to national politics because it spends little or no money outside, and its workers have no contact with government and politics. A further hampering effect of the hacienda upon Latin American development is that it has held back the rise of a middle class of businessmen, who by the very nature of their interests help to modernize a country. The dilemma of the hacienda today is that it cannot adjust to modern conditions because by its very nature it must remain as it is or cease to exist. Growing peasant demands for land, supported by rising political leaders who appeal to the peasants, may spell the end of the hacienda system.

Politics

Politics in Latin America are very different from those in North America because there are no comparable political parties. Leadership in Latin America is a personal relationship to a man, not to an office. A democratic country such as the United States divides and distributes authority to different branches of government, such as the executive, the legislature, and the judiciary. Such a system prevents one man from using power as he sees fit, but in an authoritarian society all power is usually in the hands of the leader. He cannot divide it or share it, and his ministers, the legislature, and the courts of justice all become reflections of the leader's authority.

A democratic society provides for an orderly succession to the leadership, a set of rules by which a new leader replaces a former leader. In the Latin American countries there are no rules for orderly succession, there is no legitimate or effective machinery for the transfer of power, and as consequence the *coup d'état* is frequently the method of change.

Violence

Violence is a significant factor in much of Latin America today, and it may grow as increased demands from the lower classes lead to *coups d'état*, assassinations, invasions by exiled citizens, and the guerrilla activities that have plagued Guatemala, Peru, Nicaragua, Bolivia, Venezuela, and other nations. Violence may be the only way for legitimate popular demands to have any chance of success. Another characteristic of Latin American politics and economic life has been the indifference of the upper classes to the needs of others. While standards of living may have risen markedly in recent decades, the *per capita* income has not risen proportionately, and the gap between the poorer classes and the comfortable and the wealthy has widened. The poor see what modern life can provide, and they become frustrated and alienated, and willing to listen to extremists, to *Fidelismo*, the methods and program of Cuba's Fidel Castro. The peasant demand for land may not be satisfied without revolution, and Communist groups will almost certainly be ready to provide leadership at the opportune moment.

Political Violence. The heat generated in politics is shown here as politicians in Argentina dispute the election of a provincial governor.

Moderate groups realize that unless the demands of the lower classes are met, then the extremists may get political power. The Catholic Church has recognized this, and in recent years has identified itself more with the interests of the lower classes and the forces of reform.

The Military

The role of the army has not historically been limited to purely military functions. In the early days of independence the army helped to maintain order. It also continued to contribute to national life by developing communications and transportation systems and in other civic programs. The military has on several occasions interfered in politics, partly because governments were ineffective, sometimes because existing governments demanded military assistance against extremist groups, sometimes because middle class groups wanted an authoritarian government removed. In Latin America the military has played a role not experienced by democracies, and because its forces are drawn from working and peasant classes it may play a larger part in a changing society.

One example of the military's role in Latin American politics can be seen in Brazil, where João Goulart was overthrown in 1964 by the army. Goulart had followed two presidents who had brought the country close to economic ruin, and in his struggle for political survival he leaned increasingly toward Communist support.

The army continues to rule through harsh authoritarian methods.

Argentina has been dominated by the military in politics since 1930. On four occasions the army has removed governments which in its view were not acting in the interests of the country. In 1943 the army took control and put into power Juan Perón, whose wife Evita became very popular with the poor "shirtless ones," the *demiscados*. Backed by the army and industrial workers, Perón introduced social security and raised the standard of living of the poor, but his granting of further social benefits to the poor of Argentina led to serious economic dislocation by 1955. This situation and Perón's high-handedness, the evident corruption of his government, and his granting of concessions in the Patagonian oilfields to United States companies led to an army *coup d'état* and his downfall. Two of his successors have also been removed by the army, and there is little chance that Argentina will have civilian democratic government in the near future. In November 1972, after exile in Spain, Perón returned. His arrival, acclaimed by his supporters, presented the Argentinian government with a difficult situation.

Military Intervention. Bolivian soldiers take control of La Paz in 1970.

In 1963 Peru had genuinely free elections which chose Fernando Balaúnde as president. However, in 1968 Congress opposed him and the army deposed him and took over the government.

Bolivia, with an economy based on tin, has gone through a violent series of crises in recent history. In 1952 the Amerindian tin miners under the leadership of Paz Estenssoro, an economics professor, revolted against the mine-owners, representatives of the white minority. The rising was a success, and Estenssoro sponsored a socialist program, with substantial economic aid from the United States. However, he was unable to continue his program and was forced to flee in 1964 during a series of riots. Since then the country has been ruled virtually at gun-point by a succession of military-backed regimes.

In Latin American countries the military is frequently either the government or a deciding factor in politics. Simón Bolívar's prediction when he fled into exile in 1830 that "Latin America is ungovernable; those who have served the revolution have ploughed the sea," has unfortunately proved prophetic.

4. The United States and Hemisphere Relations

The Roosevelt Corollary

Relations between the United States and Latin America have suffered tensions throughout the 20th century. The "Colossus of the North" can exert, and has exerted, great influence on Latin America in order to attain its objectives.

The Monroe Doctrine of 1823 had clearly warned Europe to keep out of the Western hemisphere, proclaiming United States intention to permit no further European colonization and no European interference in the affairs of independent Latin American nations. In 1904 the Roosevelt Corollary to the Monroe Doctrine, pronounced by President Theodore Roosevelt, radically changed the concept of the Monroe Doctrine and the role of the United States.

The corollary announced that if Latin American nations committed acts which invited European action, then the United States would intervene in Latin America. The occasion for this attitude was the Venezuelan situation in 1902, when Venezuela refused to honor her foreign debts, and Germany, Great Britain, and Italy blockaded Venezuelan ports. The United States insisted upon arbitration of the matter because Roosevelt regarded European intervention as a violation of the Monroe Doctrine. The threat of similar European intervention occurred in 1904 when the Dominican Republic failed to pay its foreign debts. Roosevelt intervened, took control of the Dominican customs houses, and from the customs income paid off the debts owed to creditor nations.

In December 1904 Roosevelt announced that "chronic wrongdoing" by nations in the Western hemisphere might compel the United States to exercise an international police power to prevent European intervention. The Roosevelt Corollary aroused the opposition of Latin American nations, which resented interference in their affairs by so powerful a neighbor.

Clark Memorandum and Good Neighbor Policy

In 1930 the United States felt obliged to announce in the Clark Memorandum that the Roosevelt Corollary was not properly a part of the Monroe Doctrine, and that the Doctrine did not concern itself with inter-American affairs but was directed only against European intervention in the Western hemisphere.

In his inaugural address of 1933 President Franklin Roosevelt referred to hemisphere relations in these words, "I would dedicate this nation to the policy of the good neighbor who... respects the rights of others." Latin America waited to see what these words actually meant. Secretary of State Cordell Hull at the Pan-American Conference in Montevideo in December 1933 committed the United States to the principle that, "No state has the right to intervene in the internal or external affairs of another." A major test came in 1938 when Mexico took over the properties of the British-Dutch and American oil companies. The stockholders demanded United States intervention, but the United States refused to act, and in time Mexico paid for the properties, although not to the satisfaction of the owners.

The Good Neighbor Policy encouraged Latin American nations to develop a multilateral policy in which all should participate. At a conference held in Lima, Peru in 1938, the republics declared that, on the suggestion of any one state, the foreign ministers of all should meet to consult on any matter "which concerned the defense of their peace, security, or territorial integrity."

Multilateral Action: The Act of Havana

By mid-1940 Germany had occupied Holland and France, and was threatening Great Britain. If the Latin American possessions of those nations fell to Germany, then the safety of the Western hemisphere would be threatened. The United States told the Axis powers in June that she "would not recognize any transfer, nor acquiesce in any attempt to transfer any geographic region of the Western hemisphere from one non-American power to another non-American power." To avoid the charge that the United States was acting alone, Secretary of State Cordell Hull requested a conference of the foreign ministers of the Latin American states.

At the meeting in Havana in July 1940, the delegates proclaimed the Act of Havana which stated that "any European possession apt to change sovereignty" be placed under temporary control by a joint committee representing all the American states, to be called the Inter-American Commission for Territorial Administration. Any attempt against any territory of any American state "shall be considered an act of aggression against the signatory states."

The United States assisted Latin America by trying to use all the Latin American products which had lost their European markets because of the war. When the United States declared war on the Axis powers on December 8, 1941, all the Central American states, Haiti, and the Dominican Republic followed immediately. In Rio de Janeiro in January 1942, a conference of ministers passed resolutions requesting all American states to sever relations with the Axis powers. Only Argentina and Chile did not respond.

Regional Defense Pact: The Rio de Janeiro Conference

At a conference held in February 1945 at Chapultepec, Mexico, the Monroe Doctrine was expanded to "make all the American republics co-guardians of the Monroe Doctrine, even against an American aggressor."

In 1947, at Rio de Janeiro, the Rio Pact established an Inter-American Treaty for Continental Defense. An armed attack on one would be regarded as an attack upon all, and each of the signatory nations "undertake to assist the attacked power."

Organization of American States: The Bogota Conference

There had existed ever since 1910 a Pan-American Union with headquarters at Washington, D.C. It was criticized by some Latin Americans as the "United States Ministry of Colonies" because the United States Secretary of State was automatically chairman of the executive board.

In 1948 at Bogota the delegates substituted for the Pan-American Union the Organization of American States, with similar purposes of consulting on common interests but with representatives of ambassadorial rank on the policy-making Council. Although the United States is by virtue of its size, wealth, and international commitments the single most powerful member, the OAS has provided the means for significant participation in hemisphere affairs by Latin American nations.

The unilateral actions by the United States in supporting the Bay of Pigs invasion of Cuba in 1961, and in sending troops into the Dominican Republic in 1965 were regarded by some Latin Americans as contradicting the intention of the Organization of American States.

5. Cuba and Castro

Corruption in Cuba

The history of Cuba after it became a protectorate of the United States under the Platt Amendment of 1901 is generally one of corruption and tyranny. In succession, Presidents Gomez, Menocal, and Zayas emptied the treasury. In 1925 President Machado was hailed as a businessman who would bring order to government. He built a personal political machine, and rewarded henchmen with contracts and concessions, with the result that when he was re-elected in 1928 students and professional

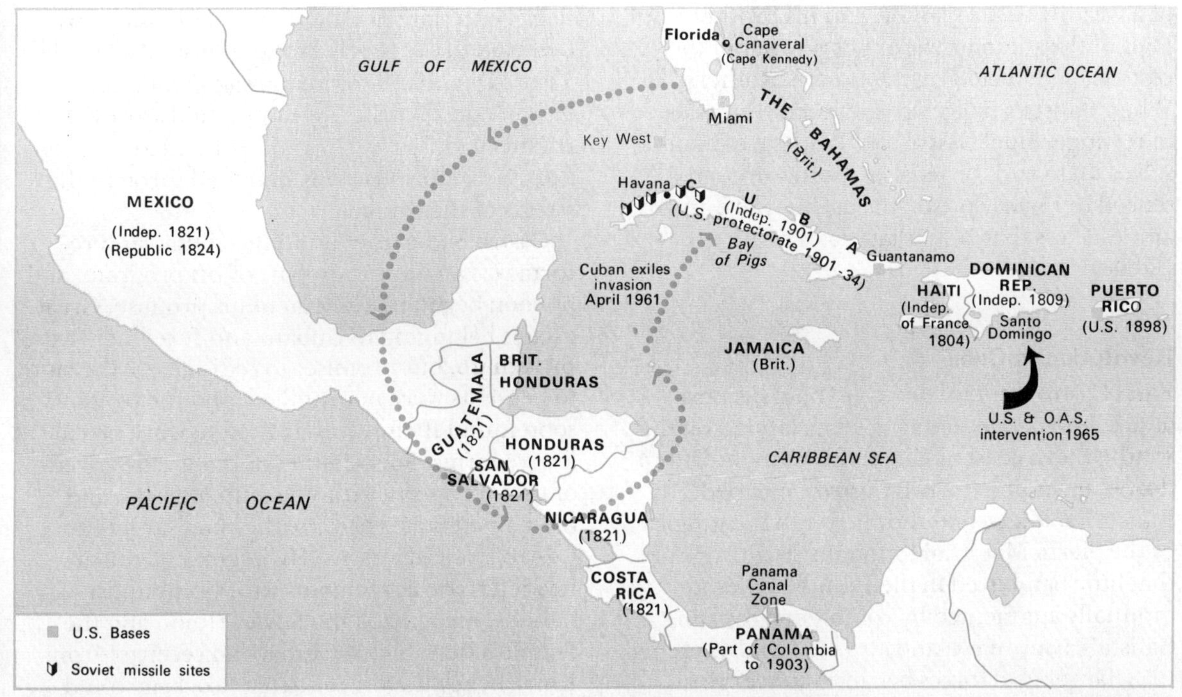

Central America. Independence to modern times. Cuba became a U.S. protectorate immediately on gaining independence. The 1962 placing of missile bases on Cuba by Russians was an obvious threat to U.S. security.

men organized against him. Government troops shot protestors in the streets and invaded homes without search warrants. Opposition groups called a general strike, the army insisted on a change of government, and in 1933 Machado took a plane for the Bahamas. A temporary government lasted only three weeks before it was overthrown by the "sergeants' revolt" led by Sergeant Fulgencio Batista, who replaced 500 superior officers with his own conspirators, and promoted himself to Colonel and Chief of Staff.

Until 1940 Batista ruled through a series of puppet-presidents, then took the position himself for four years, but at the request of President Franklin Roosevelt he permitted the election of two presidents in succession before once again taking over the position, in 1952. During the years 1944–1952 many Cubans wished Batista was back as President, because under two men the corruption became so great that one 4-year term president, on a salary of $25,000, was able to build himself a multi-million dollar house.

In 1952 Batista took over in barracks-revolt tradition, and seized the army barracks before dawn. From then on, Batista's regime was one of increasing terrorism by police and violent reaction from the people. Effective opposition against Batista began on July 26, 1953 when about 160 university students stormed the army barracks in Santiago, under the leadership of 26-year old Fidel Castro, a law student and son of a wealthy sugar planter, and his brother Raul. Half of the students were shot down, but the rest escaped, including the Castro brothers. When Batista's police used terrorist reprisals in revenge, Fidel Castro and Raul gave themselves up to end the tension. Both were sentenced to 15-year prison terms, but were given amnesty less than a year later as a result of public demand.

Revolution in Cuba

Fidel Castro went to Mexico to plan his next attack, and on December 2, 1956, landed on the southeastern coast of Cuba with 82 men. Only a dozen, including the two Castros, escaped Batista's soldiers, and they fled into the jungles of the Sierra Maestra Mountains. For two years that little band lived in their jungle hide-out gradually augmented by volunteers, resisting Batista's army, navy, and air force. In December 1958, large rebel forces began to converge on Havana. Normal life came to a standstill, Batista declared a state of emergency, and his troops deserted to the rebels by the thousands. On New Year's Day, 1959, rumor spread throughout Havana that Batista, his family, and scores of friends had fled by ship and plane; Fidel Castro's victorious army marched through the streets of the capital.

Fidel Castro makes his triumphant entry into Havana, January 1959.

Castro had earlier announced that land reform was an important part of his program, and he soon began to implement his promise. Great estates belonging to Cubans and foreigners were broken up, but promises to redistribute the land to peasants were not fulfilled, and the peasants soon found themselves drafted to work on collective farms. Foreign investors were deprived of their property without compensation, and the United States became the chief target of Castro's verbal attacks. He negotiated much-needed trade agreements with Communist nations, recognized the Soviet Union and the People's Republic of China, and received from Khrushchev the promise that "rockets would fly" to protect Cuba's independence. Castro waged a cold war on the United States and tried to stir up Latin American nations against the "imperialistic" United States. In January 1961, the United States withdrew the official recognition which had been accorded to Castro's regime two years earlier. Many American sympathizers with Castro began to change their minds.

At home, Castro announced that Cuba was a socialist state, and admitted that as a rebel he had deliberately kept his Communist sympathies hidden while fighting Batista. Domestically he may have improved the condition of the working classes, for whose children he provided schooling and technical training formerly unavailable to them. And in foreign affairs he gained much sympathy from other Latin American nations until he threatened to encourage revolution wherever he could in Latin America.

The Bay of Pigs and the Missile Crisis

Large numbers of Cuban exiles in the United States were anxious to overthrow Castro. They were subsidized by the Central Intelligence Agency during the Eisenhower administration, and about 1,500 were trained in Guatemala. President Kennedy agreed to invasion plans, provided no Americans were directly involved. But the plans were incompetently handled; Castro's intelligence agents prepared him; and on April 19, 1961, when the expedition landed on the Cuban coast at the Bay of Pigs it ran into disaster. Nearly 300 of the invaders were killed, and 1,200 were taken prisoner, later to be ransomed by private citizens in America in exchange for more than $60,000,000 in drugs and infant foods, or for about $50,000 per man. Castro's success strengthened his position at home and his image among the underprivileged people of Latin America.

Khrushchev took advantage of the apparent weakness of the United States to use Cuba as a base for ballistic missiles pointed at the United States. The prompt and decisive action of President Kennedy showed America's strength, and to some extent discredited Castro because the incident brought substantial Latin American support for the United States. (*See* IV, 6.)

The Threat of Cuba to Latin America

The sympathy that Castro had earned from other Latin American countries in resisting what was interpreted as United States interference in Cuban affairs was gradually lost as Castro advocated and encouraged wars for "national liberation" in Latin America. At first, many of these nations claimed that Castro's Communism was purely national and local, but before long it became clear that Cuba was a growing threat to her neighbors.

The willingness of Castro to permit the Soviet Union to build ballistic missile bases in Cuba exposed the Castro regime as being militantly and aggressively Communist.

In 1964 the foreign ministers of the members of the Organization of American States denounced Castro's shipment of weapons to Venezuelan rebels and called for a diplomatic and economic boycott on Cuba, with the warning that in future such action could bring military retaliation. Only Mexico refused to sever diplomatic relations with Cuba, chiefly to show her independence rather than to indicate approval of Castro.

6. United States Intervention in the Dominican Republic

Rafael Trujillo: Dictator

United States intervention in the Dominican Republic in April 1965 resulted in immediate hostile reaction in Latin America to the United States, because it was regarded as interference in a purely domestic matter. The United States believed, whether correctly or not will probably never be proved, that the Dominican Republic was in danger of a Communist take-over.

For thirty years between 1930 and his assassination in 1961 Rafael Trujillo had ruled the republic ruthlessly and as his own personal estate, salting away hundreds of millions of dollars for himself and family in Swiss banks, leaving the Dominican people little better off than in colonial days.

Many Dominicans attempted to seek help against Trujillo, while he in turn gave refuge to ousted dictators such as Batista, and was allegedly implicated in plots to assassinate Venezuela's liberal President Bétancourt. The younger officers of the Dominican Republic decided to rid the country of Trujillo, and under the leadership

U.S./OAS Intervention, Dominican Republic, 1965. The ceremony shown underlines the combined efforts of the U.S. and other American countries. The OAS flag is handed to a Brazilian general by a U.S. general.

of Colonel Barrera they ambushed and killed Trujillo on a lonely road in May 1961. Immediately the nation was torn by a struggle for power between the Trujillo family supported by the older army officers, a group of young officers, and the leftist group of Communists supported by Castro men. In January 1962 the Trujillo family and intimates fled the country, and a Council of Government ran the country until new elections could be held in December 1962, to be supervised by the Organization of American States.

Juan Bosch: Unsuccessful President

The Popular Revolutionary Party, a moderate group despite its name, outlawed the Communists from its ranks and won the election with more than 60 percent. Their successful candidate was Juan Bosch, a political science teacher, who had been anti-Trujillo for the previous twenty years. In trying to put through democratic reforms he antagonized landowners and businessmen. Bosch tried to distribute the vast Trujillo lands and estates to the peasants, but the landowners whose lands Trujillo had previously taken now expected to get them back. Businessmen who hoped to take over the many Trujillo-controlled businesses objected to the Bosch program of nationalization. Army men who had been in the plot to assassinate Trujillo feared the loss of their political power. In seven months Bosch fell from power and was exiled to Puerto Rico by a civilian and military junta. The two leaders of the *coup d'état* were Colonel Imbert, who had shot Trujillo, and General Wessin y Wessin, a fanatical anti-Communist who believed that Bosch was a Castro supporter and agent.

The temporary government under Pedro Cabral was inept, corrupt, and caught between Communist-led masses and the rightest military leaders. Elections were scheduled for September 1965, but a revolution led by Bosch supporters exploded in April. In the name of Juan Bosch weapons were passed out to street fighters who threatened to attack foreign embassies and hotels where foreigners were staying.

Intervention: The U.S.A. and the OAS Peace Force

United States troops were landed, on the excuse that American lives were in danger, and soon the city of Santo Domingo was in the hands of three different groups, with Americans in the center of town, the followers of Imbert and Wessin in another, and the port and slum area held by Colonel Francisco Camaaño Deno in the name of Juan Bosch.

Although President Johnson was criticized for unilateral action, the Organization of American States voted to send in a military force, the first such joint action in the history of Latin America. The OAS Peace Force, consisting of Americans, Brazilians, and token forces from other Latin American nations, brought about an uneasy peace, and after four months of negotiations persuaded Imbert and Camaaño to resign their "commands," and back the compromise candidate Garcia Godoy. In June 1966 a presidential election was held between Juan Bosch and Trujillo's vice-president Joaquim Balaguer, whc won by 55 percent of the total vote of 1,270,000.

The Dominican intervention may have been the initiation of a new institution, the OAS Peace Force, which could be used in similar situations in future. United States unilateral intervention raises a very important issue of whether the United States has the obligation to remain out of the domestic affairs of Latin America, even if further political and economic upheavals occur in the hemisphere. Revolutions may occur from time to time in Latin America, as they have in the past, and they may be the results of internal political and economic tensions and frustrations. The likelihood of Communist support is very probable, and the United States would be obliged to consider very carefully whether its own opposition to Communism would be sufficient and proper reason to intervene in what Latin America might regard as a purely local matter.

Brasilia. Symbol of hope or White Elephant?

Favella. Peasants flock to the cities for a better life only to join others in crowded makeshift homes on the outskirts.

7. The Alliance for Progress

During the 1950's Latin American states believed that the United States was so concerned about the Soviet Union, Communism, and the Cold War that Latin America was being neglected, in great contrast to wartime assistance by the United States. Latin America was also greatly disturbed by United States grant of loans to Perez Jímenez, the hated dictator of Venezuela, and by its treating the playboy son of dictator Trujillo of the Dominican Republic as an honored guest at an officers' school in the United States. In 1958 Vice President Richard Nixon toured through Latin America, and was stoned by university students in Lima and barely escaped from an angry crowd in Caracas, from which Jímenez had fled for his life only a few weeks earlier.

In Cuba, Castro began to change the economy radically and to confiscate foreign property. He came into conflict with the United States over this policy, turned toward the Soviet Union, and became the first Communist nation in the Western hemisphere. Castro's threat to export his revolution to other hemisphere countries forced the United States and Latin America to plan reform programs that could head off revolutionary tendencies.

On March 13, 1961, President Kennedy launched the Alliance for Progress, *La Alianza Para el Progreso,* "a vast cooperative effort, unparalleled in magnitude and nobility of purpose, to satisfy the basic needs of the American people." The Alliance was to be a joint self-help program over a period of 10 years, assisted by the United States. The Latin American nations pledged themselves to spend $80,000,000,000 over the ten years to achieve the goals of greater industrialization, wide agrarian reforms to provide land for needy peasants, primary education for all children, tax reform to make those pay who were able to do so, and other social achievement programs such as low-cost housing and health facilities. To encourage this self-help, the United States pledged itself to find $2,000,000,000 every year in external assistance, with one half to come from the United States government, and the other half from other countries and private investment.

In August 1961 the Latin American nations framed the Alliance for Progress Charter at Punta del Este, Uruguay. However, after more than five years the achievement fell far short of

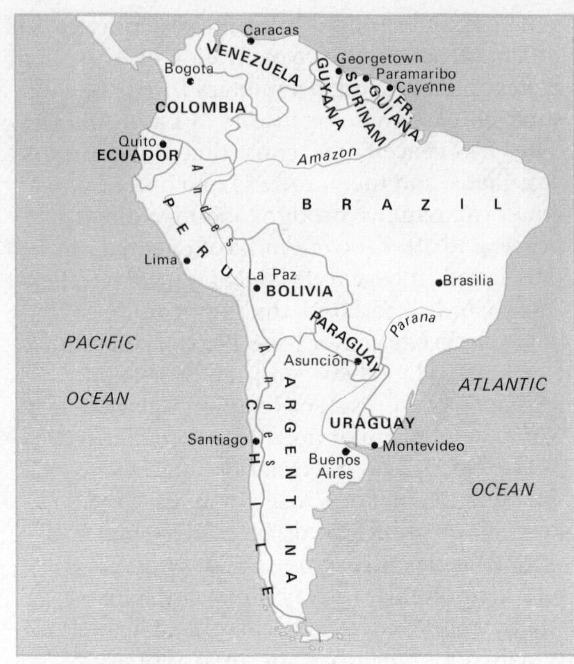

Modern Latin America

the promise. Reduction of customs duties among Latin American nations as a means of encouraging trade was disappointingly slow; several countries, such as Argentina, Brazil, and Chile, continued to have their usual financial troubles; overproduction of raw materials such as petroleum, coffee, tin, and sugar brought down the price on the world market; and private investors were discouraged by political instability in Latin America and the possibility that their property could be confiscated.

It was clear that after five years the program had fallen far behind, partly because the urban population increased so rapidly that needs became greater than before, and conditions worsened. It is estimated that of the 135,000,000 people who live in cities, about 45,000,000 live in substandard, unsanitary slums, known as *favellas* and create a health and a political hazard.

Current housing shortages are at least 20,000,000 and are increasing so rapidly that the problem is virtually impossible to solve at the present rate of building. The staggering expansion of urban population is creating similar shortages in lighting, water, and sanitation systems.

Tax reforms have been partly successful in bringing in more taxes to the government. Schools have been built, and many millions of children have benefited from school-lunch programs. Critics claim that progress has been much too slow, that too high a proportion of funds has been used to pay off the interest on foreign debts or to fight inflation at home instead of being put into projects which make jobs and help to raise living standards. Land distribution has lagged far behind the goals set.

Such an ambitious program as the Alliance for Progress can readily be criticized. So vast an undertaking cannot be accomplished in a short time and across so large a continent. The planning may have been too ambitious and may have raised hopes too quickly. President Frei of Chile raised a significant question when he asked, "Can change so long pent up, now come peacefully?"

Election of a Marxist President in Chile

For nearly 40 years Chile had been the strongest democracy in South America, with no *coups d'état* since 1932. In October 1970 Chile elected as its president Dr. Salvadore Allende Gossens, who had campaigned on an avowedly Marxist platform of nationalization of major industries and the expropriation of foreign businesses. Of political significance is the fact that Allende is the first Marxist-Leninist Communist in Latin America to be freely elected to office. Since Allende won by a plurality of only 36 percent against the National Party's Jorge Alessandri Rodriguez with 35 percent and the Christian Democrat's Radomiro Tomic Romero 28 percent, the final decision rested with the republican legislature's choice between the top two candidates. Since Tomic's program was almost indistinguishable from Allende's, the two combined with a vote of 64 percent. Congress chose Allende by 160 to 35.

Within hours of Allende's election middle-class people withdrew over $87,000,000 from banks, and by competitive bidding drove down the value of the escudo from 14½ to 55 to the U.S. dollar, and left the country in substantial numbers, fearful of a completely Communist regime.

Dr. Salvadore Allende Gossens. Voting in the elections that brought him, a Marxist-Leninist, to power in Chile in 1970.

Allende's candidacy was successful partly because economic conditions, and particularly inflation, had worsened in recent months. A major earthquake, floods, and a long drought had hindered the reform efforts of the previous president Eduardo Frei, the then leader of the Christian Democrats. He had expropriated more than 1,200 large private estates and distributed the land to 30,000 families, built more than 250,000 new housing units, and tripled the number of schools to educate 600,000 more children. During his administration, from 1964 to 1970, Frei had started the redistribution of national wealth, but basic economic conditions remained serious. Over 50 percent of the families in 1970 were living on less then $30 a month, 50 percent of the children were undernourished, the unemployment rate was 7 percent, and inflation was galloping ahead at 30 percent a year.

Although Allende claimed that he would not interfere with the democratic process, no one knew what he would do. There are many Chileans who agreed with the comment, "This could be a beautiful experiment in democracy—or it could be a concentration camp." Allende's hand may be forced by the Communists, who are well organized and have demanded Cabinet positions in return for their support of Allende. Some Chileans believe that in time the Communists will take over and deny the very freedom of speech and election that they used in order to win power.

The immediate neighbors of Chile, especially Argentina, fear that Chile may become a refuge for Communist terrorists, even a Pacific base for the Soviet Union. Concerned though the United States may be, it cannot, for military and political reasons, intervene in Chile. That country is 5,000 miles away, and intervention would arouse the resentment of other Latin American nations. Nor can the United States bring economic pressure to bear, because recent United States foreign aid has been negligible, and 90 percent of Chile's important copper exports go to Japan and Europe.

The Alliance for Progress, initiated by the Kennedy administration, has not proved successful because, among other reasons, it has moved too slowly to remedy pressing economic conditions. The annual inexorable population rise of at least 3 percent has outpaced government reform plans for more jobs, houses, schools, and general social improvements.

The declining world price of copper, severe food shortages, and persistent inflation resulted in riots in the late summer of 1972, and a widening breach between left and right.

The application of Marxist-Leninist theories has not yet proved successful in Chile.

Review Questions

Sections 1 and 2

1. In what ways has geography affected the Latin American continent?
2. In what respects was the African slave better off in South America than in North America?
3. What conditions in Latin America caused revolts against Spanish rule?
4. How did each of the following affect revolution in Latin America: Lexington and Concord; The French Revolution; Creoles; Napoleon?
5. What part did each of the following play in securing the independence of Latin America: Miranda; San Martín; Bolívar; de Sucre?
6. In what way did the Monroe Doctrine aid the young republics of Latin America?
7. Why can the phrase "independence without democracy" be properly used in Latin America of the 19th century?

Sections 3 and 4

8. How did each of the following hinder the development of Latin America: the village; regionalism; the hacienda; politics; violence as a method; the military?
9. How did the Roosevelt Corollary change the original intention of the Monroe Doctrine? What was the connection between the Clark Memorandum and the Monroe Doctrine?
10. In what ways did each of the following show increased respect by the United States for her Latin American neighbors; The Act of Havana; Rio de Janeiro Conference; the Bogota Conference?

Section 5

11. What conditions in Cuba won support for Fidel Castro?
12. What was the nature of Castro's revolution in Cuba after he had forced Batista out?

Sections 6 and 7

13. What was the political situation in the Dominican Republic after the fall of Trujillo?
14. Why did both the United States and the Organization of American States intervene in the Dominican Republic?
15. What was the purpose of the Alliance for Progress? What part were the Latin American republics expected to take in the Alliance?
16. Why does the Alliance for Progress seem not to have been successful?
17. What was the effect of Allende's election in Chile?

3

The Middle East: Conflict and Crisis

The Emergence of Modern Nations in the Middle East

The Palestine Mandate: Emergence of Israel

Israel: Land, People, and Government

Foreign Affairs, 1948–1967

Problems since the 1967 War

The Middle East has been a historic crossroads of trade and of rivalries for its control. Napoleon Bonaparte tried to seize it in order to make Britain's route to India difficult; Czarist Russia attempted to control it; and Hitler made Egypt a target of his African campaign. It is to be expected, therefore, that the modern Israeli-Arab issue should become of concern to the major powers.

During World War I Britain promised to find a "homeland" for the Jews. In 1919 the British were given Palestine as a mandate, and for more than a decade experienced no trouble over Jewish immigration into Palestine. But by the mid-1930's the Jewish population had increased to 30 percent, and the Arabs were showing their resentment and hostility. After World War II the British tried to limit Jewish immigration, but in the face of violence by Jewish extremists gave up the mandate and turned the problem over to the United Nations.

From that time on fighting between Jews and Arabs was almost continuous, erupting into the Six-Day War of June 1967. The greatest obstacles to peace since 1967 have been Israel's insistence upon retaining its territorial conquests of that war, and Egypt's equal insistence that the return of this Israeli-occupied territory is essential as a basis for peace negotiations. Renewed terrorism, such as the murder of eleven Israeli athletes at the Olympic Games, has seriously interfered with negotiations for peace.

Terms

1. Middle East
2. Fertile Crescent
3. Treaty of Sèvres
4. Étatisme
5. Babylonian Captivity
6. Pentateuch
7. Diaspora
8. Aliyot
9. Kibbutz
10. Moshav
11. Zion
12. Balfour Declaration
13. Knesset
14. Mapai
15. Mapam
16. Herut
17. Histadrut
18. Fedayeen
19. FLOSY
20. Al Fatah

People

21. Mustafa Kemal (Atatürk)
22. Mohammed Naguib
23. Gamal Abdel Nasser
24. David Ben-Gurion
25. Mrs. Golda Meir
26. Anwar Sadat
27. Hussein Ibn Talal

Places

28. Turkey
29. Egypt
30. Lebanon
31. Syria
32. Jordan
33. Saudi Arabia
34. Yemen
35. Oman
36. Fertile Crescent
37. Red Sea
38. Persian Gulf
39. Turkish Straits
40. Iraq
41. Palestine
42. Negev
43. Gulf of Aqaba
44. Tel Aviv
45. Sinai Peninsula
46. Gaza Strip
47. Sharm el Sheikh
48. Elath
49. Strait of Tiran
50. Iran
51. Kuwait
52. Southern Yemen
53. Libya
54. United Arab Republic, UAR, Arab Republic of Egypt

Events

1882–1904	The First Aliyah
1917	Balfour Declaration
1919	British Mandate of Palestine
1948	Israel Becomes a Nation
1948	Arab-Israeli War
1956	Suez Canal Incident
1967, June	Israeli-Arab (Six-Day) War

1. The Emergence of Modern Nations in the Middle East

Historic Importance of the Middle East

The Middle East is the name used today to include the region stretching from the Black Sea southward to the Red Sea, and from Egypt eastward to the Indian Ocean. It comprises Turkey, Egypt, Lebanon, Syria, Jordan, the Arabian states of Saudi Arabia, Yemen and Oman, several Trucial Sheikhdoms* along the Persian Gulf, and Iraq, Iran, and since 1948 the state of Israel. Historically, the Middle East has been important as a "bridge" from Europe to Asia, an importance demonstrated by the attempts of Napoleon Bonaparte and Adolf Hitler to win possession of it. Another historically important geographical fact is the Fertile Crescent which curves northward from the Red Sea, parallels the Mediterranean Sea, and then swings southeastward to the Persian Gulf.

Its three great river valleys have been of vital concern to various empires throughout history: the Nile in Egypt; the Orontes River flowing between the Lebanon Hills of Syria; and the Tigris-Euphrates valley of modern Iraq. The third significant factor is the modern one of oil, because the Middle East is today the world's greatest single source of petroleum, with some two-thirds of the world's reserves.

From Arabia the original Moslems spread throughout much of the region during the 7th and 8th centuries, and they almost swept aside the early Christian civilization, even penetrating France in 732. For nearly two centuries the Crusaders tried to take back from the Seljuk Turks the Holy Places of the Middle East, but they were finally unsuccessful. Then the Ottoman Turks came in from the east, captured Constantinople in 1453, and pushed northward to the gates of Vienna before they were turned back in 1683. From then until 1815 the Ottomans, who were also Moslems, controlled the Balkans, North Africa, southward along the Red Sea and eastward to the Persian Gulf.

Decline of the Ottoman Empire

Then, like other empires before her, the Ottoman Empire began to decline, and during the 19th century it had to face Russia's repeated attempts to secure control of the strategic Turkish Straits that provided the exit from the Black Sea to the Aegean Sea and the Mediterranean. This rivalry between Turks and Russians was the result of Russia's natural desire to break out of its vast but land- and ice-locked boundaries and find warm-water ports to the south. Britain, because she was afraid that Russian influence in this area would threaten and perhaps cut her communications with India, encouraged Turkey to resist Russia. While Turkey was doing so, the British and French took over for themselves several of Turkey's possessions in North Africa and the Middle East.

British and French efforts to bolster up the "Sick Man of Europe," as Turkey was called, were doomed to failure because her subject Christian peoples in the Balkans were discontented with Turkish domination. Greece had become independent in 1829, and by 1912 such Balkan states as Serbia, Bulgaria, and Rumania had also become independent. While Turkey was trying to suppress rebellions in the Balkans and resisting Russia, her possessions in North Africa were being taken from her. France seized Algeria in 1830 and Tunisia in 1881; Egypt won its virtual independence from Turkey in 1841, only to be occupied and administered by Great

*The Trucial Sheikhdoms consist of small communities which signed treaties in the 1820's and later with the British government, agreeing to a "truce" in their attacks upon British ships. They agreed to permit the British government exclusive authority in their possessions.

Britain from 1882; and Italy received most of Libya after the Turkish-Italian War of 1911. The Ottoman Empire would probably have collapsed some time in the 19th century had not the great powers intervened from time to time, each one not wishing to see another take over Turkey.

The final blow came after World War I. Turkey allied herself with Germany and suffered the consequences of the defeat of the Central Powers. By the Treaty of Sèvres in 1920 the Sultan had to renounce all rights over Palestine, Transjordan, Arabia, Syria, and Mesopotamia, and officially recognize her earlier losses in North Africa. Turkey was restricted to Constantinople and Asia Minor.

While the Allies were working out the details of the Treaty of Sèvres, Greek forces invaded the soil of their old enemy. Fired by a spirit of nationalism the Turks rallied behind their leader Mustafa Kemal, drove out the Greeks, and in 1922 deposed the Sultan and proclaimed the Republic of Turkey. Under their leader Mustafa Kemal, later known as Atatürk, Father of the Turks, the country became united, and introduced reforms to modernize the nation.

The main objective of the Turkish reforms was to separate Turkey from its ancient Asiatic-Arabic traditions and culture, and to develop her into a modern westernized state. Kemal Atatürk's reforms were directed against all the institutions which could perpetuate the old order. The spiritual leadership of the caliph, the religious leader, was abolished, religious courts were denied any influence in civil matters, the Latin alphabet was introduced, and the capital removed from ancient Constantinople to the new capital of Ankara.

The constitution of 1937 was based on a program which included republicanism as the form of government, nationalism based on common citizenship instead of upon religion or race, populism or equality before the law, and *étatisme* or participation by the government in the national economy. This break with the past set Turkey on the road to becoming a modern nation.

Egypt

Egypt in 1914 was nominally a part of the Ottoman Empire, ruled by a khedive who in theory recognized the authority of the Turkish Sultan, but who in fact was controlled by the British. When Turkey joined with Germany in World War I, the Suez Canal and the naval base at the eastern end of the Mediterranean were of increasing strategic importance to the Allies.

The ruling khedive, sympathetic to the Turkish cause, was deposed by the British and replaced with an Egyptian sultan whose country now became a British Protectorate. A delegation of Egyptians, desiring independence, unsuccessfully tried to represent Egypt at the Peace Conference in 1919. The leaders were exiled for their temerity, but in 1922 Great Britain gave Egypt its independence under its sultan, now raised to the rank of king.

Britain retained her right to defend the Canal and to exercise with Egypt her authority in the Anglo-Egyptian Sudan. Egypt was still subject to British intervention through the High Commissioner who watched over British interests. British troops remaining in several Egyptian cities and the Canal Zone were a source of conflict until 1936, when the High Commissioner was withdrawn, and the British troops were restricted to the Canal Zone only. In 1936 Farouk I came to the throne, but personal extravagance, corruption in public office, and delays in promised reforms led to an uprising in 1952.

The Society of Free Officers selected Major-General Mohammed Naguib as commander-in-chief and forced Farouk's abdication. Naguib became Prime Minister of a temporary government until the republic was instituted with him as its first President and Prime Minister. In 1954, Lt-Col. Gamal Abdel Nasser, the principal influence behind the army *coup* of 1952, removed Naguib and succeeded him as Premier. Two years later, in 1956, Nasser was elected President by an overwhelming vote, with a constitution providing for freedom of speech, press, and religion, under a democratic, republican form of government.

Iran

An agricultural civilization existed in this region six thousand years ago. Cyrus the Great founded the Persian Empire here in 550 B.C. In the 19th century Persia lost vast territories to Afghanistan and Russia, and the discovery of oil in 1901 led to Anglo-Russian rivalry and the division of Persia into zones of influence. The present Pahlevi dynasty was founded in 1925 by a *coup d'état*. In 1935 the name of the country was changed from Persia to Iran.

In 1953 the Shah decided that after twelve years of constitutional rule the country had made too little progress. He took over power for himself, started the "White Revolution" or the "Revolution from the Throne" by dividing his own lands among the peasantry, building dams and irrigation systems, power plants, and factories.

In 1961 he suspended the constitution in order to speed up land reform, decreeing that all land in excess of one thousand irrigated acres and two thousand unirrigated acres must be sold to the government at the valuation previously placed upon the land by the owners for taxation purposes.

Subsequent reforms gave workers a share in factory profits, extended rights to women and improved health and education services. Much remains to be done to raise income and to improve the mortality and the 80-percent illiteracy rates.

In October 1967, after ruling since 1941, the Shah was officially crowned Emperor of Iran, having "earned" the crown instead of simply "inheriting" it. Social security measures provide accident, sickness, and retirement benefits, and free medical care and hospitalization for insured persons.

Iraq

This country dates back seven thousand years to Sumerian civilization, and is said to have been part of the Garden of Eden. It became part of the Ottoman Empire in the sixteenth century, and remained under Turkish rule until World War I. Made a British mandate in 1920, it became independent in 1932. Revolution in 1958, preceded by eight earlier *coups*, deposed the king. This was followed by recognition of the Soviet Union and the People's Republic of China.

Despite large income from oil, the people of Iraq remain poor and illiterate, and aware of the great benefits from oil income enjoyed by their Iranian neighbors.

Jordan

The Hashemite Kingdom of Jordan was formerly a part of the Turkish Empire until 1916. The present East Bank of the river Jordan was set up as Transjordan in 1916, as a British sphere of influences. In 1928 Britain recognized it as independent, but retained financial and military control until 1946, when it was proclaimed the Kingdom of Transjordan.

In 1948 fighting broke out with Israel, and in the subsequent armistice Transjordan acquired the West Bank and changed its name to the Hashemite Kingdom of Jordan, with Hussein Ibn Talal as its king.

Kuwait

The young, small nation was settled by Arab tribes in the 18th century, was nominally a province of the Turkish Empire, but requested and received British protection when its sheikh feared absorption by Turkey, and was recognized by Britain as an independent state in 1961. Kuwait has no drinking water, but enough oil—about one-fifth of the world's reserves—to make one person in every 230 a millionaire, in a population of 700,000. Proportionately, this would be 900,000 millionaires in the United States.

A feudal wilderness, it ranks today only slightly below the United States in per capita income.

It is a capitalist welfare state with free education through the university, free medical service, free telephone service, token rents, and one of the world's highest ratios of doctors and hospital beds. In 1961 it requested British aid against Iraq, which claims Kuwait as a province.

Muscat and Oman

A backward area on the Gulf of Oman and the Arabian Sea, the Sultanate of Oman is one of the least-known areas of the world. It is a dictatorship, although the present ruler, who deposed his father in 1970, promises a modern government. Oil reserves have only recently been developed; their sale should increase the annual revenue greatly.

Saudi Arabia

Officially a kingdom, its flag is green with a white sword below the Arabic inscription, "There is no God but God, and Mohammed is His Prophet." As a political unit it dates from the 18th century when the Saud family gained control; it was named the Saudi Arabian Kingdom in 1932.

Known until recently for the annual pilgrimage to Mecca, the capital of Saudi Arabia, with more than 300,000 pilgrims in 1966, the country was economically transformed by the discovery of oil in the 1930's. Half of the income from oil, developed by foreign companies, goes to the government, which means the king, since there is no legislative body.

Southern Yemen

Officially the People's Republic of Southern Yemen, this collection of some twenty former sheikhdoms, sultanates, and emirates, was officially proclaimed a nation in 1967. With no industry, no natural resources, no railroad, and only an occasional paved road, this young nation was born from the fighting between a native National Liberation Front and the Egyptian-supported FLOSY, Front for the Liberation of Occupied Southern Yemen.

Although in theory governed according to the principles of Islam and "scientific socialism," Southern Yemen is ruled by decree. Slavery of African descendants was officially abolished in 1968.

Yemen

Officially the Yemen Arab Republic, this forbidding area along the Red Sea is known in Arabic as the Right Hand, because this is the direction of the country as one stands in front of the Kaaba in Mecca. In classical times it was the site of the rich mercantile Kingdom of Saba or Sheba. It was under Turkish domination for four centuries until World War I.

In 1958 Yemen joined the United Arab Republic of Egypt and Syria to form the federation of United Arab States. When Syria withdrew, President Nasser of Egypt dissolved his association with Yemen, claiming that it was reactionary. By a *coup d'état* in 1962 a revolutionary government came into power, supported by

Nasser. Saudi Arabia supported the deposed ruler, and for six years Egypt spent millions of dollars unsuccessfully supporting its candidate. Not until 1970 did civil war end with a coalition government of monarchists and republicans.

2. The Palestine Mandate: Emergence of Israel

Historical Jewish Connection with Palestine

The present situation of unrest between the Arab world and the state of Israel, which became an independent nation in 1948, can only be appreciated against the background of history.

Some thirty-two centuries ago the tribal ancestors of the Jews migrated into Palestine and for twelve centuries occupied it as their home. According to Jewish tradition, the children of Israel came to Palestine forty years after their exodus from Egypt, about 1250 B.C., under the leadership of Joshua. The word Israel was another name for Jacob, whose battle with the Angel of God (recounted in Genesis 32:24–28), gave him the name Israel, meaning He Who Struggles with God. Historical evidence shows that a group of tribes called Israelites came from the Syrian desert into lands lying along the eastern seacoast of the Mediterranean. Under pressure of attacks from common enemies the several tribes of Israelites banded together to form a kingdom under Saul, and extended their territory under the kings David and Solomon to include the entire region between Egypt and Assyria. It was Solomon who built the Temple of Jerusalem which gradually became the center of Israelite religion and national life. When Solomon died, the ten northern tribes formed their own kingdom of Israel, and the two smaller tribes or kingdoms formed their own kingdom of Judah, with Jerusalem their religious center.

In 721 B.C. the Assyrians destroyed Israel, carrying off many of its citizens, later to be known as the "ten lost tribes," who disappeared from history. Judah accepted the suzerainty of the Assyrians, who were in turn conquered by the Chaldeans. In 586 B.C. the Chaldeans swept into Judah; they destroyed the Temple and carried off the people to Babylon, in what is called the Babylonian Captivity. There the Jews managed to preserve their religion with the help of famous prophets like Jeremiah and Daniel whose words now form part of the Old Testament. When Cyrus the Great, founder of the Persian Empire, offered the Judeans the opportunity to return to Palestine in 538 B.C. some 40,000 did so, and in time built the Second

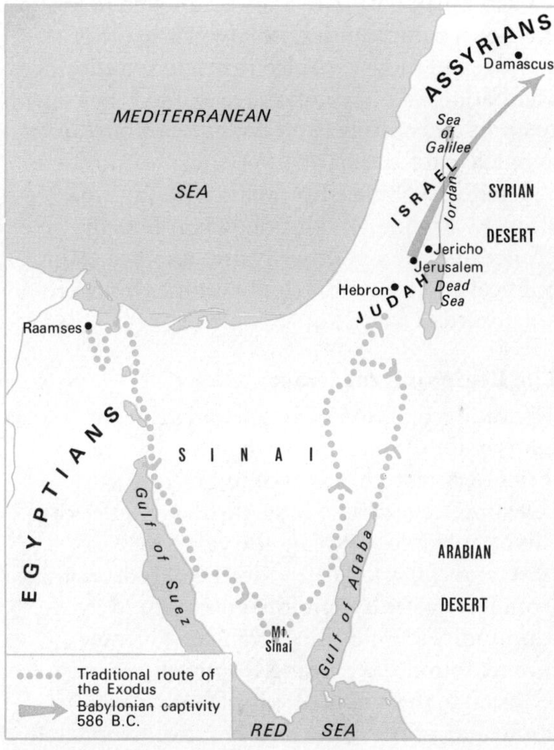

Biblical Palestine

Temple. Very little is known about the people during the next four hundred years, but it was during this time that the Pentateuch, from the Greek *pente*, five, and *teuchos*, book, the first five books of the Old Testament, was written and became the center of Jewish life.

From 63 B.C. the Romans ruled this land as their province of Judea, which was roughly the region of King Solomon's kingdom of several centuries earlier. Disturbed by increasing taxation from Rome, and a growing sentiment for nationalism, the Judeans revolted in 66 A.D., and in 70 A.D. were finally crushed by the Romans, who burned the Second Temple. Later revolts ended in further slaughter and ultimately to the dispersal of the Jews, the Diaspora, to other lands. Over the centuries Jews in Europe were usually compelled to live in their own communities, isolated from other people, and they were also restricted to specified occupations. As a result, they retained their own customs and culture, and had little opportunity to participate in the life of people around them.

Their first chance for emancipation came after the French Revolution, when Jews in France and then in other countries were given political and economic opportunities but were not accorded social equality.

The Beginnings of Israel

The modern nation of Israel had its beginnings in the 19th century when the first of a series of Aliyot, or waves of migration into Palestine, began. The first Aliyah (singular of Aliyot) took place during the years 1882 to 1904, and consisted of about 25,000 Jews, mainly from Russia, who went into an existing Jewish community in Palestine of 25,000. The newcomers found the existing community quite opposed to their idea of a Jewish national homeland, and in time they became assimilated into the older community. A great Jewish migration of more than 2,000,000 took place over the next twenty years, with most of the migrants going to the United States. The small number which went to Palestine came in as pioneers dedicated to working on the land.

These people set up two distinctive institutions that are characteristic of today's Israel, the *kibbutz* and the *moshav*. The *kibbutz* (plural, *kibbutzim*) is a communal agricultural settlement that is owned in common by the group. The *moshav* is a co-operative village of people who own land individually but work together for common interests.

The Balfour Declaration and British Mandate

During the post-war years of 1925 to 1939 another wave of about 350,000 immigrants from Poland and Central Europe brought the skills and learning of business and professional people who did much to develop the industry and education of Palestine. Many of these people were encouraged to come because the Balfour Declaration of 1917 stated the British government's intention of providing "a National Home for the Jewish people," which many believed foreshadowed the hope of the Zionists who wanted the resettlement of the Jews in Palestine. The term Zion referred to the hill in Jerusalem which was the site of the royal residence of David and his successors; it signified the re-establishment of the Jewish nation.

By the mid-1930's the situation in Palestine had become tense because the Balfour Declaration seemed to have made two contradictory promises. When Foreign Secretary Balfour had stated that his government "will use their best endeavors to facilitate the achievement" of a National Home for the Jewish people, he had qualified the promise by saying that the pledge was made "without prejudice" to the rights of non-Jewish communities in Palestine.

By 1936 the Arabs in Palestine, who had

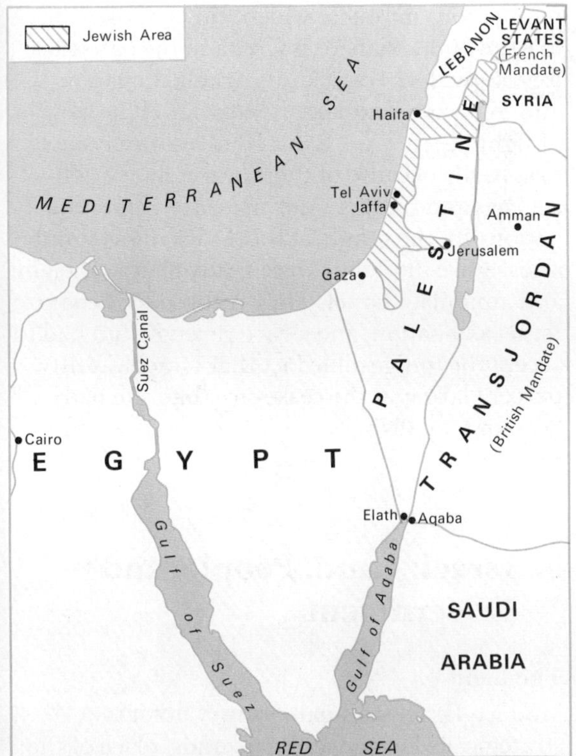

Palestine after World War I. By the treaty of Versailles, 1919, Britain and France received mandates over Palestine and Syria.

actually welcomed Jews in the 1920's, now objected to the great wave of immigrants that threatened to engulf them. In 1919 the Jewish population had been no more than 65,000. By 1933 it had risen to about 215,000, but it was still no threat to the more numerous Arabs. But the Jewish persecution by Hitler resulted in an influx of another 165,000 between 1933 and 1936, with Jews making up about 30 percent of the population in Palestine.

British Proposals for Palestine

Arab extremists decided to take action by attacking Jewish settlements. In self-defense the Jewish settlers organized their own forces, which eventually became the well-organized military *Haganah.* The situation was rapidly getting out of hand and, as World War II loomed nearer in Europe the possible conflict threatened British oil and communications in the Middle East.

A conference of Arabs and Jews in London in early 1939 proved to be fruitless, so the British government issued a White Paper, or policy statement, proposing the end of their mandate and the establishment within ten years of an independent Arab-dominated Palestine. For the next five years Jewish immigration was set at a maximum of 75,000. Upon the outbreak of World War II the Jewish community, knowing that their interests could be served better by Britain than by the Arabs, joined the British forces and gained both military experience and a cache of clandestine weapons.

When the war ended the United States urged upon Britain the admittance into Palestine of 100,000 Jews. In 1947, unable to find a settlement that satisfied both Jews and Arabs, Britain submitted the problem to the United Nations, which appointed a Special Commission on Palestine. A majority of the commission recommended partition of Palestine into Jewish and Arab states; a minority recommended a federal state including both Jewish and Arab communities. The Arabs violently objected to both recommendations, and in doing so they made a tactical error in rejecting the federal plan. Had the Arabs accepted it, they could have controlled the Jews, who would have lost public sympathy had they rejected either plan. In November 1947, the plans were referred to the United Nations, which decided, by a two-thirds majority, upon partition.

Civil war broke out in December, and the United Nations was powerless to act. The Palestine Jews bought arms from Czechoslovakia, while the United States unrealistically called upon the United Nations to give up the partition plan, and urged Britain to keep the mandate over Palestine.

Independence and War, 1948

On May 14, 1948, at 4 p.m. David Ben-Gurion read the proclamation of independence, "In the Land of Israel, the Jewish people came into being." By the decision of its own people the state of Israel was an independent nation. It was recognized almost immediately by the United States. Arab reaction was immediate and violent. In Cairo a spokesman for the Arab League said, "This will be a war of extermination and a momentous massacre which will be spoken of like the Mongolian massacres and the Crusades." Egypt, Jordan, Iraq, Saudi Arabia, Lebanon, and Syria attacked Israel, but after eight months of fighting, they were forced to ask for a cease-fire, partly because of their own military deficiencies and partly under pressure from other nations. In the minds of the Arabs it was simply a cease-fire until they were ready to attack again and annihilate Israel. They refused to recognize Israel as a nation, and swore revenge, but had to accept the indigestible fact that Israel was fifty percent larger at the cease-fire than she had been in May 1948.

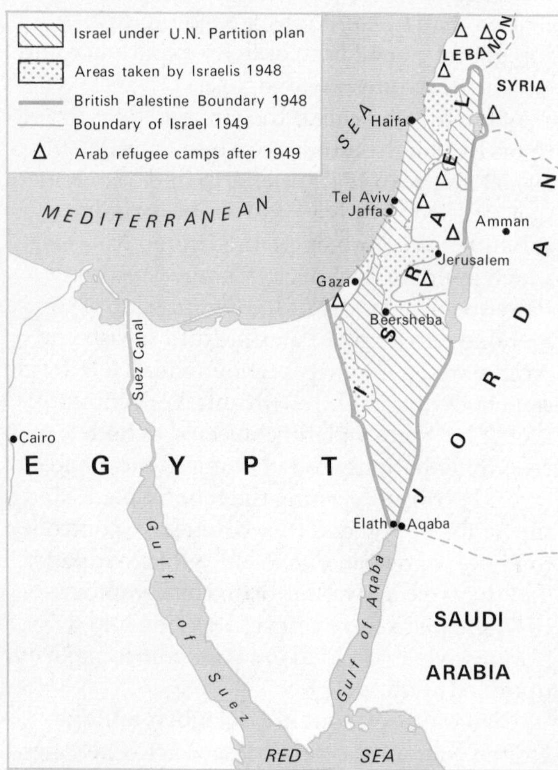

Israeli Independence, 1948. The map shows both the United Nations *plan* and Israeli action.

3. Israel: Land, People, and Government

The Land

Modern Israel is a small country but it is strategically located at the meeting-place of the three continents, Europe, Africa, and Asia, and it controls the only land route between Egypt and the Fertile Crescent. On the land side it is surrounded by the Arab states of Egypt, Jordan, Syria, and Lebanon. It stretches only 265 miles from the northernmost point, Metulla, to the Red Sea port of Elath in the south. The narrowest point is near Elath, only six miles between Egyptian and Jordanian borders. The country's greatest width is only 70 miles, from the Dead Sea toward the coast. Only 7,993 square miles in area, about the size of New Jersey or Massachusetts, it is a land of great physical contrasts. The most luxuriant of its several distinct regions is the narrow 115-mile strip along the Mediterranean, where most of the people live, and where Israel's heavy industry is concentrated.

A central chain of hills runs from Lebanon in

the north to the Negev desert in the south. In the northern region of the hills, around Nazareth, the Arab population of Israel lives in small communities.

The Jordan River rises in Israel, is fed by streams from Lebanon and Syria, and, until the Israeli-Arab war of June 1967, flowed across Jordan into the Dead Sea. Four nations have so vital an interest in its waters that the Jordan has been a constant cause of friction between Israel and these three neighbors. Half of the land of Israel consists of the Negev desert, a triangular land mass extending from the Judean Hills to the Gulf of Aqaba. The northern part around Beersheba is being put under cultivation, and as the River Jordan water project is extended southward, more of the desert will be cultivated.

Israel is developing her own natural resources of oil, magnesium salts which are available in large quantities in the Dead Sea, and important phosphate deposits in the Negev. Through great effort Israel has put much of her land under cultivation, and its farms can produce enough foods, except meat and grain, to feed its people. Israel's great agricultural problem is the shortage of water supply in the south, but she is diverting water sources in the north and has entered into an agreement with the United States to build in the near future a nuclear unit to desalinate sea water.

The most important cities are Jerusalem, for religious reasons, and the important ports of Haifa, Elath, and the twin-city of Tel Aviv-Jaffa, the first all-Jewish city in the world. Nearly 20 percent of Israel's total population lives in this cosmopolitan city, which is the cultural center of the country.

The People

The total population in 1970 was 3,004,000, of whom 2,561,000 were Jews, 328,000 Moslems, and 115,000 were Christians and Druzes. Between 1948 and 1964 more than 1,000,000 immigrants came into Israel from more than 80 countries, with over half of them from Asia and North Africa. These new Jewish immigrants have created a difficult problem because their social background and culture differ so greatly from the existing Jewish community. These "Oriental" Jews, as they are called, came from such countries as India, Turkey, Iraq, Iran, and Egypt, and they brought with them their own social customs. Their educational standards are generally lower than those of the older Jewish community, and for several reasons they have become the economically underprivileged group; with generally lower incomes, and lower literacy, they lack the skills and educational standards necessary for professional, civil service, and managerial careers.

Israel is a Jewish state with not only non-Jewish minorities but also Jewish groups who differ in religious practices from the official religion, and who therefore can become divisive political forces.

One distinctly minority group is the Druze people of about 40,000, whose origins are still uncertain and whose closely-guarded religion is believed to be a combination of Moslem, Jewish, and Christian traditions. The Druzes have adopted Arabic as their language, but they have kept their separate identity. Extremely loyal to Israel, they fought as the only non-Jewish unit in Israel's war for independence. The 75,000 Christians include Arab Christians, Greek Orthodox Christians, and Quakers.

The majority of Israel's Arabs are Moslems, and overnight in 1948 they became a minority in the new nation. Although Israel has done much to educate and improve the living standards of these Arabs, they are always a potential problem because they regard as brothers the Arabs living in Arab nations across the border.

Government

Officially the nation is Medinat Israel, the State of Israel, a parliamentary republic with a president, a prime minister, and a single-chamber legislature of 120 members, called the Knesset. Its members are elected for 4-year terms by universal suffrage, it elects the president, whose duties are formal and ceremonial, and has the power to dissolve itself. The prime minister is chosen by the party, or coalition of parties, which has the majority in the Knesset.

The first man to hold that position was David Ben-Gurion, who was born in Russia in 1886, founded a Zionist movement in his home town, and in 1905 emigrated to Palestine. Before World War I he studied in Greece and Turkey, and while vacationing in Palestine when war broke out in 1914, he was exiled with other Zionist leaders. He spent several years in the United States working for the Zionist movement, returned to Palestine, served as Secretary of the General Federation of Labor until 1935, and from then on was the leader of the *Mapai*, the Israel Labor Party. He was responsible for many of the important political decisions which shaped Israel's future, and also for the Defense Forces which played a very significant part in defending Israel in the first few months of her existence.

Golda Meir. Israel's tough woman prime minister.

Levi Eshkol became Prime Minister in 1966, and led his country through the Six-Day War of 1967. He was succeeded by Mrs. Golda Meir, who has served her people during the past fifty years.

Born in Kiev, in the Russian Ukraine, in 1898, she was brought by her family to Milwaukee in 1906. As a young girl she planned to become a teacher, but after graduation from teacher's college she became a staff member of Poale Zion, a small Yiddish-speaking faction of the Labor Zionists. In 1921 she decided to emigrate to Palestine because she felt that "Jewish people had the right to one spot on earth where they could live as a free independent people." That same year she married and persuaded her husband to sail with her on the third aliyah, wave of migration. In Palestine she lived and worked for a time in a kibbutz, then worked for the Histadrut, and became a delegate on the Women's Labor Council. She was one of the signers of the proclamation of independence of the State of Israel on May 14, 1948, and was the only woman member of the first legislature.

She was appointed by Ben-Gurion as Minister for Foreign Affairs in 1956, and served until 1966 in that office. In March 1969 the Cabinet and the leaders of the Israel Labor Party passed over other candidates and selected her as Prime Minister. In the general elections of October 1969 her party failed to win a clear majority, and she was obliged to choose her cabinet from six parties. The need to satisfy the interests of the several groups has complicated her arduous task of negotiating with the United Arab Republic.

One great weakness of Israel's political system is its use of proportional representation in the Knesset. A list of candidates for the 120-member legislature is prepared by each party which contests the election, and in proportion to the number of election votes received, each party is represented in the Knesset. In 1961 there were 24 parties with candidates up for election, and 11 of these parties returned one or more members. Unlike a two-party system, the proportional representation method does not "waste" votes. But whereas the two-party system seldom has even an effective third party representation, in Israel's system of representation there are numerous splinter groups. This may appear to be more democratic than a two-party system, but actually an Israeli government must consist of a coalition of at least two parties, probably more. Consequently, each party may have to give up some of its principles in order to persuade other parties to join it. Voters may therefore find that the party they voted for has changed significant parts of its platform.

The Arab issue has proved to be one which greatly affects Israeli politics. For example, the *Mapam*, United Workers' Party, favors the rights of Arabs in Israel, while the *Herut*, Freedom Party, favors the expansion of Israel to include Jordan west of the Jordan River, and is therefore anti-Arab. Although in foreign affairs the Herut is violently anti-Russian, there is a Communist Party which is decidedly pro-Soviet. A government formed by a combination of Mapam, Herut, and the Communists would have a very difficult time formulating domestic or foreign policy.

Another political problem is religion. A strong religious minority wants a theocratic state, one run by Church authority, while the larger group insists upon a secular state in which religion is separated from politics. The theocratic supporters want to enforce strict dietary laws, control the education of the state, and even enforce their religious beliefs and doctrine throughout Israel. The problem is somewhat complicated by the fact that during the Diaspora, when Jews were scattered through many countries, each Jewish community of necessity developed its own local religious and cultural institutions. Although four religious parties received only 15 percent of the seats in the 1961 election, they have been able to exert considerable influence by joining with the Israel Labor Party which controlled 30 percent of the seats.

Co-operatives and State Ownership

The Histadrut is the General Federation of Labor, but it is also the owner of industrial plants and co-operatives. In the 1920's Histadrut encouraged its members to make jobs by organizing themselves into producers' co-operatives, to organize their own selling outlets, to start their own businesses and hire their own members, and to sell their produce and manufactured goods collectively instead of competing with each other. By 1963 Histadrut employed some 200,000 workers, and produced nearly 75 percent of the nation's food.

The government also plays a significant role in the country's economy. It owns and operates railroads, builds highways, irrigation and drainage facilities, and owns more than half the shares in many businesses which produce electric power and develop mineral resources. There are two main reasons for government participation. One is the belief in the Zionist state, a country into which Jews may immigrate; this means unrestricted immigration and the need for government assistance in finding and making new jobs. The second reason is that Israel has had to depend upon foreign financial contributions to develop farms and build industries. The United States has given financial aid and technical assistance; West Germany has given Israel large sums as reparations for seizure of Jewish property by the Nazis, and has also paid "restitution," or what could be called "conscience money" for the millions of Jews deliberately killed in Germany's extermination camps. But this foreign assistance cannot be counted on indefinitely. Another of Israel's economic problems will be to find growing markets for its goods in order to obtain money for further internal improvement. Israel will probably have to cut down demand for products by its own citizens, keep wages at a steady level, and be ready to face competition on the foreign world market. Government ownership and controls will probably increase rather than lessen.

4. Foreign Affairs, 1948–1967

The Suez Canal Incident, 1956

After the 1948 war with her Arab neighbors, Israel hoped that she could come to terms with them. But these hopes proved fruitless because the Arabs had no reason to be conciliatory. Raiding parties from Egypt were repeatedly sent across the frontier to plunder and kill, and by 1956 Egypt, Syria, and Jordan had signed a military agreement which the Israelis were convinced was directed against them. By 1956 other events had made Israel desperate. In 1954 Great Britain and Egypt came to an agreement which prepared for the evacuation of British troops from the Suez Canal. In 1955 Egypt arranged an arms agreement with the Soviet Union.

As a counter-measure the United States offered to finance in Egypt the much-needed Aswan Dam to increase arable land for the growing population. Israel, unable to buy arms from the United States or Great Britain, believed herself to be deserted by friends while Nasser of Egypt was planning to encircle her. Egypt recognized Communist China, and arranged to buy Soviet military equipment through Czechoslovakia. The United States appeared to use these actions as sufficient reason to withdraw her offer to help finance the Aswan Dam project. The Soviet Union quickly offered to help Egypt to build the dam. In October 1956 the Soviet Union was busy suppressing a revolt in Hungary, and the United States was occupied with the presidential election campaign. Israel decided to strike her enemy before being invaded herself. On October 29, 1956, she crossed the

Suez, 1956. French and British troops in the canal area.

frontier and moved into the Sinai Peninsula. Immediately, Britain and France issued an ultimatum to Israel and Egypt that unless fighting stopped within twelve hours, and all forces withdrawn ten miles from the Suez Canal, their own forces would attack.

Nasser rejected the ultimatum, President Eisenhower appealed to Britain and France to halt their projected invasion, and the United Nations drafted similar resolutions. For the first time Great Britain, supported by France, used her veto in the Security Council, and for the first time the United States and the Union of Soviet Socialist Republics aligned themselves against Great Britain and France.

On October 31 Anglo-French air forces attacked Egyptian installations along the Canal, and this was followed with troop landings. By November 5 the Israelis were in occupation of the Gaza Strip and the Sinai Peninsula, had reached the Canal and pulled back the ten miles demanded by the British and French. After repeated appeals from the United Nations, Prime Minister Eden of Great Britain agreed to a cease-fire, but he defended his attack on Egypt as a means to prevent "a forest fire" from spreading to "a large war."

The Israelis withdrew from most of the territory they had occupied; they agreed to withdraw from the southern tip of the Sinai Peninsula, from which the Egyptians had blocked the Gulf of Aqaba, only when the United States morally committed herself to support Israel's right of "innocent passage," the right of merchant ships to sail through the Gulf to the Israeli port of Elath.

So severely was British and French prestige shaken that Nasser with impunity denounced Egypt's 1954 treaty with Britain by which Egypt would take over complete control of the Canal after seven years. He seized all British installations in 1956.

The Israeli-Arab War, June 1967

During the 1948 Arab-Israeli war more than 650,000 Arabs fled from Palestine to neighboring Arab countries, where they became refugees and displaced persons awaiting the day when they could go back to their homeland. Their tragedy is that nations have done little to remedy their situation, a pitiful existence eked out on meager rations doled out by the United Nations and relief agencies. Some observers claim that oil-rich Arab countries could have resolved the problem had they wanted to. The refugees are a political asset to the Arabs who claim that the Jews must be driven out of Israel and the country turned over to the Arabs. The realistic political fact is that for 25 years the Arab people have

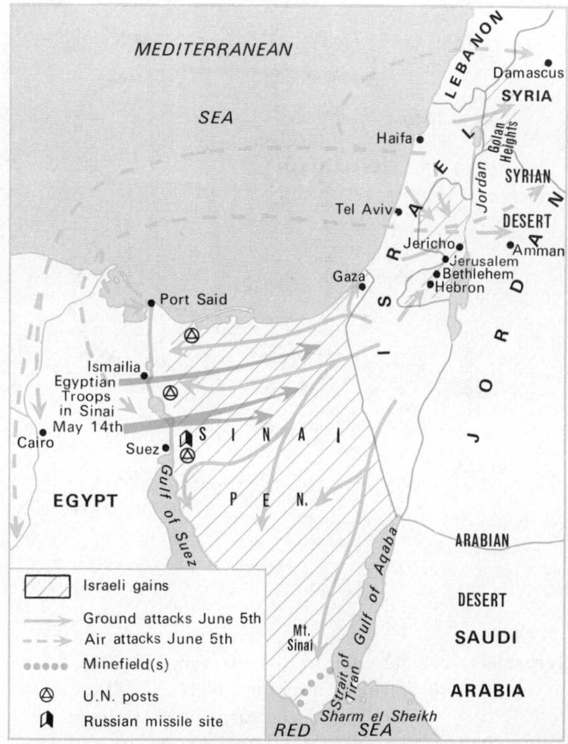

The Arab-Israeli War, 1967

nursed their hatred of Israel and waited for the day when it could be driven into the sea.

On May 14, 1967, Nasser started to move 80,000 Egyptian troops and armor into Sinai and demanded the withdrawal of the United Nations troops stationed as a deterrent along the Egyptian-Israeli frontier. The United Nations forces withdrew on May 19. On May 22 Nasser closed the Gulf of Aqaba and completely bottled up Israel's southern port of Elath, and announced, "The Israeli flag will not pass through the Gulf of Aqaba . . . if the Israelis want to threaten us with war they are welcome." Two days later the Egyptians placed mines across the 4-mile-wide Strait of Tiran, the entrance to the Gulf, and sowed mines in the Gulf. On May 26 Nasser warned Israel that an attack on Egypt or Syria would mean all-out conflict in which the Arabs' "main objective will be the destruction of Israel."

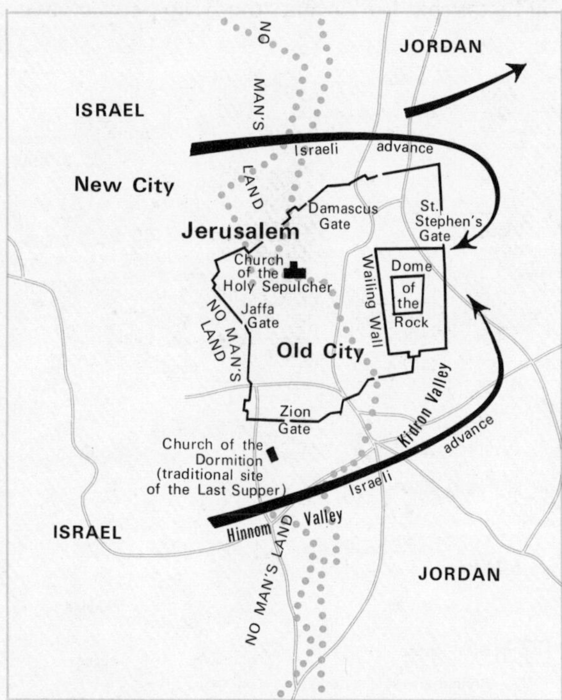

Jerusalem, 1967. Jews and Arabs both regard the Old City as their religious shrine. Before the 1967 war the Old City was partly a "no man's land" and partly Arab territory, although the lines were constantly in dispute. The capture of the Old City was a major objective of the Israeli forces.

Israel decided that she had no choice but to strike before being attacked. On June 5 Israeli planes flew out into the morning darkness over the Mediterranean, came in below radar level and struck at more than a dozen airfields in Egypt, Syria, and Jordan. Nasser immediately called for assistance. Syria shelled northern Israeli towns from hills overlooking the Sea of Galilee, while Jordan opened a second front by bombarding Jerusalem and shelling Tel Aviv with long-range guns.

Israel quickly seized the Biblical towns of Jerusalem, Jericho, Hebron, and Bethlehem, took over all of King Hussein's kingdom of Jordan west of the Jordan River, and occupied the entire Sinai Peninsula, including the fortress of Sharm-el-Sheikh which blockaded the Gulf of Aqaba.

On June 10 the United Arab Republic accepted the United Nations cease-fire proposal, and the next day it broadcast that the Six-Day War was ended.

Was the war inevitable, and why had it ended so quickly and in such a complete victory for the Israelis? The basis of the Middle East conflict of 1967 and the continuing tension in the months since then is the refusal of the Arabs to accept the existence of the State of Israel. The Arabs have deep roots in Palestine and a moral claim to the land. They seized the country in the 7th century, wrested it back from the Crusaders, and for more than 13 centuries lived there and were the vast majority of the population. Palestine has sacred meaning for Moslems, for tradition says that the Prophet visited Heaven by a ladder of light from the place marked today

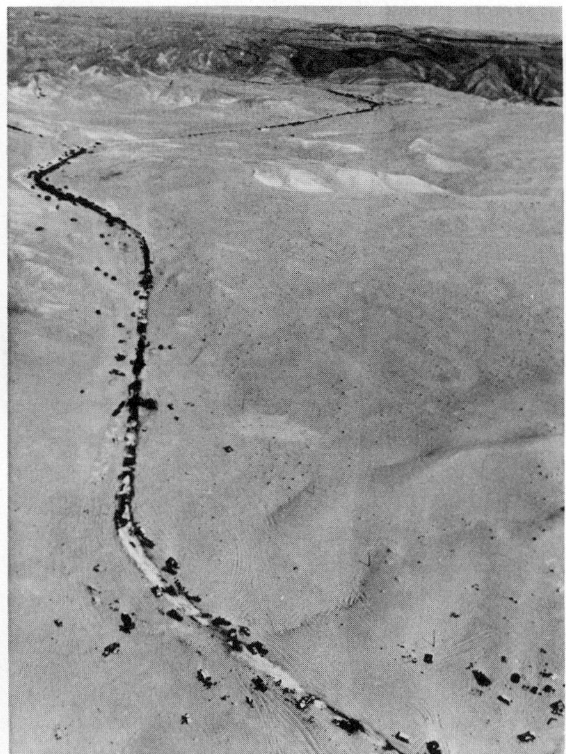

Egypt Defeated. Lines of tanks and trucks abandoned and destroyed in the Sinai Desert.

Israeli Soldiers show joy after taking the Old Quarter of Jerusalem from the Jordanians in 1967. The Dome of the Holy Rock mosque, in the background, was not damaged in the fighting.

by the Dome of the Rock in Jerusalem. Perhaps the real tragedy of the Arabs is their inability to use the skills of the Israelis to make the Middle East a prosperous region.

Nasser proved his ability to begin to solve Egypt's problems by planning the Aswan Dam, emancipating women, and even attempting to find a solution for the Israeli problem. But other Arab nations have been unwilling to join together for common purposes, and Nasser seems to have been diverted from practical solutions by the aspiration to become a leader of all Arabs.

The Arabs have been too long subject to foreign domination to develop a sense of cooperation and nationhood. Their loyalty to family and tribe does not encourage a real sense of being a nation with a distinct identity. Even when attacked by a nation of only 2,600,000 people, the four immediate neighbors Egypt, Lebanon, Syria, and Jordan with a total population of 40,000,000 people could not defeat a little nation one-sixtieth their combined size. Realistically, the presence of Israel cannot physically threaten the combined forces of all Arab nations. Arab hatred is caused by other factors. Israel has accomplished so much in so short time. Israel is a modern state which symbolizes much of what the Arab world resents but sorely needs. The Arab people are being inevitably drawn into the modern world, and could raise themselves to a prosperity they have not known for many centuries if they adopted Israel's techniques for developing desert land. But Arab "justice," as the extremer elements call it, demands the elimination of the Jewish state.

5. Problems since the 1967 War

The United Nations states that "there should be no territorial gains by conquest," and that Israel should be willing to negotiate on that basis. The flaw in the argument is that the Arab nations have been not only unwilling to recognize the existence of Israel, but have also insisted on maintaining a state of belligerence. There were, however, hopes that these attitudes could be modified.

Israel's Dilemmas

Israel's announced conviction that her safety depended upon the retention of all the territory she occupied in June 1967 has created several problems for herself. One of these is unemployment. Before the war Israel was already suffering a serious four percent unemployment rate in a labor force of 950,000. The problem was worsened by the addition to her Arab population of another 1,000,000 from the occupied areas. The acquisition of Jordan west of the river brought in 800,000 Arabs, half of them the regular population, the other half earlier refugees from Palestine. The Gaza Strip had another 300,000 Arab refugees, and the territory taken from Syria another 15,000.

The very nature of the Jewish nation is seriously threatened by a growing sense of nationalism among the Arabs within Israel's borders; the addition of over a million more Arabs in the occupied territories created an approximate proportion of three Arabs to every five Jews. Already Israel is facing the internal problem of the discontented "Oriental" Jews who resent their inferior position in Israel. The threat of the complicating Arab problem cannot be ignored by Israel when considering whether or not to surrender part or all of her 1967 conquests.

The Problem of Displaced Arabs

In 1948 about 650,000 Arabs fled from the new State of Israel; by May 1967 that number was said to have doubled, although this figure may be exaggerated, since ration cards of dead Arabs are not turned in; the extra food is far too valuable. The United Nations Relief and Works Agency has been feeding these refugees since they fled to Syria, the Gaza Strip, and Jordan in 1948. On an annual budget of $39,000,000 UNRWA spends 9 cents per day for dry foodstuffs for each refugee. This niggardly ration is only a little more than half what the poorest person eats in the Middle East.

The actual number of refugee Arabs is probably no more than 10 percent of all people displaced by World War II, but the Arabs are in a politically sensitive part of the world. Unfortunately they have been used for political purposes, and their misery has been prolonged to arouse fierce antagonism against Israel. Arab nations refuse to permit the refugees to move freely, partly because of their political use as refugees, and partly because they could prove

Arabs in Israel are subject to frequent searches by Israeli troops.

to be politically embarrassing if they moved into other Arab states. Although Arab nations have generally argued that to accept them would be to admit that Israel is a nation, several of the Arab states have other good reasons to keep them out.

Lebanon opposes admitting them because at present the country is almost equally divided between Christians and Moslems. Arab refugees would create a Moslem majority, and since the Lebanese constituion demands that the president must be a representative of the country's largest sect, the present Christian leader would be replaced by a Moslem.

Syria could face a serious aggravation of her present economic and political instability if she admitted refugees.

Egypt, faced with a rapidly-rising birthrate that already threatens the agricultural gains to be made by the Aswan Dam, cannot absorb refugees. Jordan, faced with the loss of her fertile land across the Jordan River, is no longer economically viable without financial help from outside.

The U.S.S.R. and the Middle East

For more than 150 years Russia has had military and strategic interests in the Middle East. Czarist Russia's attempts to control the Turkish Straits were blocked by Great Britain and Germany in the late 19th century. With the Revolution of 1917 Russia was concerned at first with sheer existence, and then it was striving to build itself up as the leading Communist nation. The years immediately after World War II were occupied with the Cold War against the West, but after the death of Stalin in 1953 events in the Middle East provided the Soviet Union with the opportunity to play an active role there. Arab antagonism to Israel, and a growing sentiment among the Arabs for nationalism gave the Soviet Union the chance to weaken the influence of the western powers. The Soviet Union could advance its strategic interests and its objective of spreading Communism at the same time, by encouraging the relatively "have-not" Arab nations to become envious of their oil-rich neighbors and by fostering Arab unity against the common enemy Israel.

Western influence in the Middle East could be further threatened if Israel was presented as the agent of foreign powers, particularly the United States, which the Arabs blamed for the continued existence of Israel. The Soviet Union could also use western oil interests as a weapon against the West, claiming that the oil resources which could be used to raise the standard of living of the Arab people, had been seized by seven of the largest United States and British oil companies.

For ten years before the Israeli-Arab War of June 1967, Russian technicians and military experts were "advising" Egypt and Syria on military matters. The swift Israeli victory was a blow to Soviet expectations and a loss of prestige in the eyes of the Arabs. The Soviet Union evidently misjudged the military capabilities of both Arabs and Israelis, and it was not prepared for a direct confrontation with the West. Despite this setback, the Soviet Union is giving even more military equipment to Arab nations, and the Soviet Mediterranean fleet is clearly demonstrating its presence by appearing in Arab ports.

This policy gives the Soviet Union such allies as Egypt, Algeria, and Syria, which are important in the Soviet Union's bid for power in the Mediterranean. Other strategic Arab nations are Somalia, which controls the Gulf of Aden approaches, and Egypt, the Sudan, and Yemen, which control the shores of the Red Sea. The Soviet Union has in recent years become aware of the importance of sea power, and it is ready to challenge United States sea power in the

Mediterranean. However, the Soviet Union had made no apparent attempt to encourage the creation of one Arab state or even a federation of Arab states, because such a consolidation could weaken Soviet influence. It is in the interest of the Soviet Union to foster local rivalries and anti-Israeli sentiment but not to risk a major war in this highly explosive area.

Soviet-Egyptian Treaty

Since Middle East oil is cheaper than Russian oil, it would be to Russia's advantage to be in a position to restrict oil supplies to the West.

The "friendly, unofficial visit" to the United Arab Republic in May 1971 of Soviet President Nikolai Podgorny, accompanied by the Soviet Foreign Minister and the Deputy Defense Minister, resulted in a diplomatic and political *coup* by the Soviets. The 15-year Soviet-Egyptian Treaty included the Russian pledge to continue aid to the United Arab Republic and to continue its objective of the recovery of "all Arab territories occupied by Israel." The new treaty appeared to give the Soviet Union added prestige in the Mediterranean, and to reduce Washington's influence in Cairo. But events in July 1972 changed that situation.

Ouster of Soviet Advisors

Twice in 1972 President Sadat went to Moscow to demand the fulfillment of an earlier Soviet pledge to provide MIG-23 fighter planes and ground-to-ground missiles. Twice Sadat was rebuffed. Because of this he was convinced that the Soviet Union did not intend to build up Egypt's military force to the capability of challenging Israel. He also believed that at the Moscow Summit meetings Brezhnev had agreed to withhold offensive weapons from Egypt, as a way of avoiding a possible Middle East confrontation between the United States and the Soviet Union.

At home Sadat faced increasing resentment for his indecisive no-war, no-peace policy of the past several months. Resentment among his army leaders became serious, because although Russian technicians were helping Egypt, they were aggravating Egyptians with their disdain and antagonism toward Arabs. So serious were disputes on some bases that joint mediation committees had to be formed.

In July Sadat announced that he had ordered Russian military advisors out of the country, and that Egyptians would take over all bases and equipment. The situation was not such a setback for the Russians as it at first appeared, because they were allowed to continue using naval facilities at Alexandria, Port Said, and Mersa Matruh, and to keep their own naval personnel there.

The United States and the Middle East

The United States was one of the very first nations to recognize the State of Israel in 1948, and since that time American citizens have made heavy private financial contributions to support Israel economically. As a consequence, American popularity and prestige among Arab states is decidedly low, particularly since the United States has been supplying Israel with military planes, and has promised more.

In recent years United States interest in the Middle East has been to avoid involvement in the tensions between Israel and Arab nations. The United States has shown its concern over further possible conflict in that area, and would prefer to avoid involvement that could lead to confrontation with the Soviet Union. Neither major power could benefit from such a confrontation, with all its possible consequences.

The Fedayeen: Arab Guerrillas

A growing threat to negotiations since 1968 has been the activities of the *fedayeen*, the "men of death" who have conducted what Arab countries proclaimed as a *jihad* or Holy War against Israel.

The best-known and probably the largest group of several is Al Fatah, which has conducted frequent raids on Israeli territory, with the purpose of terrorizing and killing. To the Israelis the fedayeen are thugs and terrorists, committed publicly to the extermination of the State of Israel. Their methods have been brutal and in several instances included the bombing of cinemas, school-yards, and crowded markets.

Their victims have been indiscriminately women and children and whoever has happened to be in their line of fire. One avowed aim of the fedayeen has been to goad Israel into retaliation and further expansion of its boundaries because, according to Yassir Arafat, leader of Al Fatah, the very process of Israeli expansion would bring reaction from countries whose borders were threatened. In 1968 Arab terrorists staged over 1,000 incidents and killed more than 900 Israelis.

Civil War in Jordan, 1970

The civil war which broke out in Jordan in September 1970 between the guerrillas and the Jordanian army was inevitable. From 1968 to 1970 several successive Jordanian cabinets and the eleven guerrilla organizations that make up the Palestine Liberation Organization, PLO, were in chronic conflict. By the summer of 1970 the guerrillas were practically joint rulers of Jordan, setting up their own laws, carrying weapons in defiance of government prohibition, and openly defying King Hussein and his government.

A basic cause of guerrilla opposition to Hussein was resentment that the king did not show sufficient regard for his Palestinian people who make up 65% of the population of Jordan. So tense did the situation become that three times since 1968 small though actual wars broke out, with that of June 1970 resulting in the death of 200 people in three days of fighting.

The Jordanian Civil War. Loyal Jordanian troops display a picture of King Hussein as they patrol Amman in 1970.

In August 1970, an assassination attempt on Hussein infuriated the Jordanian army, particularly the Bedouins who are contemptuous of the Palestinians and resentful of the growing power of the guerrillas. Hussein had given in to the guerrillas because he believed that a showdown with them would result in civil war. The army came very close to mutiny in 1970 when Jordanian premier Abdel Rifai made an agreement permitting the guerrillas to operate openly in the capital of Amman, and keeping the army outside the city. So humiliated did the army feel that one tank commander, while on review maneuvers for Hussein, flew a woman's undergarment instead of the official pennant on his aerial. When asked by Hussein why he did this, he snarled in reply, "We have all become women."

The hijacking of three planes to Jordanian

Fedayeen Guerrillas dance on top of the wreck of one of the three jetliners they had hijacked to Dawson Field and destroyed after releasing the passengers and crews. Hijacking of jetliners for political purposes became a major international problem in 1970.

soil in September 1970 was the final humiliation for the army, because the units which immediately surrounded the grounded planes were ordered by Hussein to do nothing more. So outraged were Hussein's Bedouin troops that they intimated they might depose him. Hussein found himself with no choice but to take decisive action if he wished to avoid mutiny. He fired and replaced the prime minister, and appointed Field Marshall Habas Majali as commander-in-chief of the army and military governor of Jordan, with orders to "act immediately to undo hostile planning."

Claiming that in twenty-four hours the guerrillas would be cleared out of Amman, Majali moved tanks and artillery into the city. Majali had badly miscalculated guerrilla resistance. The fighting lasted for 10 days, refugee camps were ruthlessly shelled because they were said to be harboring guerrillas, and estimates were that at least 20,000 people were killed. Wounded were left unattended on the streets for days. Shortages of water and food, outbreak of disease, and atrocities by Hussein's Bedouin troops left a bitter resentment among the population of Jordan.

Fedayeen Expelled from Jordan

Jordan was particularly open to trouble because in 1948 when the State of Israel was created, of the more than 1,000,000 Arabs in Palestine only 160,000 chose to remain in the new nation of Israel. Some went into the Gaza Strip held by Egypt, and others to the West Bank of the Jordan River, then made a part of Jordan. Some 700,000 ended up as refugees in 54 refugee camps scattered throughout Jordan, Syria, and Lebanon. There they remained for more than 20 years, forgotten by the world, and deliberately abandoned by other Arab nations as pawns in the Arab struggle against Israel.

These became the hundreds of thousands of refugees from whom the fedayeen were recruited and may in the future continue to be recruited. Nevertheless, the example of commando activities against Jordan's Hussein has caused concern in other Arab countries. Not only can they threaten the internal stability of these nations, but they can become a serious obstacle to possible peace in the Middle East.

One extremist group of the Palestine Liberation Organization, the PLO, is the fanatical Popular Front for the Liberation of Palestine, the PFLP, led by George Habbash, who has challenged the leadership of Yassir Arafat. Habbash, a Christian and a Marxist, stole the spotlight with his airplane hijackings in 1970 in Jordan. Habbash has attempted to win radical support with his pronouncement, "What we want is a war like the war in Vietnam." Such extreme views as Marxism and continued war may by no means be welcome in other Arab countries. Iraq has all but banned commandos from her soil, Syria has watched them closely, and the United Arab Republic has expelled several hundred "undesirables" who included guerrillas.

In 1971 Hussein had no choice but to drive the guerrillas out of Jordan completely. They were setting up their own self-governing soviets in the Jordanian territory they controlled and blatantly challenging Hussein's authority. Driven from their Jordanian bases, and severely restricted in Syria and Iraq, they chose Lebanon as their headquarters in fifty square miles of the rocky Arkub area. From there they could continue their attacks on Israel, because the Lebanese dared not take action against them for fear of reprisals against the government.

In March 1972 the situation changed completely after guerrilla ambushes killed five Israeli citizens. The Israelis warned the Lebanese government that it must accept responsibility for guerrilla activity, and launched the heaviest land and air attack since the Six-Day War. Tanks and troops moved into "Fatahland," as the Arkub has been called ever since the Lebanese government allowed the Al Fatah guerrilla group to make a base there. For four days the offensive continued, and as soon as the Israeli attacks ceased, Lebanese tanks and troops went in, "this time to stay."

Guerrilla fighting will continue because the fanatical Popular Front for the Liberation of Palestine will not give up. Their purpose is not only to destroy Israel but to overthrow what Habbash considers to be corrupt and conservative Arab governments. "We don't want peace," he said. "Peace would be the end of all our hopes." If a third world war would be the only way to destroy Israel, Zionism, and Arab

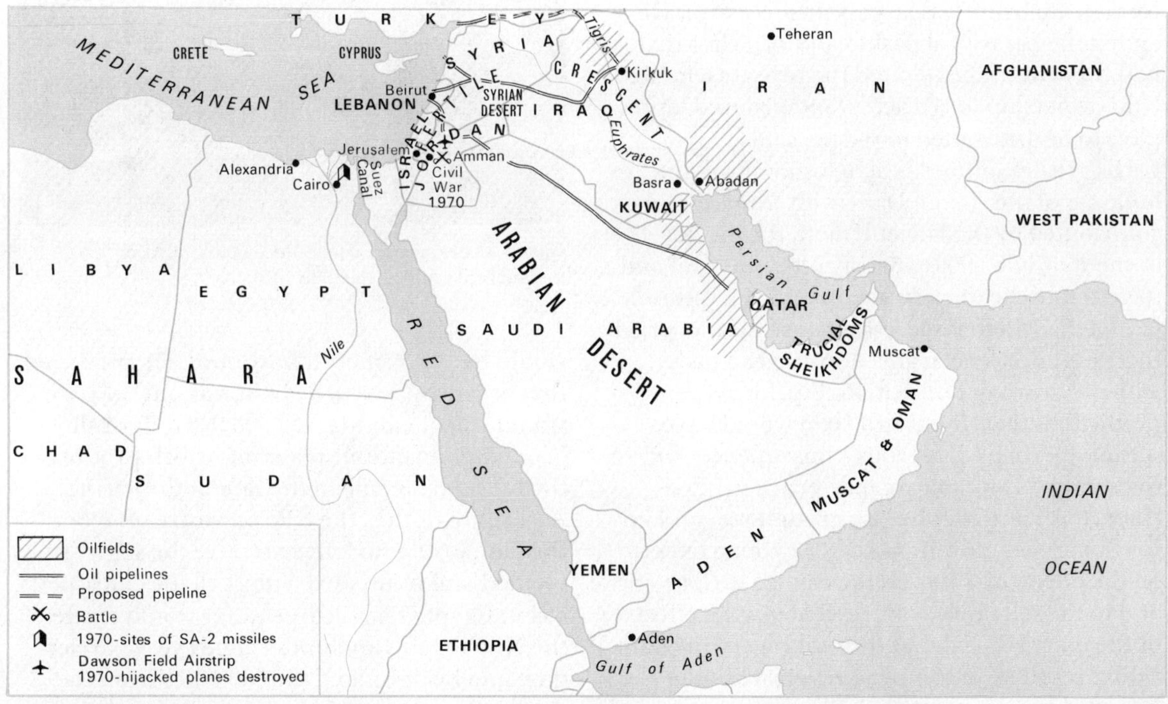

The Middle East, 1972

reactionism, "then we wish for it" says Habbash.

Their determination to spread terrorism world-wide was shown at Munich, Germany, with the deliberate assassination of eleven members of Israel's team at the Olympic Games, and with the mailing of letters containing bombs to Jewish leaders in Europe, Canada, the United States, and Australia.

Nasser's Achievements and Failures

In 1952 Gamal Abdel Nasser played a significant role in overthrowing the corrupt and inefficient government of King Farouk. Nasser's success in the *coup d'état*, and his promises to bring prosperity to Egypt and to provide leadership in the Arab world were not fulfilled when his sudden death at the age of 52 in October 1970, stunned the Arab world. In domestic affairs Nasser achieved moderate success, but in foreign affairs he was largely unsuccessful. He ended the parasitical pasha-landlord class that had for centuries exploited the peasants, limited land ownership to 208 acres, and ordered larger plots to be distributed to the peasants.

His greatest domestic achievement was the building of the Aswan Dam, with funds largely contributed by the Soviet Union, for the development of 1,500,000 acres of cultivable land and to generate cheap electric power. Even this project has had limited success because the increased food supply has been able only to keep pace with the growing population. Furthermore, predictions that the Aswan Dam would have serious, perhaps disastrous, consequences for the country's agriculture may prove to be correct. A few weeks before ground was broken for the project a distinguished Egyptian expert on the effects of water on the earth's surface and in the soil publicly warned about the effects of the dam. He said that the building of the dam would result in "a complete reversal of time-honored Nile irrigation policy" and that it would be "extremely hazardous." He predicted that because it was to be built without sluices it would trap an annual 134,000,000 tons of silt "containing volcanic materials which produce the most fertile soil on the face of the earth." As a result of this, the Nile downstream from the dam would no longer receive the silt which formed and nourished almost all the cultivated soil in Egypt. The silt-free water would erode the Nile's banks and undermine every barrier-dam and bridge along the 600 miles from the Aswan Dam to the Mediterranean. Further-

Gamal Abdel Nasser. The central figure of Arab nationalism until his death in 1970.

more, changes in underground water movements would cause such losses in the lake forming behind the dam that Egypt would almost certainly end up with less water.

Much of what the Egyptian expert predicted has happened, for it has recently been estimated that 6,000,000 acres of cultivated land now need fertilizer. The delta coastline has been eroded by sea currents, and millions of acres are threatened with permanent damage because of the rise in salt content of the soil. Although only a disappointing 300,000 acres had recently been reclaimed, another 700,000 acres have been converted to agricultural land through canal irrigation. However, the United Arab Republic now faces the problem that underground drains and pump installations necessary to combat the salinity of the soil would cost as much as the dam itself, and this would not remedy the major problem of the loss of valuable silt downstream.

The United Arab Republic is suffering from the failure to industrialize. Egypt's present population of 34,000,000 is expected to be 50,000,000 by the year 1980, with little hope that industrial development will be able to provide jobs for these millions. The lack of industrial development is partly to be blamed on Nasser, for in his professed intention to eliminate foreign domination over Arabs he discouraged foreign capital and engaged in disastrous foreign exploits. He intrigued against his neighbors, drove Syria out of the United Arab Republic by his domineering methods, engaged in two disastrous wars against Israel, and spent needed resources on a thoroughly unsuccessful war against Yemen. One of his most serious miscalculations was the acceptance of Syria's contention that Israel was about to attack Egypt. Nasser ordered the United Nations peace-keeping forces out of the controversial Gaza Strip, later expressing great surprise that Secretary-General U Thant of the United Nations took him at his word and removed the troops. Egypt's subsequent mobilization led to Israel's pre-emptive attack in June 1967, and the Six-Day War.

Nevertheless, for all his errors of judgment and his inability to raise the standard of living of his people, Nasser gave to Egypt and to men throughout the Arab world a sense of personal and national pride. Not only Egypt but most of the Arab world lost a man who will be difficult to replace. None of his potential successors appears to have the personality to step into his shoes.

Nasser's unsuccessful foreign exploits led him to want to avoid war in the future, and although the Soviet Union in all probability does not want to see a showdown between Israel and the Arabs, the interests of the Soviet Union in the Middle East can be served by "controlled tension," which provides the excuse to "support" Egypt with arms and technicians.

Cease-fire Talks

In July 1970 Soviet-made surface-to-air missiles, the S-A 2's, were moved secretly to within eleven miles of the west bank of the Suez Canal, thus threatening Israeli defenses on the east bank. Tensions grew alarmingly, but in late August the Israelis and Egyptians were persuaded to accept a 90-day cease-fire proposed by the United States and the Soviet Union. In September 1970 Israel charged, and the United States corroborated the accusation, that the Egyptians and Russians were building more missile sites and moving old ones nearer to the Canal, in violation of the "standstill" agreement that neither the United Arab Republic nor Israel should improve its military position during the cease-fire.

Very few talks were held between the two adversaries during the 90-day period; the truce was extended another 90 days in early November, but the same basic obstacles to real negotiations remained. The United Arab Republic continued to refuse to attend any talks until Israel agreed to withdraw from all the territory it had occupied in 1967. Israel countered with her refusal to talk until her status as an independent nation was recognized by the United Arab Republic. Such recognition would be a contradiction of Arab insistence that Palestine historically belongs to the Arabs. Israel insisted that the territory she occupied in 1967 is strategically essential for her very safety.

The Sinai, useless as land, is an important buffer zone. Israel might be persuaded to withdraw from it only if it was internationalized under the protection of a peace-keeping force supplied by other nations.

A very strategic area captured by Israel is the Golan Heights from which for twenty years the Syrians have shelled kibbutzim in Israel. It is unlikely that Israel will agree to return it without absolute guarantees that the area is demilitarized.

Another strategic point is Sharm-el-Sheikh, where the Gulf of Aqaba meets the Red Sea, and from which Egyptian guns once controlled the Strait of Tiran, which provides the one water access to the vital port of Elath, Israel's only outlet to the Indian Ocean. It is probable that Israel will refuse to give up this important point without ironclad guarantees that her shipping has free access to and from Elath.

The most emotional conquest of the 1967 war is East Jerusalem. For the first time in nearly 2,000 years the Wailing Wall, the remains of Solomon's temple compound, was held by Jews. Israel has vowed never to give it up, but the issue is complicated by the fact that Jerusalem is sacred also to Moslems and Christians.

Until December 1970 there seemed little chance that either nation was willing to budge from its intransigent position. Then the apparent deadlock was broken that same month when Israel agreed to resume indirect talks with the United Arab Republic and Jordan through Gunnar Jarring, the United Nations mediator. Israel's willingness to resume talks came the day after a very pessimistic report from Cairo, where President Anwar Sadat, successor to Nasser, stated for the first time his peace terms with Israel. She must give up "every inch" of territory captured from the United Arab Republic in the 1967 war; the United Arab Republic would be prepared to "negotiate" Israel's "right of passage" through the Strait of Tiran and the Gulf of Aqaba; Israel's use of the Suez Canal would depend upon the settlement of the Palestine issue.

Despite these apparently non-negotiable terms, Israel agreed next day to resume talks, but nothing was accomplished when the second 90-day cease-fire period ended in February 1971. President Sadat refused to extend the cease-fire further, probably because influential Egyptians believed that a further extension would simply harden Israel's determination not to compromise, and might even encourage it to make further demands upon the United Arab Republic.

Sadat's Peace Proposal

Then, surprisingly, Sadat offered terms for negotiation that opened new diplomatic channels for a Mid-East settlement, and in fact accomplished more in six months than Nasser had done since June 1967. As a condition for opening the Suez Canal he proposed "partial Israeli withdrawal," which he defined as "a line behind El Arish," a 90-mile withdrawal from the Canal which would remove Israeli troops from almost the entire Sinai Peninsula. In return he promised to open the Suez Canal in six months, and agreed to the probability of an international force to be stationed in Sharm-el-Sheikh, so vital to Israeli shipping to Africa and the Far East.

In February Sadat forced Israel upon the political defensive by informing United Nations special envoy Gunnar Jarring that the United Arab Republic was prepared to sign a peace agreement with Israel, which would mean recognition of the existence of the State of Israel. This has been one of Israel's major demands, unconditionally denounced by Nasser for more than three years.

In his public pronouncements since taking office Sadat has freed Egypt from commitments previously accepted by Nasser. Immediately after the 1967 war Arab leaders met in a Khartoum summit conference and there pledged themselves never to negotiate with Israel, never to reach a peace agreement with Israel, and never to recognize its existence as a nation. Sadat has instead made it quite clear that he wants a peace treaty, and that he is ready to recognize the existence of Israel.

Unlike Nasser, Sadat has taken great care not to be the spokesman for the Arab world, and has made it evident that he is concerned with the United Arab Republic alone. In his speech revoking the cease-fire he made no reference to Jordan or Syria, the other two nations whose territory was occupied by Israel.

Whatever the success of Sadat's proposals may be, he has forced Israel to reconsider its intransigent position of refusing to give up any of the territory it occupied in 1967. Furthermore, Sadat has won support from the nations which fear that an unsettled Middle East could escalate into an area of major conflict.

Hussein's Peace Proposal

The first concrete proposal for peace in the Middle East was Hussein's plan of March 1972. He proposed to turn Jordan and the Israeli-occupied West Bank area into a United Arab Kingdom of two semi-autonomous regions, with "any other Palestinian territories to be liberated." This referred to the Gaza Strip, an area formerly administered by Egypt.

Each of the two parts, Jordan and the West Bank, would elect a legislative council which would choose its governor-general. The Palestinian capital would be the old Arab sector of Jerusalem. Finances, defense, and foreign affairs for the United Arab Kingdom would be administered by a national government in Amman, the capital of Jordan, presided over by Hussein.

Reaction was predictable. Mrs. Golda Meir denounced the suggested surrender by Israel of any part of the Gaza Strip or Jerusalem. While she sarcastically denounced Hussein for "crowning himself King of Jerusalem," she did concede that "this plan affects Israel's most vital interests."

The Israeli parliament passed a resolution that the government should "continue to negotiate with Jordan." It may be conjectured that Mrs. Meir's attitude was deliberate and political, because immediate Israeli acceptance of the plan would have suggested that Israel and Jordan had collaborated.

Factors against the Proposal

One factor which may work against Hussein's plan for the West Bank is the increased prosperity of the Palestinians there. Five years after the Six-Day War and the Israeli occupation of the area, the earlier terrorism has given way to planning for the future.

This apparent success is no doubt in large part the result of Israel's immediate use of force and harsh punishment against Palestinian terrorists. Hundreds were imprisoned, and the homes of suspected terrorists were blown up. A call by commando chieftain Yassir Arafat for "a week of flaming vengeance" on the fifth anniversary of the Six-Day War brought no response in the West Bank.

Another obstacle to Hussein's plan may be the very liberal Israeli medical assistance and welfare payments to needy Arab families, even the families of terrorists. Israel has been largely responsible for an economic upturn in the West Bank, where the gross national product has risen more than 10 percent annually, wages have risen by nearly 18 percent, and unemployment has dropped. It is doubtful that Hussein could meet such conditions, but he may have one factor on his side. The Palestinians feel themselves to be second-class citizens in their native land.

The problem has recently become complicated by the threat of Colonel Muammar Kaddafi, strong man of Libya, to use Libyan embassies around the world as recruiting offices to enroll volunteers for the future struggle with Israel. Libya has a billion-dollar income from oil to support the Palestinian cause.

Review Questions

Section 1

1. Why is the Middle East sometimes referred to as the "bridge" from Europe to Asia?
2. Why did Kemal Atatürk wish to modernize and westernize Turkey? How did he do it?

Section 2

3. Has past history given the Jewish people any claims to the land of modern Israel?
4. In what ways did the problem of Palestine become increasingly difficult after 1930?
5. Does the blame for the 1947 situation in Palestine rest with Britain, the Arabs, the Jews, the United Nations, or a combination of two or more?

Section 3

6. How have the following geographical factors affected the relations of Israel with other nations: the size of Israel; the location of Elath; the Jordan River?
7. What are the main "racial" problems faced by Israel today? In what ways are they problems?
8. In what ways has the system of proportional representation complicated Israel's politics?

Sections 4 and 5

9. What conditions in the Middle East caused Israel to attack Egypt in 1956? Did the invasion of Egypt by Britain and France seem to be justified?
10. Why has Israel insisted upon retaining Jerusalem, the Gaza Strip, and the Sinai Peninsula?
11. What dilemmas has Israel faced since her victory over Egypt in 1967?
12. What have been traditional Russian interests in the Middle East? What are Russia's interests today?
13. In what ways did each of the following further aggravate the tense Middle East situation: (a) general activities of the fedayeen, (b) the hijacking of planes and other acts of terrorism, (c) violation of the cease-fire standstill agreement by the United Arab Republic?
14. How does each of the following appear to have affected the Middle East situation: (a) the death of Nasser, (b) the accession to the presidency of the UAR of Anwar Sadat, (c) the 1971 Russo-Egyptian Treaty,

4

India, Pakistan, and Bangladesh: A Subcontinent Divided

The British took over the administration of India from the East India Company after the Sepoy Mutiny of 1857, and ran it as a British colony. Early in the 20th century India demanded independence and accepted the leadership of Mohandas Gandhi in his campaign of non-violent non-co-operation, or passive resistance, to force Britain's hand. Concerned with probable Hindu domination if India was granted independence, the Moslem population organized as a political party under Mohammed Ali Jinnah to demand separate statehood.

In 1947 the two nations of India and Pakistan won their independence, amid terrible slaughter as Moslems left India, and Hindus sought safety in India. Pakistan was physically divided by a thousand miles of India between West Pakistan and East Pakistan.

Dissension between West and East Pakistan led to the declaration of independence by East Pakistan, as Bangladesh, and resulted in civil war between the two, conducted with savagery by West Pakistan.

Relations between the nations of India and Pakistan were embittered from the day of independence over the strategic province of Kashmir, which each claimed as its territory, and over which they were to fight.

In foreign policy India was for several years neutralist and non-aligned, but China's attacks on its northern frontier modified its neutralism. Pakistan, at first pro-Western, later turned toward Communist China — an enemy of India.

Terms

1. Monsoon
2. Urdu
3. Bengali
4. Hinduism
5. Reincarnation
6. Nirvana
7. Vedas
8. Dharma
9. Islam
10. Caste
11. Varna
12. Brahman
13. Kshatriyas
14. Vaishyas
15. Sudras
16. Untouchables
17. Communal Representation
18. Amritsar Massacre
19. Swaraj
20. Salt March
21. Moslem League
22. Sikhs
23. Panchayat
24. Awami League
25. Bangladesh
26. Mukti Bahini
27. Jihad

People

28. Dravidians
29. Aryans
30. Asoka
31. Mohandas Gandhi
32. Jawaharlal Nehru
33. Mohammed Ali Jinnah
34. Lal Shastri
35. Indira Gandhi
36. Ayub Kahn
37. Yahya Kahn
38. Mujibur Rahman
39. Zulfikar Ali Bhutto

Places

40. India
41. Nepal
42. Bhutan
43. Sikkim
44. Ceylon (Sri Lanka)
45. Himalaya Mountains
46. Pakistan
47. Islamabad
48. Hindustan
49. Rivers Indus, Ganges, Brahmaputra
50. Bay of Bengal
51. The Deccan
52. Western and Eastern Ghats
53. Jammu-Kashmir
54. West Pakistan
55. East Pakistan
56. Bangladesh

Events

1917 British promise of Greater Participation in Government for Indians
1919 Amritsar Massacre
1920 Demand by Gandhi for Indian Independence
1930 Salt March
1935 Government of India Act
1947 India Independence Act
1950 Occupation of Tibet by Communist China
1962 China-India Border Incidents
1964 Death of Nehru: Shastri becomes Prime Minister
1966 Tashkent Conference: Death of Shastri
Mrs. Indira Gandhi becomes Prime Minister
1971 India-Pakistan War
Bangladesh declares Independence

1. Land, People, Religion, and Caste System

The Land

The subcontinent of India* is a vast land mass of 1,680,000 square miles, less than half the size of the continental United States but with nearly three times its population. It is called a subcontinent because it is a part of Asia, the world's largest continent, and it is also a peninsula stretching nearly 2,000 miles southward into the Indian Ocean. India and the small countries of Nepal, Bhutan, Sikkim, and the island of Ceylon, are collectively called South Asia.†

In one respect the subcontinent of India is one geographical unit because, except for a few mountain passes, it is almost completely cut off from the continent of Asia. This has meant that India throughout history has never been quickly overrun by foreign invaders. But within its own frontiers, India consists of three main geographical areas: the mountain, the plain, and the plateau.

Except for the province of Kashmir, geographically the least important of these three regions is the Himalaya Mountain region of the northeast. It is in this mountainous region that the new nation of Pakistan is building its capital Islamabad, to be completed by 1976. The city is being built in this rugged Western Frontier region for security reasons.

The most important region is the Hindustan Plain, a flat lowland area extending west to east across India in a belt from 150 to 300 miles wide. Here are India's three great rivers, the Indus, the Ganges, and the Brahmaputra, making a great fertile plain which is the world's largest alluvial area of land, formed when soil is deposited by moving water. The Ganges River rises in the Himalayas and flows eastward for 1,500 miles into the Bay of Bengal. The Brahmaputra River rises in the far northeast corner of India, and flows westward to join the Ganges on the Bay of Bengal.

Because the Ganges basin receives so much rainfall and provides water for irrigation and the raising of such crops as cotton, sugar, rice, and wheat, over 125,000,000 people live in this part of the plain, concentrated in one of the most densely-populated regions of the world. Despite the dense population, there are few towns, and most of the people live in the thousands of small villages. Most of this delta region, with its population of 125,000,000 people and the city of Calcutta, is today in the nation of India.

The Western Plain is watered by the Indus River and its five tributaries, which flow west and southward into the Arabian Sea. Here was the home of India's first civilization of Harappā, in a region which was once wet and fertile, but which over the centuries has become dry and dusty.

The Hindustan Plain, or simply Hindustan, the Land of the Hindus, is the region where India's civilization and great empires originated. On the southern edge of Hindustan are several ranges of hills which separate it from a great plateau called the Deccan, surrounded on three sides, west, east, and south by ranges of rugged hills that isolate the Deccan from the coastal regions. The Deccan is a land that ranges from forests and arable lands to scrub country burned under scorching suns in the spring, and then lashed under the torrential rains blown in by

---

*The term India is used in the early sections to describe the whole subcontinent consisting of the nations of India and Pakistan, which did not become independent and separate nations until 1947, and Bangladesh in 1971.
†Bhutan and Sikkim are protectorates of India: Nepal and Ceylon are independent nations.

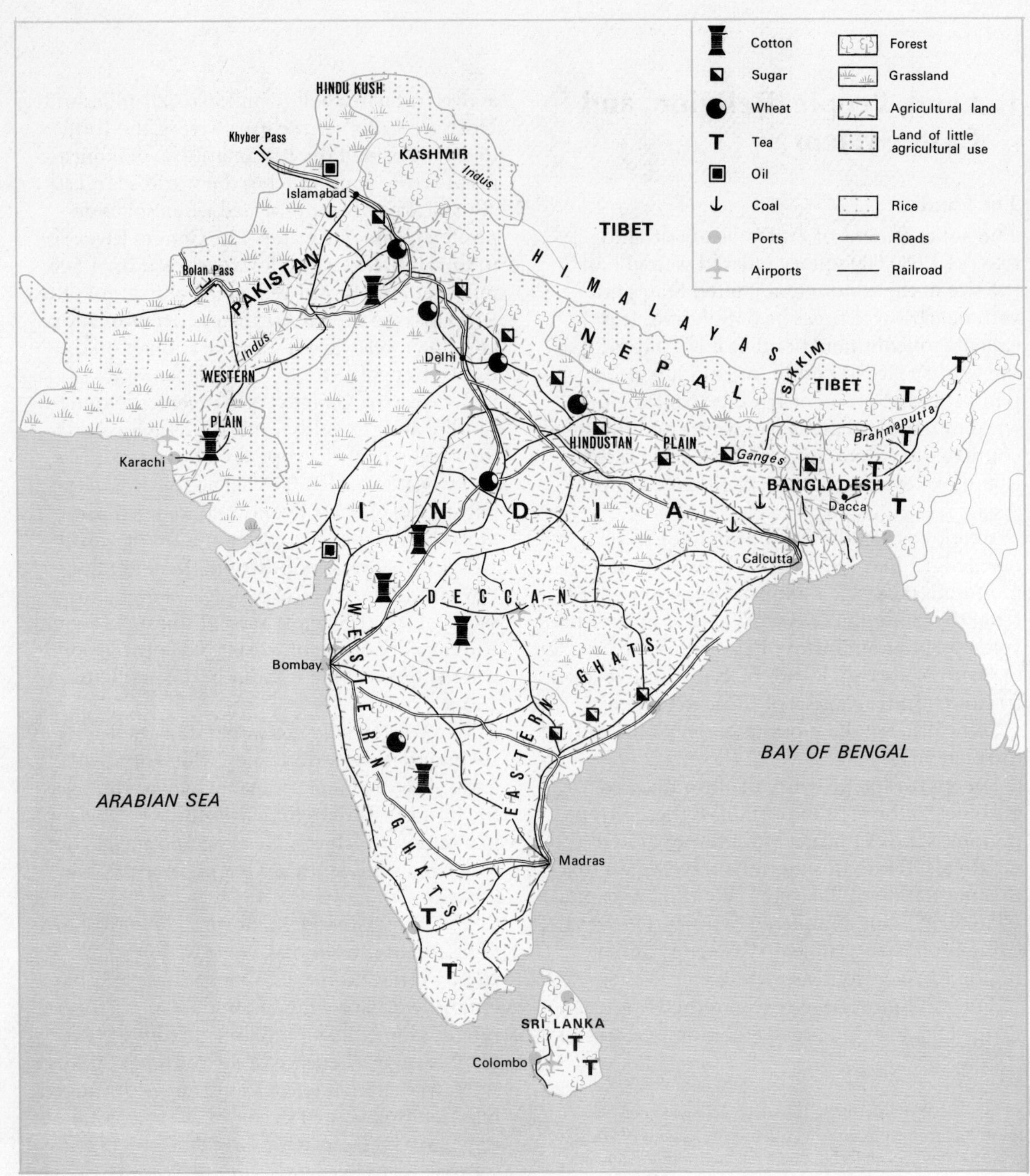

India, Pakistan, Bangladesh, and Sri Lanka. Land and resources.

monsoons, the winds that come in across the sea from the west. Frequently the sun-baked lands cannot absorb the rains, which turn into floods and sweep away people and farms. This region was long occupied since prehistoric times by people called the Dravidians, who have kept their culture and their language for more than 2,000 years.

Fringing the Deccan are the Western Ghats and Eastern Ghats, so named from the ghats or passes which break through the ranges of hills, and beyond them are the narrow coastal strips which are fertile and heavily settled, producing rice as the main crop. It is from these coastal strips that many thousands of Indians have migrated to Africa, Malaysia, and the South Pacific.

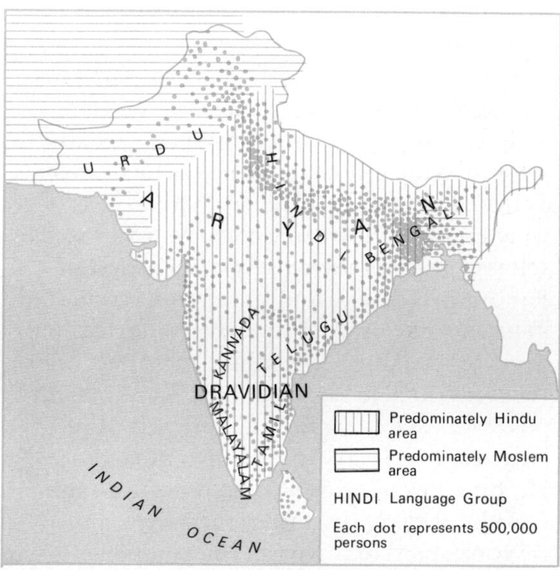

India and Pakistan. People, language, and religions.

The People

Over the centuries so many people have migrated into India from Central Asia, the Middle East, and Southeast Asia that "race" has come to mean little more than distinction between Dravidians and Aryans, and even this distinction has become less evident through intermarriage between dark Dravidians and light Aryans. Some Negroid characteristics are to be found in people living in the hills, and people with Mongoloid features are found in the northern region bordering on China and Central Asia.

Language

The national language is Hindi, spoken by about 160,000,000 people, and followed closely by the four regional languages spoken by 150,000,000 Dravidian people. Urdu is spoken by Indians of the north and by the majority of Moslems living in modern West Pakistan. Another important language is Bengali, spoken in the region around the lower Ganges River and its delta. Of the 14 officially recognized languages of India, ten are Aryan, and four are Dravidian. This diversity of languages makes difficulties for a nation attempting to unify its people, and has hindered the operation of the central government. Sanskrit is the language of religion and literary expression, and is spoken and written by the educated classes.

Religion

Hinduism is the dominant religion of India, practiced by more than 80 percent of the population, who accept its principle of the reincarnation or continual rebirth, and its aim of reunion of the human soul with the Supreme Being. Hinduism is very much a puzzle to Western man because it seems to have one basic contradiction. Hinduism has one God, Brahma, the eternal spirit or Supreme Being, but each family or individual can have his own god or gods, although each one is believed to be simply one of the infinite aspects of Brahma as seen by different people. Actually, Brahma is also expressed in terms of three gods: Brahma the Creator, Vishnu the Preserver, and Siva the Destroyer.

The Hindu believes that all things, including man, are repeatedly born or "reincarnated." The cycle or chain of life constantly repeats itself just as the insect lays an egg, which becomes a chrysalis, then a caterpillar, then an insect which repeats the cycle. Similarly, man's soul or self is repeatedly reborn. Another aspect of Hinduism is that a Hindu's religion is reflected in his every act in daily life. His rising, bathing, dressing, cooking, and eating are all part of his religious ritual in search of Brahma. The only possibility of ending the endless cycle of reincarnation is finally to reach Nirvana, the Hindu's idea of heaven or union with Brahma. Only by obeying strict rules through many reincarnations may Nirvana be attained.

Hinduism has no single system of belief, for it has no Bible or Koran, but it does have a literature of four books called the *Vedas*, which set forth the hymns, the teachings, and the rituals. These writings reveal the basic culture of the conquering Aryans who, as a cattle-raising rather than a farming society, left almost nothing else by which the archaeologist can reconstruct Indus civilization. The Aryan priests collected in great detail all the religious beliefs and practices of their people.

The thousand years between 1500 B.C. and 500 B.C. are called the Vedic Age, after the four great *Vedas*. The first great book is the Rig Veda, "Royal Knowledge," containing more than one thousand hymns, prayers, and ceremonial rituals. The other three books are the *Yajur Veda* of technical instructions for priests, the *Sama Veda* and *Atharva Veda* of rituals, incantations, and magical spells. There are other writings about heroes, but the Vedas are the religious books.

The important fact about the Vedic period is that the Aryan conquerors had to decide how to deal with the greater number of defeated native Dravidians, and at the same time retain their own racial identity. They solved the problem by organizing the caste system, by which people were born into permanent, fixed positions in society that could not be changed until another rebirth or reincarnation occurred.

Asoka

One of the most famous of the early rulers of India was Asoka, who lived about 250 B.C. Asoka was converted to Buddhism, an offshoot of Hinduism, but he seems to have been tolerant of both Buddhism and Hinduism. He was inspired by the ideal of non-violence and was perhaps the only powerful ruler in human history who actually apologized to a conquered people after a bloody war, and then issued Edicts carved on stone which renounced war as a policy. These amazing Edicts, only deciphered since 1837, also included moral directions and practical advice on all aspects of life and government, following the principle of Dharma which was, according to Hinduism, dutiful or conscientious action adopted to the caste and station in life of each human being.

Islam

India was repeatedly invaded from the north by Scythians, Huns, and others, who ruled the areas they conquered, but in time came to accept the Hindu religion and the caste system of the people they conquered.

Not until the Moslems came to India did another religion challenge Hinduism. Three times the Moslems came into India: in the 8th century with the Arabs; with the Turks in the 12th century; and with the Afghan-Turkish wave in the 16th century. The simplicity, equality, and security of Islam challenged Hinduism, but actually Islam made only a few converts.

The successive waves of Moslem invaders

PETER CLAYTON

Above. Mexican Aztec mosaic mask of Quetzalcoatl who represented the God of Fire.

PICTUREPOINT

Above. The Statue of Justice in Brasilia. President Kubitschek inaugurated the first buildings in 1958.

Below. Hidden high on the mountain tops of Peru the lost city of the Incas, Machu Picchu, was recently discovered by the American archaeologist Hiran Bingham.

JOHN BULMER/UNIPHOTO

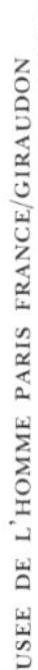

MUSEE DE L'HOMME PARIS FRANCE/GIRAUDON

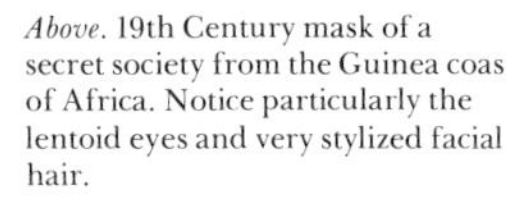

Above. 19th Century mask of a secret society from the Guinea coast of Africa. Notice particularly the lentoid eyes and very stylized facial hair.

PETER CLAYTON

Left. Classic Maya jade carving from Teotihuacan, with Maya dignitary, c1200 AD.

GIRAUDON

Right. 19th Century wooden mask from the Ivory Coast. The decoration above the head may have been horns but such masks often represent different things amongst the various tribes in the area.

GUIMET MUSEUM PARIS FRANCE/GIRAUDON

Above. Miniature from a story originating in Java in the 12th Century AD, about the adventures of Prince Inaung, which became a popular fairy tale in south east Asia during the 19th Century.

Right. Japanese print c1793.

GIRAUDON

Below right. Temple of Dawn in Bangkok, Thailand. Built 1844.

Below. Chinese bronze figures of Chou wrestlers 6th Century BC.

PETER CLAYTON

GERALD CUBITT/UNIPHOTO

JOHN BULMER/UNIPHOTO

JOHN BULMER/UNIPHOTO

Above. Vast cities of temples exist in Cambodia from a lost civilization between the 12th–15th Century, such as Ankor Wat.

Left. The ceremonial dress for the initiation ceremony of a Buddhist monk.

Below. Taj Mahal Mausoleum, east of Agra, India. Built by Shah Jehan for his favorite wife c1648.

JOHN BULMER/UNIPHOTO

established kingdoms in northwestern India, which became bases for their attacks on other parts of India. These Moslem Arab conquests might have remained simply as outposts of Arabian or Turkish empires had it not been for Genghis Khan and his Mongols. In the 13th century Mongols began their incredible sweep across the Asian continent from Japan to Hungary. They took ancient Central Asian trading centers, and raged into Baghdad killing, looting, and burning the famous libraries.

One of the Moslem regions which escaped the Mongol invasion was northern India, which then became a refuge for gifted Moslem scholars and wealthy businessmen. For three centuries northern India became a mixture of Hindu and Moslem states, until a third wave of Moslem invaders came in the 16th century. This time the invaders were Turkish Moslems from the modern Russian Turkestan, today a republic of the U.S.S.R., whose leaders claimed descent from Genghis Khan, and who were therefore Mongols, corrupted to Mughal or Mogul, the name given to the Mughal or Mogul Empire; this was one of India's greatest dynasties, whose first emperor was Babur, and whose descendants spread Mughal control over all India except in the southern tip beyond the junction of the Western and Eastern Ghats. One of Babur's successors was Akbar, who was sufficiently statesmanlike to realize that since he was governing a multi-religious and a multi-racial empire, he should be tolerant of the Hindu religion and customs, although he himself was a Moslem.

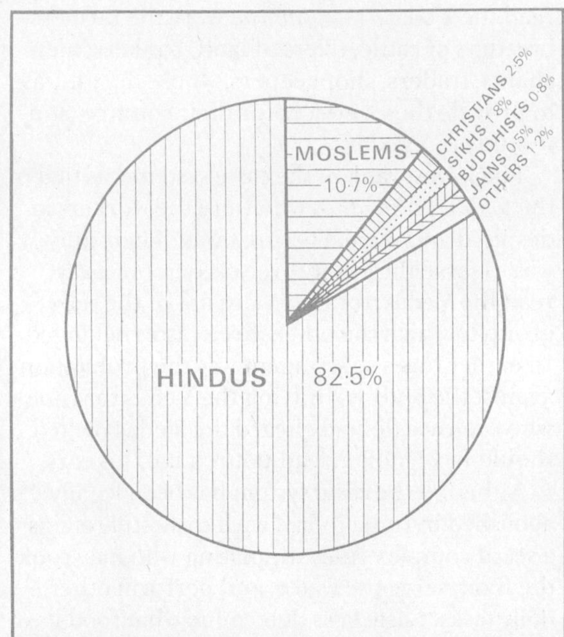

Indian Religions

Hindu converts to Islam were relatively few despite the ease with which a man could become a Moslem, simply by expressing his willingness to submit to Allah. The basic conflict between the two religions was the way in which man faced the sorrows and hardships of life. Islam insisted that the faithful must submit to the will of God and accept whatever sorrow came a man's way. Hindus, who believed in reincarnation of a soul in another body, accepted their obligation to improve their lives, and not passively accept what came. Some Hindus who did become Moslems were motivated by the opportunity offered to a Moslem to rise quickly in professions by skill and ability. The Hindu caste system prevented this, but the Hindu was usually unable or unwilling to attempt to break out of his caste. Other Hindu converts to Islam were either captives or conquered people who were forced to accept the customs, even to eat the food, of their conquerors, under circumstances which contradicted the basic beliefs of their Hindu religion. They were actually outcasts from their castes because they had violated the basic rules.

The Caste System

Historically, the Hindus believed in the caste system, and although the origin of the system is obscure, it probably goes back to the Aryan conquest of the Dravidians. The Hindu word for caste is *varna*, which also means color, and suggests that the light-skinned, light-haired Aryans regarded the dark-skinned, dark-haired Dravidians as inferiors. Certainly one of the chief concerns of the Aryans was to perpetuate their separate identity.

There were four main castes, although these were subdivided into more than 3,000 subcastes based on occupations. Land was important to the Aryan invaders, and they consequently appropriated it from the natives and made farming a legitimate and respectable Aryan occupation. Handicrafts and menial tasks were assigned to the subject races.

Yoga: A Fakir. Lying on a bed of nails this man is able, through meditation, to overcome the pain and achieve spiritual ease.

Society could function in an orderly fashion and without violent disturbances only if man rigidly followed the occupation or task destined for him by the caste into which he was born. If distinctions in society were to be maintained, then rigid rules of behavior must be followed. So it was claimed that at the time of the Creation, society consisted of four distinct and carefully graded and segregated classes. Whatever legend may suggest, the probable historical fact is Aryan control of the Dravidians.

The highest caste in Hindu society was that of the *Brahmans* or *Brahmins*, whose duty it was to study the Vedas, teach them to others, and perform all the necessary rituals and sacrifices. These formed the highest caste, as priests did in other societies, and they strictly enforced the caste distinctions. The next caste was the *Kshatriyas* who were the rulers and warriors whose duty it was to defend the country, and to read the Vedas. The *Vaishyas* were the farmers, breeders of cattle, tillers of land, bankers, merchants, traders, shopkeepers, whose duty it was to provide these services for their country, and to study the Vedas.

The lowest rank in the caste system was that of the *Sudras* or *Shudras*, who were the workers in despised and menial occupations. Their duty was to serve the other three classes, but *not* to read the Vedas, for they were not of the select group to which the other three castes belonged. In earlier times so stringent was the prohibition against the Sudras studying the Vedas that one who even accidentally heard the Vedas recited should have molten lead poured into his ears.

Although the caste system has been legally abolished in India today, each caste still retains a set of complex rules stipulating who may cook the food, serve the water, and perform other daily tasks. Caste laws determine what food its members may eat, who may marry whom. Within the castes are rigid subdivisions into some 3,000 subcastes in which every occupation has a place. There are castes for gardeners, laundrymen, washerwomen, pottery-makers, thieves, bankers, and hundreds of others.

Below the four main castes are more than 60,000,000 "out castes" who are literally outside a caste. Historically they have performed the meanest and most unpleasant tasks in society, and traditionally they have been forbidden to mix in any way with even the Sudras. If the shadow of an Outcast or Untouchable should fall upon the food or the person of a Brahmin, the food is uneatable, and the Brahmin will probably believe that he has to bathe himself. Untouchables may still be obliged to live outside the limits of a village and be denied the right to use the village well.

Mahatma Gandhi fought on behalf of the sixty million Untouchables as human beings, and deliberately broke the laws of his caste, the Vaishya, by mixing with them. Through his efforts, legislation has now made it a criminal offense to show discrimination against the Untouchables, although discrimination is still practiced is some rural communities. As India becomes industrialized, the caste system will become less rigid, because skills and ability will become more important than caste distinctions. If India is to change and progress she must reduce caste differences which create handicaps to modern society. Fixed status and occupations may interfere with the economic improvement of society by preventing the flow of talent and skills and by preventing political unity.

The worst aspect of the caste system was its deliberate segregation of people and its basic belief in the inequality of man. An extreme example was that of the Chandala caste whose members could not leave their segregated quarters without striking a wooden clapper to warn others of their contaminating approach. Life was one continuous humiliation for the Untouchables, and was made more intolerable by their own conviction that their condition was unchangeable for themselves and for their children.

2. Independence and Partition

Early British Control

British interest in India began with the charter granted in 1600 by Queen Elizabeth to the East India Company. In 1773 the British government began to restrict the authority of this company, and after the Sepoy Mutiny of 1857 the government abolished company control and took over its territories in India. In 1858 the British government appointed a new cabinet minister, the Secretary of State for India, and gave him authority over India. Under the new type of administration the British authorities developed irrigation schemes, reclaimed land for agriculture, and so improved India's communications that by 1914 she had the best road system in Asia.

In 1876 Parliament proclaimed Queen Victoria as Empress of India, and in so doing made all the people of India subjects of the British Crown. But almost nothing was done to give Indians any participation in government.

The unification of India by Britain led inevitably to a growing feeling of nationalism among the people, and this led to increasing demands by Indians for participation in the government. A new and more vigorous breed of nationalist leaders from the educated middle class wanted the ideals of the West adapted to Indian society. Educated Indians resented the fact that British administrators favored the European minority, and denied Indians the rights enjoyed by Englishmen.

In 1885 a British civil servant who had served as an administrator in India organized the Indian National Congress, a political group requesting that India "be governed according to the idea of government prevalent in Europe." The leaders were asking for nothing more than increased Indian participation in government. They were not asking for home rule or limited self-government, and certainly not for independence.

But a small group in the National Congress Party believed that Britain was concerned only with profits, and had no interest in the welfare of the Indian people. They demanded a policy that would lead to independence. The possibility of a united Indian front was threatened by the large Moslem population, because the Congress Party appealed mainly to educated Indians, and since the Moslems kept to their traditional beliefs in Islam, very few Moslems were sufficiently educated to qualify for government positions.

When the Congress Party advocated voting rights for all Indians, the Moslems realized that they would be in the minority. They therefore supported "communal representation" which would apportion a guaranteed number of political positions to each religious and ethnic group. To further these aims they organized the Moslem League in 1906, which soon came under the able leadership of Mohammed Ali Jinnah.

Mohandas Gandhi

Another man who was soon to exert great influence in Indian politics was Mohandas Gandhi, born in western India, and a Hindu of the merchant or Vaishya caste. After finishing his law studies in London he returned to India, and then in 1893 went to South Africa to fight on behalf of the many Indians who had migrated to work in South Africa. During the twenty years of fighting for Indian rights there, he developed his theory of civil disobedience and passive resistance, for which he served several jail sentences.

Gandhi returned to India in 1914, and before the end of World War I he was demanding self-government for India. The war temporarily healed the differences between Hindus and Moslems because British attacks on Turkey outraged the Moslems. Turkey was the home of the Caliph, the spiritual leader of all Moslems. Believing that Britain was attacking their religion, they were drawn to the Hindus by common opposition to British rule. By declaring themselves in favor of communal representation, the Hindus won over the Moslems to the cause of Indian independence. It was during the early war years that the Indian poet Tagore gave Gandhi the title of Mahatma or Great Soul.

India's hopes were raised when the British Secretary of State for India announced in 1917 that Britain would give India a greater share in government "with a view to the progressive realization of responsible government in India." Whatever this meant to Great Britain, to Indians it was a promise of self-rule.

Unfortunately, extreme Indian nationalists had committed acts of violence during the war, and the British government passed legislation in 1919 authorizing officials to arrest and try in secret any Indians accused of political crimes. In great indignation at this violation of rights enjoyed by British people, Mohandas Gandhi organized *hartals* or one-day strikes in which no Indian worked. Not unexpectedly, the hartals led to riots, and to retaliatory use of British troops, culminating in a tragic incident which increased Indian bitterness toward Britain. In 1919 at Amritsar, in the Punjab, hundreds of Indians, ignoring British orders, gathered in a walled enclosure for a political meeting. General Dwyer gave orders to his troops to fire upon the crowd. Repeated volleys killed 400 persons and wounded another 1,200. The commanding general was ordered back to England, where he

Mahatma Gandhi

was censured by an investigating committee but was commended by the House of Lords.

Mohandas Gandhi, convinced that nothing short of *swaraj*, or complete independence, could be acceptable to India, called for a campaign of non-violent non-co-operation, or passive resistance, against the British authorities. In 1920 he asked Indians to have nothing to do with any government services or agencies, such as the use of British courts, or working in the civil service for the British. The riots that resulted from this boycott led to Gandhi's arrest and a six-year jail term. Released after serving two years, he organized a boycott of British textiles, spun his own thread as an example to Indians to make their own cloth. Gandhi refused to accept any position in politics because he did not wish to be limited by any particular party platform. The role of political leadership of the Congress Party fell to Jawaharlal Nehru, son of a wealthy lawyer, who had been educated in England. A member of the Brahmin caste, Nehru served as president of the Indian National Congress, and demanded not only independence but a complete break with England as a sovereign republic without any ties to the British Crown.

The Salt March

The widening gap between India and Britain was dramatized in March 1930 when Gandhi deliberately flaunted the British salt tax levied upon all inhabitants of India. Gandhi wrote to the Viceroy, whose salary was $84,000 a year, telling him that civil disobedience would commence in nine days as a protest against the position of the Indian peasant under British rule. "Even the salt he must use to live is so taxed as to make the burden fall heaviest upon him."

On March 12, 1930, Gandhi and his 78 followers started out from his village, and walked for twenty-four days across country, from village to village, to the seashore 200 miles away. Gandhi walked the entire distance, despite his age of sixty-one years. The attention of all India was now upon the man who was deliberately about to break British law by making salt and not paying a tax on it. By April 5 his followers had grown to several thousand. The next morning he dipped into the sea, walked back to the beach, and picked up some salt left by the waves.

Automatically he became a criminal because he possessed salt not bought from the British salt monopoly. All around India's long seacoast villagers inspired by Gandhi's example gathered up sea water and boiled it down for salt. In Bombay salt was made on the roof of the Congress Party headquarters, while 60,000 persons watched. Hundreds were arrested and jailed in Bombay, including Nehru, who received a six-month prison sentence. Across India more than 100,000 people, including Gandhi, were arrested and jailed.

The Salt March and its consequences had been so dramatic that the British knew they had to make more concessions. By the Government of India Act of 1935 they introduced reforms which would lead to eventual dominion status for India. At this point in time, the earlier Moslem fears were again aroused. Out of the eleven provinces of India, eight were dominated by Congress Party ministries which refused to allow non-Congress Party people any positions. Mohammed Jinnah had hoped that in provinces with large Moslem minorities, the Congress Party would appoint a few Moslems to cabinet positions. When Congress refused, Jinnah was faced with two alternatives. Either he could lead the Moslems into the Congress Party and admit that Congress represented all Indians, Hindus and Moslems alike, or he could stay out of Congress Party and work for a separate Moslem state when India became independent.

When Britain went to war with Germany in 1939, the Viceroy of India proclaimed India to be in the war, without consulting any Indian leaders. The India Congress Party determined to push its demand for complete Indian independence, and to refuse to co-operate if the demand was rejected. Jinnah immediately seized upon this situation to demand that India be divided into two parts, one to be called Pakistan, and to be an independent nation for the Moslems.

With the loss of Malaya and Singapore to the Japanese in 1942, the British tried to appease India by promising dominion status or home rule at the end of the war. Gandhi opposed this half-way measure, and started another campaign for independence, resulting in the arrest and jailing of some 60,000 Indians. From this moment until independence in 1947 Mohammed Jinnah worked for separate independence for Moslem areas, and neither the Moslem League nor the Congress Party would make any concession to the other.

Independence, 1947

The disastrous set-backs suffered by Britain in Asia during World War II convinced the government that it could no longer resist independence movements. The defeat of Churchill and the Conservative Party by the Labour Party in the election of July 1945 ended the rule of the man who said that he had not become His Majesty's minister "to preside over the liquidation of the British Empire." In February 1947, the Labour government announced that it would withdraw from India, and set up a plan for the creation of two nations of India and Pakistan.

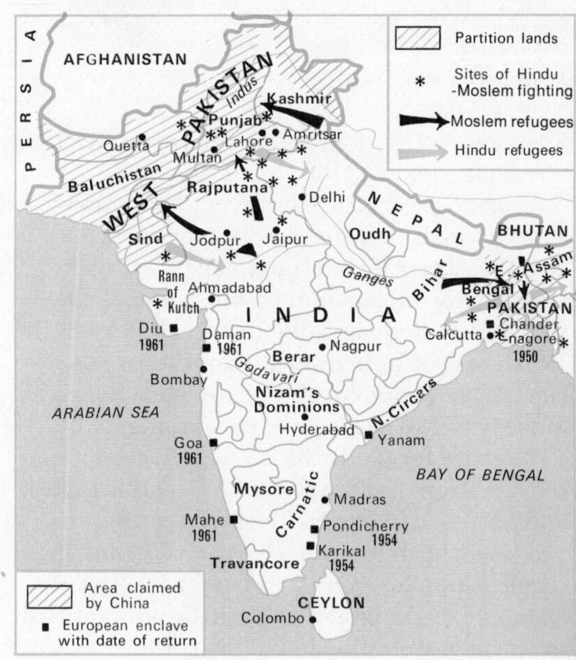

The Partition of India, 1947

Gandhi denounced partition as a "spiritual tragedy," although he appeared not to appreciate Moslem fears of Hindu domination. When Nehru criticized Moslem opposition to the terms of partition, Jinnah called upon the Moslems for direct action. Within a few days nearly 20,000 people lost their lives in Hindu-Moslem riots.

The British saw no practicable solution to the problem, and in July 1947 passed the India Independence Act which provided for the transfer of authority to India and Pakistan in August. With the withdrawal of British authority, and in the absence of effective local authority, centuries-old, deep-seated religious hostility exploded into incredible violence. Within nine months of partition 16,000,000 refugees fled from crazed mobs, Hindus from Pakistan, and Moslems from India. Between 500,000 and 1,000,000 people were slaughtered with unbelievable barbarity.

Gandhi was horrified by the killings and went on a hunger strike to persuade Hindus not to kill Moslems. To climax the dreadful situation, a Hindu fanatic shot and killed Gandhi, charging that Gandhi's consideration for Moslems was a treacherous act against Hinduism.

Why Was India Partitioned?

For two centuries Hindus and Moslems had lived together in increasing friction, but were temporarily linked in common opposition to British rule. Almost all today's Moslems on the subcontinent are descendants of low-caste Hindus who converted to Islam, which emphasizes individuality and equality under a single deity, to escape the rigid social and economic restrictions forced upon them as "Untouchables" by the Hindu caste system.

The origin of the differences between the two groups goes back centuries to almost 1,500 B.C., when fair-skinned Aryans invaded from the north and subjugated the dark-skinned Dravidian inhabitants. Then, after the rise of the Mohammedan faith and its crusading expansion across Europe, invading Turks, Persians, and others from Central Asia conquered the subcontinent and established the Moslem faith. By the seventeenth century the Hindus were a subjugated minority under firm Moslem rule. But by the eighteenth century the Mogul Empire was in decline and the British were establishing their rule over large areas of the subcontinent. With British rule came a Hindu renaissance, with Hindus serving as civil servants for the British and becoming the country's lawyers, doctors, teachers, engineers, philosophers, and poets.

As hopes for India's independence grew brighter, Mohammed Ali Jinnah determined to win independence for the Moslems, whose 160,000,000 could become a political minority in an Indian nation ruled by 320,000,000 Hindus.

By 1937 he was firmly committed to the two-nation principle, which although reasonable in theory had decided practical problems. It was impossible to divide the subcontinent so that all Moslems lived in one area, and all Hindus in another, because a large number of both groups lived in the Punjab in the west and in Bengal in the east.

Anxious to grant independence, the British accepted Jinnah's demands and set up the physically divided Moslem nation of West Pakistan and East Pakistan, separated by one thousand miles of India. The two republics came to independence to face the enormous problems created by the several million refugees who moved from each new nation to the other.

To complicate matters, more than 500 prince-ruled states, which covered half the land of India and no longer had British protection, had to be absorbed. These princely states varied in size from 200 acres, about the size of New York's Central Park, to others of more than 80,000 square miles. They finally surrendered their independence to India and Pakistan in return for financial provisions. The one problem was the province of Jammu and Kashmir, with a long frontier on Communist China's border, whose ruler was a Hindu but whose people were 80 percent Moslem. The Maharajah refused to join Pakistan and did not want to join India. When troops from Pakistan invaded Kashmir, the Maharajah requested help from India. Nehru, Prime Minister of India, referred the issue to the United Nations, requesting that Pakistan be condemned as the aggressor, but promising that the people of Kashmir would be allowed to decide the issue by popular vote under United Nations supervision. The promise was not kept, and for more than twenty years the problem of Kashmir was to remain a repeated cause of conflict between India and Pakistan.

Problems of Partition

Why did Jammu-Kashmir become so bitter an issue between the two new republics? Because at the time of partition both regarded Kashmir as a buffer against Communist China, although later on Pakistan became friendly with China. The basic issue was, and still is, that Kashmir's rivers supply water for the Indus irrigation network that serves both nations. Each is afraid that the other could control exclusively this vital water supply.

Partition created also enormous economic problems. The two "wings" of West and East Pakistan were separated by one thousand miles of India without any land corridor to join them; and East Pakistan cut off almost completely the Indian province of Assam from the rest of India. The very efficient railroad system built by the British was divided between the two nations, which were unable to agree to joint administration. Pakistan was the better food-producing area, India had the major coal and industrial resources, but the two could not co-operate economically for their common good.

3. India since Independence

The Government of India

The government of India is a federal union of seventeen states, based upon parliamentary democracy; each state has its own limited powers, and within each state is a number of districts each divided into villages. The constitution has adopted the British concepts of equal rights before the law and representative self-government, and the American concept of separation of judicial powers from executive and legislative powers.

The president is elected for five years by the members of parliament and state legislative assemblies, with essentially ceremonial functions, but with the power to advise his ministers and to suspend the constitution if a national emergency arises.

The effective political leader is the prime minister who is, like each of his cabinet, an elected member of parliament, and selected as the leader of the majority or the coalition party.

While he lived, Nehru maintained his leadership because he was revered by his people. After his death in 1964, his successor for a brief time was Lal Shastri, followed by Indira Gandhi, daughter of Nehru but no relation of Mahatma Gandhi.

Nehru's Domestic Policy

Nehru was responsible for the social and economic clauses in the constitution. Caste discrimination was legally forbidden, every child was to be given the opportunity for education to age fourteen, food production was to be raised, and the country was to be industrialized.

In 1952 Nehru started the first of three Five-year Plans that were to be devoted to land reform for peasants, increased agricultural production, rural development, improved transportation, and the development of industries. Most of these projects needed a great deal of government financial assistance, and while Nehru approved of private enterprise, he believed that much of India's economy would have to be owned and operated by the government. The major emphasis was upon agriculture because for several reasons crop yield per acre was one of the lowest in the world. Farms were too small, labor was inefficient, fertilizer and improved seed were too expensive, and too many peasants produced only enough to feed themselves very inadequately.

Unfortunately, the attempts of the government to raise the standard of living have been rather unsuccessful, largely because the tremendous increase in population has wiped out the gains. This increase is not simply a rise in births but a decrease in deaths through improved medical facilities and improved famine relief methods.

The lack of money has forced the government to cut back on many of its projects to raise living standards, and unless India can obtain large foreign loans and gifts, her financial future is not very hopeful.

Problems Facing India

With the death of Nehru in 1964 the politics of India changed because the power of the Congress Party, which had been in office since 1947, began to decline. It had retained power largely through the personal magnetism of Nehru, who had led his people to independence. But by 1964 the Congress Party did not represent the new generation which knew little of the fight for India's independence, and was insistent upon solutions to the country's serious domestic problems. Lal Shastri, a veteran of pre-independence days, succeeded Nehru, but he lacked his predecessor's prestige, and was unable to prevent factional splits within the party. Upon his death in 1966 Mrs. Indira Gandhi became Prime Minister and leader of the Congress Party. Despite her wide political experience she was unable to prevent the further decline of the party, which suffered losses in the national elections of 1967.

Hampered by four years of slender majorities in coalition governments, Mrs. Gandhi successfully appealed to the voters in the March 1971 national elections and won a two-thirds majority which gave her Congress Party immediate political power. But with that power comes much greater responsibility, for the size of the

Indira Gandhi with Senator Edward Kennedy in New Delhi.

vote shows that the voters expect her to make good her campaign promises, a task which probably could not be accomplished by any Indian political leader, however large the parliamentary majority.

One of the staggering statistics is that according to estimates the 1961 population of 480,000,000 will increase to 625,000,000 by 1976.

Already the population growth has wiped out almost all the economic progress of the past two decades. Despite the creation of more than 12,000,000 new jobs in the years 1961 to 1966, unemployment has risen by about 50 percent, and prospects for the future are no less pessimistic.

The largest democratic nation in the world faces other problems of staggering proportions: starvation living standards for millions, communal and caste persecution, businesses strangled by bureaucratic red tape, and socialist condemnation of free enterprise, and a serious economic situation. Indian money faces further devaluation, prices have been rising out of control, and much-needed business is seriously hampered by controls. Unemployment is serious because 6,000 extra men come into the jobs market every day of the year; in a country badly needing the use of skilled workers and technicians there are thousands of jobless qualified engineers; more than 1,000,000 highly-educated people and millions of partly-educated people are without work. Feudal land-ownership has bred violence and terrorism because government promises of land reform have proved to be empty. These are some of the challenges that Mrs. Gandhi and the Congress Party face.

India's 25th Anniversary

Despite these difficulties, India has progressed much farther than many observers believed was possible twenty-five years ago. Factories that did not exist then are now turning out computers, jet planes, and atomic reactors. And for the first time in history India has enough food to prevent starvation and face the drought which has come to India every five years. India is for the first time self-sufficient, although the term self-sufficiency is relative.

One half of India's 569,720,000 people live on less than $3 a month; 15 percent of hospital cases are patients suffering from malnutrition; and according to a finance minister, "Eighty percent of the downtrodden have remained virtually untouched by the development process."

As leader of India, Nehru emphasized the country's development from the top by industrialization, dams, and electrical power projects as a means to raise the standard of living. Gandhi stressed the need for development from the village level upward, land reform in peasant interests, and the building of roads. Prime Minister Indira Gandhi admitted that in the past "direction was not adequate for the needs of the people."

She proposes to remedy that situation in the next Five-year Plan announced at India's Twenty-Fifth Anniversary of Independence. It will attempt to improve rural development, create jobs to reduce unemployment, improve public health and education, and build homes for landless farm workers.

The world's largest democracy has proved its ability to live through the stresses that independence partly inherited and, in part, were the consequences of independence.

The Indian Village

The basic unit of Indian political organization is the village. There are more than 550,000 villages in India, and four out of five of the population live in villages, each of which is like a world apart, and with very little influence upon or knowledge about life and events outside its limits. Very gradually this isolation is breaking down. Traditionally, the village has been run by the few men with caste or money, who maintain their power by handing down decisions on almost every aspect of village life. Old traditions die hard, but gradually a semblance of democracy is taking hold through participation by villagers in their own affairs. A traditional local *panchayat* or Council of Five runs village affairs, but today the villagers have a voice in the selection of the group, which sends representatives to a district organization of several villages, and in turn to an organization of several districts. This participation in larger political groups is essential for the development of India and Pakistan. Men must learn to work with other people, and with political parties; they also must learn to break down caste restrictions and accept compromise. Because the Untouchables now have political rights, their votes will count in elections, and their humiliating identification as outcasts of society will in time disappear.

A Contraception Clinic. An Indian government social worker meeting with village women to instruct them in birth control techniques. The program backed by WHO is crucial in the effort to stop the colossal increase in India's population.

Villagers are still incredibly poor, and existence for several hundred million Indians is still constant hunger, sickness, and misery. Most of them eat little but rice and wheat, since the vast majority of them are Hindus and are strictly forbidden to eat beef. The cow is sacred to the Hindu, and it may not be killed, or any part of it used when it dies because it perhaps contains the reincarnated soul of a human being. Recent estimates indicate that India has over 250,000,000 cows, some of which provide milk and dung for fuel but which also are an economic burden upon the country. The food the cows eat could feed people. Hindu citizens criticize their government for allowing non-Hindus to kill cows and use their hides for export. They would in all probability rise in violent protest if the government supported the slaughtering of cows.

Gradually villages are getting wider contacts through a national program of road building, primary schooling, and a village radio which brings national and world news to the people.

4. Foreign Policy of India and Pakistan

India

Nehru, who was India's leader for seventeen years after partition, gave the country his direction in foreign policy. He believed that India's role was to act, as far as possible, as a mediator between nations, and to avoid any action which could increase friction between the democracies and the Communist bloc.

Although Nehru frequently criticized United

States foreign policy, his attitude was not one of support for Communism or opposition to the United States, but a policy of neutralism, of not taking sides with any great power.

India and Communist China

For more than a decade after the Communists came to power in China in 1949, Nehru was convinced that India and the People's Republic of China could maintain friendly and peaceful relations with each other. India was one of the first nations to recognize the People's Republic of China, and Nehru consistently supported attempts to admit that nation to the United Nations, because he was convinced that the efficiency of the United Nations was decidedly blunted by the exclusion of a nation representing one quarter of the world's population.

Furthermore, the island of Taiwan, officially representing China on the Security Council, was the only permanent representative of all Asia. To Nehru, and to many others, this did not make political sense. Nehru considered India to be the best spokesman for all colonial people of the world who were beginning to win their independence.

Although Nehru refused to join any collective security organization which the United Nations supported, he did join the United Nations in condemnation of North Korea's attack on South Korea in 1950 as outright aggression. It was Nehru who warned that if United Nations crossed the 38th parallel into North Korea, this might bring Communist China into the conflict.

The occupation of Tibet by Communist Chinese troops in 1950 disturbed Nehru, but not until the Chinese brutally suppressed a rebellion in Tibet did he admit that India was in possible danger from the People's Republic of China. The danger became very real in the early 1960's when Chinese troops occupied Indian border posts and extended their operations until, in October 1962, full-scale fighting broke out between Indian and Chinese troops on the northwestern frontier bordering on Kashmir, and on the northeastern frontier bordering on Tibet in the Ladakh area of Kashmir.

Indians in Captivity, 1962. These Indians are shown at prayer in a Red Chinese camp following their capture by Chinese forces.

Disillusioned with neutralism, Nehru sharply reversed his policy of non-alignment, and appealed to the United States for aid. India's enemy Pakistan immediately protested that sizeable military aid from the United States to India would be an "unfriendly act" while the Kashmir problem remained unsolved. The People's Republic of China, the aggressor on India, astutely sent letters to twenty-four African and Asian countries asking for their influence "to facilitate a peaceful settlement of the Indian-Chinese boundary question on a fair and reasonable basis," and in November offered a cease-fire to India.

The Soviet Union took the opportunity to advance its interests on the subcontinent by sending some aid to India, making political overtures to Pakistan, and acting as host in the Russian city of Tashkent, where Indian and Pakistani representatives attempted to settle the Kashmir controversy.

Portuguese Colonies in India

Ever since independence in 1947, Nehru had been determined to get possession of several "foreign enclaves" in India In 1954 France gave up five small pieces of territory, but Portugal refused to give back to India three little colonial possessions she had held for several centuries. On December 18, 1961 Nehru invaded Portuguese Goa, Damao, and Diu. On December 19 the Security Council voted 7 to 4 for cease-fire, but the Soviet Union, supported by the United Arab Republic, Liberia, and Ceylon, vetoed any action.

In the United Nations, Adlai Stevenson, Ambassador for the United States, criticized the Indian Defense Minister V. K. Krishna Menon who, "so well known in these halls for his advice on matters of peace and his tireless enjoinders to every one else to seek the way of compromise," was on the border of Goa inspecting his Indian troops at the zero hour of invasion. Krishna Menon defended his action, saying "we consider colonialism as permanent aggression. We did not commit aggression."

Moscow praised India for the "liberation," and Nehru stated, "We did not do anything wrong . . . the Soviet Union appreciated our stand: we thank them for that." This action and attitude shocked many friends of India, which had repeatedly condemned force when used by others.

The Kashmir Controversy

Kashmir remained a constant source of friction despite the cease-fire line of 1949, by which India occupied the southern area of Jammu-Kashmir, and Pakistan the northern region.

In 1964, after repeated border incidents, Nehru claimed, "Legally Jammu and Kashmir has been Indian territory and continues to be" and added that the issue of Kashmir was an internal matter for India alone to settle. He conveniently ignored his earlier promise to allow the people of Jammu-Kashmir to decide the issue for themselves.

Fighting broke out again in April 1965, and continued throughout the year. Communist China demanded that India dismantle her military fortifications in Kashmir, and the Soviet Union, acting the role of mediator, invited Premier Lal Shastri of India and President Ayub Khan of Pakistan to meet in Tashkent in Central Asia in January 1966. There the two leaders accepted the Tashkent Agree-

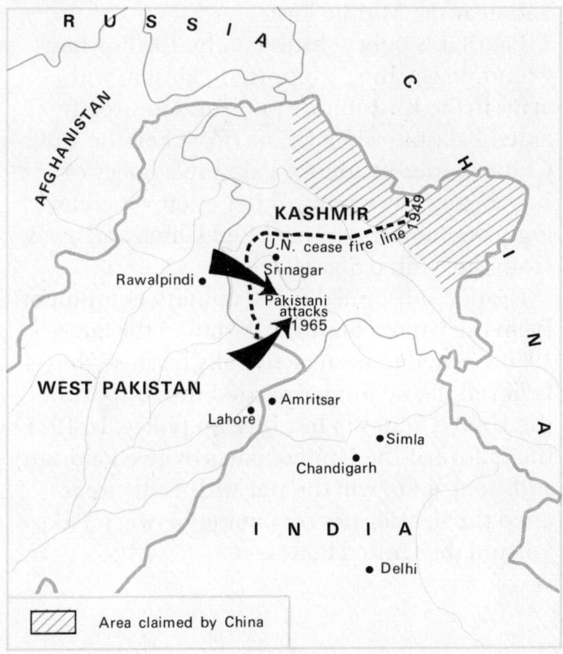

Jammu-Kashmir

ment, stating their intentions to find ways to settle the Kashmir problem peacefully.

Pakistan

During the immediate years after independence, Pakistan became virtually an ally of the United States. Pakistan's friendship was born of a need for military support against its neighbor and potential adversary India. Pakistan allowed the United States to establish radar stations and airbases on her soil because, as both India and Pakistan realized, this friendship strengthened Pakistan's military defenses against any possible attack by India.

Pakistan willingly became a member of SEATO, the South East Asia Treaty Organization of allies in common defense against Communist aggression in Southeast Asia, and of CENTO between Iraq, Iran, Great Britain, Turkey, and Pakistan for common defense in and near the Middle East.

Pakistan's policy shifted in the 1960's when Communist China supported Pakistan with arms in the Kashmir dispute, and indirectly aided Pakistan when China provoked the India-China border incidents. Pakistan's policy of supporting any enemy of her enemy increasingly oriented her toward Red China and away from the United States.

Despite substantial aid in military equipment from the United States, Pakistan in the late 1960's ceased to be an active ally because she believed she no longer needed the support of the United States in her foreign policy. In 1971 the failure of the United States to give Pakistan sufficient aid to win the war with India weakened the slender ties remaining between Pakistan and the United States.

5. Pakistan since Independence

The new nation of Pakistan* was described by some observers as a "political phenomenon" because at its creation it was a nation divided into two parts separated by a thousand miles of India, a nation apparently based upon the common bond of religion. In fact, however, West Pakistan and East Pakistan were racially and culturally divided. West Pakistan, with Urdu its main language, considers itself to be by origin and culture close to the Middle East, while East Pakistan, with its own Bengali language, regards itself as Asiatic.

Pakistan became independent in 1947 without any tradition or experience in government. A further problem was the immediate settlement of almost one-fifth of the population of West Pakistan who had fled from India as refugees. Unfortunately for the Pakistan economy, many businessmen and professional people were Hindus who fled to India at the time of partition.

Mohammed Ali Jinnah, whose personal leadership and efforts had led to the creation of the separate Moslem state of Pakistan, died in 1948 without having had time to create a strong political party or to name a successor to carry on effective government policy just at a time when it was most needed.

The Dictatorship of Ayub Khan, 1958–1969

After years of bitter struggle for power among rival political groups, a Constitution was adopted in 1956, changing Pakistan from a dominion of the Commonwealth to the Islam Republic of Pakistan. In 1958 General Mohammed Ayub Khan emerged from a military coup as the "strong man." Determined to remain in power,

---

*The word Pakistan means place of the pure, *pak* meaning place and *istan* meaning pure.

he suspended the Constitution, declared martial law, and assumed leadership as president. In 1962 he proclaimed a new constitution which gave him virtually unlimited power. The presidential and assembly elections were indirect; 120,000 "basic democrats," elected by the voters, elected the president, the members of the National Assembly, and the provincial assemblies.

General discontent with his Constitution and with Ayub's personal rule gave him the opportunity to declare a state of emergency in September 1965, a suspension of popular rights that remained in effect until late 1969. Further trouble threatened from East Pakistan which felt itself to be treated as a colony of the central Pakistan government.

In January 1969 a coalition of six parties known as the Pakistan Democratic Movement, PDM, announced its intention to boycott the national elections to be held later that year because it refused to "participate in the farcical and fraudulent elections under the present wholly unacceptable Constitution."

Opposition in East Pakistan

In Dacca, the capital of East Pakistan, and in Rawalpindi, demonstrators protested against the treatment of East Pakistan, and demanded the ouster of Ayub Khan. By the beginning of February 1969 more than 30 people had been killed in demonstrations. Ayub Khan announced that he would not be a candidate for the presidential election scheduled for March 1970, and acknowledged the justice of the criticism of indirect elections and the lack of authority of the national and provincial assemblies.

In East Pakistan, where unrest, demonstrations, and strikes increased, the demand for autonomy, local self-rule, grew louder. At the head of the protest movement was Sheikh Mujibur Rahman, leader of the Awami League, who stated East Pakistan's grievances. Although industrial production had increased 160 percent between 1960 and 1968, and agricultural output was 40 percent greater, industrial wages had declined, and *per capita* income remained among the lowest in the world, with 75 percent of all households existing on less than $500 a year. Although East Pakistan, with some 78,000,000 or 57 percent of the nation's population, accounted for two-thirds of the country's foreign earnings through tea and jute sales, the province received between only one-third and one-half of the government's investment and development funds. Rahman demanded autonomy for the province of East Pakistan, and the dividing of West Pakistan into four provinces, with all governmental powers except defense and foreign affairs transferred to them.

The Regime of Yahya Khan

In March 1969, Ayub Khan resigned from the presidency, and turned over all power to the commander-in-chief of the army, General Yahya Khan, who immediately proclaimed martial law and dissolved the national and provincial assemblies.

Yahya Khan hoped that the East Pakistan demand for autonomy, and the possible threat of secession, could be halted by a new Constitution and elections to be held in the fall of 1970.

Determined to be fair to the Bengalis of East Pakistan, although he was himself a Pathan from West Pakistan, Yahya Khan assigned the number of seats in the National Assembly in proportion to the national population.

East Pakistan with its 75,000,000 people would have 169 seats, and West Pakistan with its 64,000,000 would have 144 seats in the 313-member Assembly. Yahya Khan confidently expected that Sheikh Mujibur Rahman, charismatic leader of the Awami League in East Pakistan, would win only about 100 seats, and that the other 69 members from East Pakistan would line up with the West Pakistan members to form a clear majority for West Pakistan.

To Yahya Khan's consternation Mujibur Rahman won 167 of the 169 East Pakistan seats; Zulfikar Ali Bhutto, leader of the People's Party in West Pakistan, won a disappointing 83 of the 144 seats. Mujibur Rahman had an overwhelming majority in the National Assembly, and a mandate from the people of East Pakistan to secure self-rule for them.

Then came the event which precipitated civil war in Pakistan. Out of the Bay of Bengal roared the cyclone of November which flooded the plains of East Pakistan and killed more than 250,000 Bengalis. Because the government in Islamabad was slow in providing relief for flood victims, the Bengalis believed that President Yahya Khan, a Punjabi from West Pakistan, was deliberately indifferent to their suffering.

Dissatisfied with the results of the election, Yahya Khan announced the postponement of the meeting of the Assembly scheduled for December. Mujibur Rahman, with a mandate from his people for some degree of autonomy for East Pakistan, announced his Six Points program which proposed to give East Pakistan control of the raising and spending of its own taxes, and control over its own foreign trade.

Cyclone–Tidal Wave, 1970

East Pakistan's Demand for Independence

The overwhelming political victory and the Awami League demands were wholly unacceptable to Yahya Khan, who was pledged to defend the independence and integrity of Pakistan against India, and unacceptable also to the army, which was unwilling to be dependent upon appropriations from a non-martial Bengali majority from the Eastern "wing" of Pakistan.

Immediately after the elections, Yahya Khan announced that the Assembly had 120 days in which to work out a *unitary* Constitution, and that it faced dissolution if it did not meet that deadline and if he did not approve of the new Constitution. Opposition mounted in East Pakistan, which would lose any hopes of self-government if a unitary Constitution was adopted, so twice Yahya Khan postponed the opening date of the Assembly.

Mujibur Rahman's answer to Yahya Khan's postponement of the new parliament was to call a general strike in East Pakistan, where hundreds of Pakistan soldiers and opponents of Bengali independence were murdered. Rahman then upped his demand from autonomy to independence, and on March 15, 1971 announced that he had taken over full control of East Pakistan, and had there suspended the collection by the Islamabad government of income taxes, excise and customs duties, and sales taxes. On March 23, "resistance day" in East Pakistan, the green, red, and gold flag of Bangladesh, the Bengali Nation, was displayed.

In retaliation, Yahya Khan ordered the arrest of Mujibur Rahman and his officials on charges of treason, and struck viciously at East Pakistan with his army, which deliberately and ruthlessly slaughtered hundreds of thousands of Bengalis, needlessly destroyed towns, irrigation pumps, tea plantations and jute mills, and unleashed an indiscriminate reign of terror which sent millions of refugees fleeing into India.

The magnitude of the disaster in East Pakistan suggests deliberate genocide of the Bengalis by the Punjabis of West Pakistan. Estimates indicate that at least a quarter of a million East Pakistanis have been deliberately slaughtered, and that by August 1971 over 8,000,000 had become refugees in India. It is as if the entire population of New York City, or the combined populations of Massachusetts, Rhode Island, New Hampshire, Vermont, and Maine had become homeless.

On April 12, 1971, East Pakistan declared itself to be the independent People's Republic of Bangladesh.

6. The India-Pakistan War, 1971

For India the situation presented both an economic threat and the political opportunity to humiliate its enemy Pakistan with whom it had fought three times since partition.* Pakistan's ruthlessness was costing India $2,500,000 a day to feed the refugees, and this financial burden could continue as long as Pakistani troops remained in East Pakistan. India permitted the Bengali guerrilla freedom fighters, the Mukti Bahini, to be organized and trained on her soil; border clashes between Indian and Pakistani troops repeatedly occurred on both frontiers, and the tension heightened.

Then in December Yahya Khan made a fateful decision. He ordered a blitzkrieg-type attack similar to that made by the Israelis against Egypt in the Six-Day War in 1967. He sent 200 bombers through the mountain passes into India to destroy the important Indian airbase at Agra, southeast of New Delhi. The surprise attack was badly bungled, and prime minister Indira Gandhi had the excuse to declare that Pakistan had launched a full-scale war against her nation. India had the opportunity to humiliate the Pakistani army, assist Bangladesh to actual independence, and further weaken her enemy.

Within two weeks India occupied 1,500 square miles of Pakistani territory, captured more than 60,000 troops in East Pakistan, and recognized the independent nation of Bangladesh. On December 16 the commander of Pakistan's 60,000 troops surrendered, and the next day Yahya Khan accepted India's cease-fire proposal.

The Bangladesh Rebels, Mukti Bahini

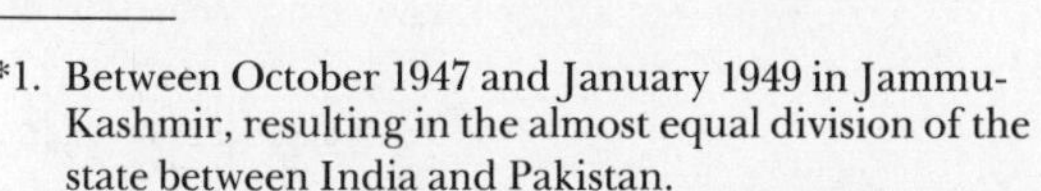

*1. Between October 1947 and January 1949 in Jammu-Kashmir, resulting in the almost equal division of the state between India and Pakistan.
2. Between April and June 1965, in the Rann of Kutch, on India's southwest frontier.
3. For three weeks inside Kashmir in late 1965.

7. Effects of War

Pakistan

Within hours of defeat Yahya Khan resigned as president and appointed as his successor deputy prime minister Zulfikar Ali Bhutto, head of the Pakistan People's Party which had been defeated in the 1970 elections by Mujibur Rahman and the Awami League. A rabid anti-India, pro-Communist China politician, who is believed to have influenced Yahya Khan to set aside the elections, Bhutto immediately declared himself to be chief martial law administrator, and minister of defense, foreign affairs, the interior, and of inter-provincial co-ordination. Pakistan had exchanged military dictatorship for civilian dictatorship.

In his first address to the nation Bhutto announced himself to be "the authentic voice of the people of Pakistan," conveniently ignoring the elections of late 1970 and the fact that Mujibur Rahman, then under arrest in West Pakistan, was the majority leader. He further ignored political facts by insisting that East Pakistan "remains an inseparable and indissoluble part of Pakistan."

But he soon had to face realities. East Pakistan was independent, and he did not have the resources to wage a sustained war against India. Mujibur Rahman, legally elected as political leader of Pakistan in 1971, could no longer be kept a prisoner in West Pakistan. Economically, Pakistan had to face the problem of survival, because it was almost bankrupt. The eastern "wing" of Pakistan had once provided exportable raw materials and a market for the western "wing's" industrial products.

The success of Bangladesh could encourage Pakistan's minorities who live in Baluchistan,

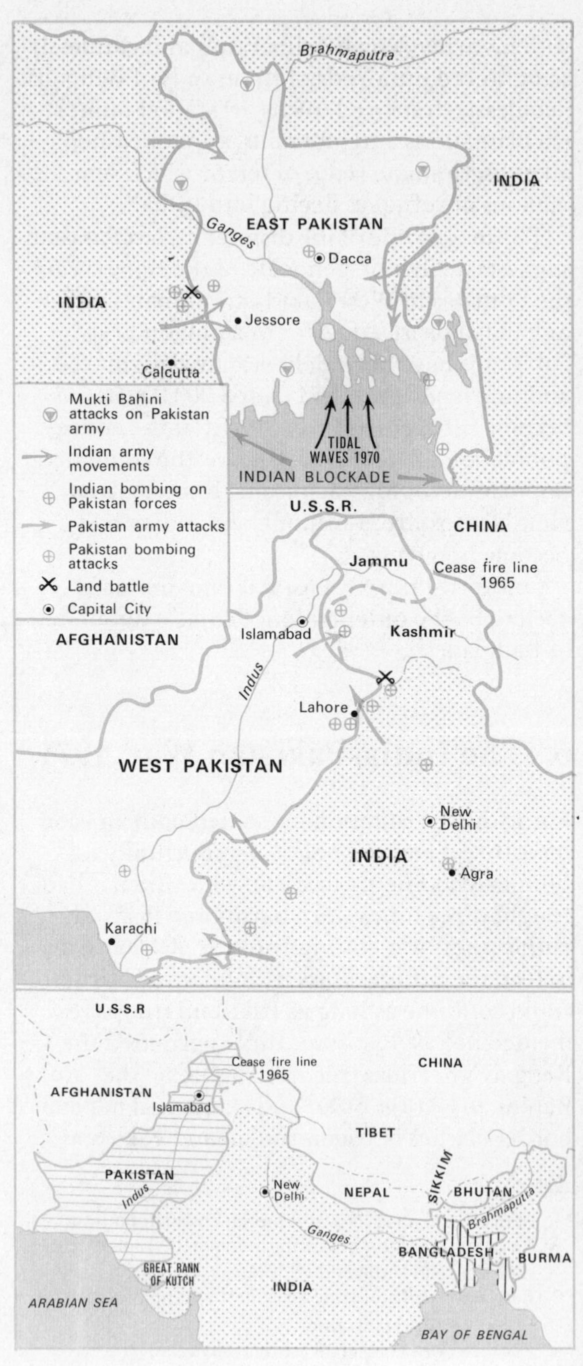

The Emergence of Bangladesh, 1971–1972. The India-Pakistan War.

Sind, and the Northwest Frontier Province to demand concessions of self-government or even independence. In the Frontier Province a National Awami (People's) Party of several million Pathan tribesmen has denounced Bhutto as a bully, and its leader, Khan Abdul Wali Khan, supports a separatist movement, and has shown great interest in the possibility of forming with fellow-Pathans in neighboring Afghanistan a new state called Pakhtoonistan.

A further problem which could weaken Bhutto's position is India's military occupation of parts of Pakistan's border region, and the 90,000 Pakistani prisoners-of-war in India. Bhutto will have to make concessions to India to get the prisoners home, concessions such as the recognition of Bangladesh, and the acceptance of the Kashmir cease-fire line.

Bhutto's relations with his army were not improved by the announcement in early April 1972 by Mujibur Rahman that his nation was planning a Nuremberg-type war-crimes trial of hundreds of Pakistani soldiers. Such a humiliation for Pakistan, after the bitter military defeat, could lead to an attempt of the army to regain the political power it had before the war with India. The fear of this is probably the reason for Bhutto's purge of some 1,300 officers.

Bhutto has attempted to quieten rising popular discontent with promises of land reform, and with plans to provide large-scale public-health services and an educational program for Pakistan's 40,000,000 illiterate adults, programs which take vast sums of money that Pakistan does not have.

India

India suffered serious financial strain from the cost of feeding the millions of refugees that fled across her frontier from East Pakistan, and from the costs of war. India's immediate problem after the war was to persuade the millions of refugees to return to Bangladesh. India also had the moral obligation to help rebuild the nation she had helped to create.

India has little to fear from Pakistan, despite Bhutto's earlier threat of a *jihad* or holy war against India, and she is in a much better bargaining position to win concessions on the Kashmir problem.

Internally, India faces possible future difficulties from her Bengali minority in West Bengal province, which may be encouraged by the example of Bangladesh to demand rights of self-government.

Bangladesh

In mid-January 1972 President Ali Bhutto of Pakistan released his politically embarrassing prisoner, Sheikh Mujibur Rahman, the undisputed political leader of the self-declared nation of Bangladesh.

Enthusiastic crowds welcomed the return to Dacca of *Bangabandhu*, the Friend of Bengal; in decisive terms Mujibur Rahman asserted his command over Bangladesh: "Ours will be a secular, democratic socialist state."

Within a few days he announced a provisional constitution setting up a parliamentary-type government, with essential power resting in the Prime Minister and his appointed Cabinet. Then he promptly resigned the ceremonial office of the president, to which he had been appointed while still under arrest in West Pakistan, and took for himself the politically powerful office of Prime Minister.

Bangladesh announced itself to be a member of the British Commonwealth, and within a few months was recognized by over fifty nations, including the United States.

The young nation is faced with serious economic and social problems seldom experienced by a newly-independent country. It is estimated that of the total population of some 78,000,000

Mujibur Rahman, returning to his newly-formed country after imprisonment in West Pakistan.

at least 20,000,000 are destitute, including the 10,000,000 refugees who are expected to return from India. The chaos of destruction caused by the war in a country with one of the world's highest population densities – 1,300 to the square mile – and with one of the lowest per capita incomes in the world, an appallingly inadequate $30, will take years to rebuild.

An estimated 6,000,000 homes were destroyed; hundreds of thousands of families had neither animals nor tools to cultivate their land; seventy-five percent of the nation's industry was not working because of wrecked and looted machinery, and the lack of skilled workers, raw materials, and capital; the wartime destruction of railroads, bridges, and roads prevented the transportation of products for export and vital food supplies for the people; and some areas suffered from an almost complete lack of ready money because banknotes and coins were stolen or deliberately destroyed by Pakistani troops.

Another difficult problem was the future of some 1,500,000 Biharis or non-Bengali Moslems who emigrated from India to East Pakistan in 1947, and who were accused of recent collaboration with the Pakistani army. They feared the vengeance of the Bengalis, and demanded to be sent to Pakistan.

However, the main problem is economic because, as the Swiss United Nations chief in Dacca reported, the destruction in Bangladesh is greater than that suffered by Europe in World War II. In 1971 he reported that for 1972 it would take at least $1,000,000,000 to prevent widespread starvation and put Bangladesh merely on the road to recovery. In 1973 there was fear in Bangladesh that economic assistance to Vietnam might reduce its own aid.

Peace Negotiations

In July 1972 India's Prime Minister Indira Gandhi and Pakistan's President Zulfikar Ali Bhutto agreed to "put an end to the conflict and confrontation" that have involved the two nations since partition.*

They agreed to consider the resumption of diplomatic relations broken off in December 1971, to observe the Kashmir cease-fire line of December 1971, and to withdraw their military forces to the pre-war common boundary. No third power took part in the negotiations because earlier mediation by third powers has pleased neither nation.

India made a major concession by returning some 5,000 square miles of Pakistani territory, but kept a few strategic salients in Kashmir. This province remains a potentially explosive

*1947–49 in Kashmir; 1965 in the Rann of Kutch; 1965 in Kashmir; 1971 in East Pakistan.

issue because Bhutto insists that the future of Kashmir, whose population of 4,500,000 is predominantly Moslem, should be decided by a plebiscite to determine whether the people agree to India's claim to the province.

A complicating factor in future relationships on the subcontinent is the future of the 91,000 military and civilian prisoners still in Indian hands. Because the majority of them surrendered to a joint India-Bangladesh command, Prime Minister Rahman of Bangladesh insists that his nation must participate in negotiations. However, Bhutto, unrealistically refuses to recognize the new nation. Mujibur Rahman proposes to try some of the prisoners, including the former commander in East Pakistan, on war-crime charges. Pakistan denounces such trials, and warns that they could lead to reprisals against the 400,000 Bengalis who work in Pakistan.

Review Questions

Section 1

1. What have been the effects of the following geographical features upon India: its isolation; the Ganges and Indus Rivers; the Indus River and tributaries; the Hindustan Plain.
2. What are the main religious beliefs of Hinduism? How did Hinduism and Islam differ in the way in which their followers faced sorrows and hardships?
3. Was there any reason for the development of the caste system? Did the caste system ever serve any useful purpose?

Section 2

4. On what political issue was the National Congress Party split? Why did the Moslems not support the Congress Party demand for votes for all Indians?
5. What situation led to Gandhi's leadership? Was his "non-violent non-co-operation" effective?
6. Why did the Salt March oblige the British to make concessions?
7. Why did the Moslems demand partition? Why did Gandhi not prevent partition?

Sections 3 and 4

8. What problems did partition create between India and Pakistan?
9. Why did Nehru favor Five-year Plans and socialism?
10. Was Nehru's policy of neutralism successful? How did Nehru contradict himself in his foreign policy?

Sections 5, 6, and 7

11. Did West Pakistan's treatment of East Pakistan since partition justify East Pakistan's decision to declare independence?
12. Was Yahya Khan or Mujibur Rahman more to blame for the outbreak of civil war? Were there any possible grounds for compromise that could have avoided civil war?
13. For what reasons did India go to war with Pakistan? Were these reasons valid, or could war have been avoided?
14. What have been the effects of war upon India and Pakistan, and independence upon Bangladesh?

5

China: From Empire to Republic

Early China

Brief History to Modern Times

The Revolution of 1911

China's past history has been very different from that of Europe, where change and strife were common occurrences for several centuries. While Europe experienced the Renaissance, the Reformation, and the Commercial Revolution, China remained comparatively peaceful, orderly, and unchanging. The "Middle Kingdom," as the Chinese called their country because they believed it to be the center of the universe, had little to do with the outside world, and when European nations forced their way into China they found what they regarded as a "backward" nation. Culturally, China was far ahead of Europe for several centuries, and its "backwardness" in the 19th century was essentially its lack of the scientific and technological development that Europe was experiencing. Europeans gave the name China to the country from the old Ch'in dynasty or ruling family.

The interference of European nations in China during the 19th century aroused resentment among the Chinese people against the foreigners and against their own royal family which had permitted the indignities of treaty ports and concessions. In the eyes of the people the Emperor had lost the "mandate of Heaven" and they were justified in demanding his abdication.

The problem that faced China after the Rebellion of 1911 was to set up a viable republic in a country which had no experience of self-government. The Rebellion of 1911 was only the beginning of significant changes which today are still continuing.

Terms

1. Middle Kingdom
2. Confucianism
3. Ethics
4. Taoism
5. Buddhism
6. Ch'in Dynasty
7. Tang Dynasty
8. Mongol (Yuan) Dynasty
9. Manchu Dynasty
10. Chinese Guild
11. Family Responsibility
12. Kuomintang
13. The "Double Ten"

People

14. Confucius
15. Buddha
16. Genghis Khan
17. Kublai Khan
18. Marco Polo
19. John Hay
20. Sun Yat-sen
21. Yuan Shi-k'ai

Places

22. Yellow River
23. Yangtze River
24. Shanghai
25. Nanking
26. Hankow
27. Chungking
28. Hsi River
29. Sinkiang Province
30. Mongolia

Events

1894–1895 Sino-Japanese War
1899 First Open Door Note
1900 Boxer Rebellion
1900 Second Open Door Note
1911 Revolution
1912 Republic of China

1. Early China

Geography

Mainland China today is the third largest country in the world, with an area of about 3,700,000 square miles, exceeded in size only by the Soviet Union and Canada. Six out of every seven of its people are crowded into the fertile east central section, which is about one-third of all China. This is equal to crowding three times the entire population of the United States into the land east of the Mississippi River. Its land borders consist mostly of mountains and deserts, and it has 7,000 miles of coastline on the Pacific Ocean.

Three rivers of China have dominated the life of its millions of people since ancient times. In the north the Yellow River or Hwang Ho flows for 3,000 miles across the North China Plain from northwest to the east coast, and provides millions of people with their livelihood. Six times in China's history it has changed its course, causing serious damage but providing the area with the fertile silt or yellow soil which is carried down stream and makes the land rich for crops of rice, wheat, and millet. The Yangtze River, over 3,000 miles long and navigable for 1,000 miles, is the fifth largest river in the world and bisects China from west to east. Along its banks are some of the great cities of China: Shanghai on the east coast; Nanking, once the capital; Hankow; and Chungking, far to the west and the capital of China during the war with Japan from 1937 to 1945.

In the far south the Hsi (shee) River,* with the port of Canton at its mouth, provides irrigation for two and sometimes three crops of rice and sugar a year.

The heartland of China throughout its history has been the east central area which was called China Proper, reaching in the north from the 1684 mile-long Great Wall of China southward to the borders of modern Burma, Laos (lah'ohs), and Vietnam, and westward to Sinkiang (shin' ji ahng') and Tsinghai (dzing' hye').

An important province of China is Manchuria, some 600,000 square miles in area, and the home of the Manchus who conquered the Chinese Empire in the 17th century and provided the last dynasty until the abdication of the Manchu emperor in 1912. During the first half of the 20th century Manchuria was the object of Russian and Japanese expansion because of its great fertile plains and its large deposits of coal and iron ore.

Larger than Manchuria is the vast expanse of Mongolia to the northwest, divided into the southern section called Inner Mongolia, a part of China today, and Outer Mongolia which was recognized as independent in the 1940's.

Northern China, hot in the summer but bitterly cold in winter, suffers from inadequate rainfall but is able to raise wheat as its principal crop. South China is warm during most of the year, has ample rainfall from the monsoon winds which blow in from the Pacific Ocean during the summer months, and is the rice-growing section of China with at least two crops a year. Central China can raise the crops typical of both north and south but specializes in tea and the mulberry trees which provide food for the silkworm.

Philosophy and Religion

The outstanding characteristic of China has been its cultural continuity for so many centuries, based particularly upon the teachings of Confucius who was born more than five centuries before Christ, and who lived at the same time as Buddha in India; Confucius was also almost a contemporary of the great Greek philosopher Socrates. Born to an aristocratic family descended

---

*Phonetic pronounciation is included in Chapters 5 and 6 to assist readers.

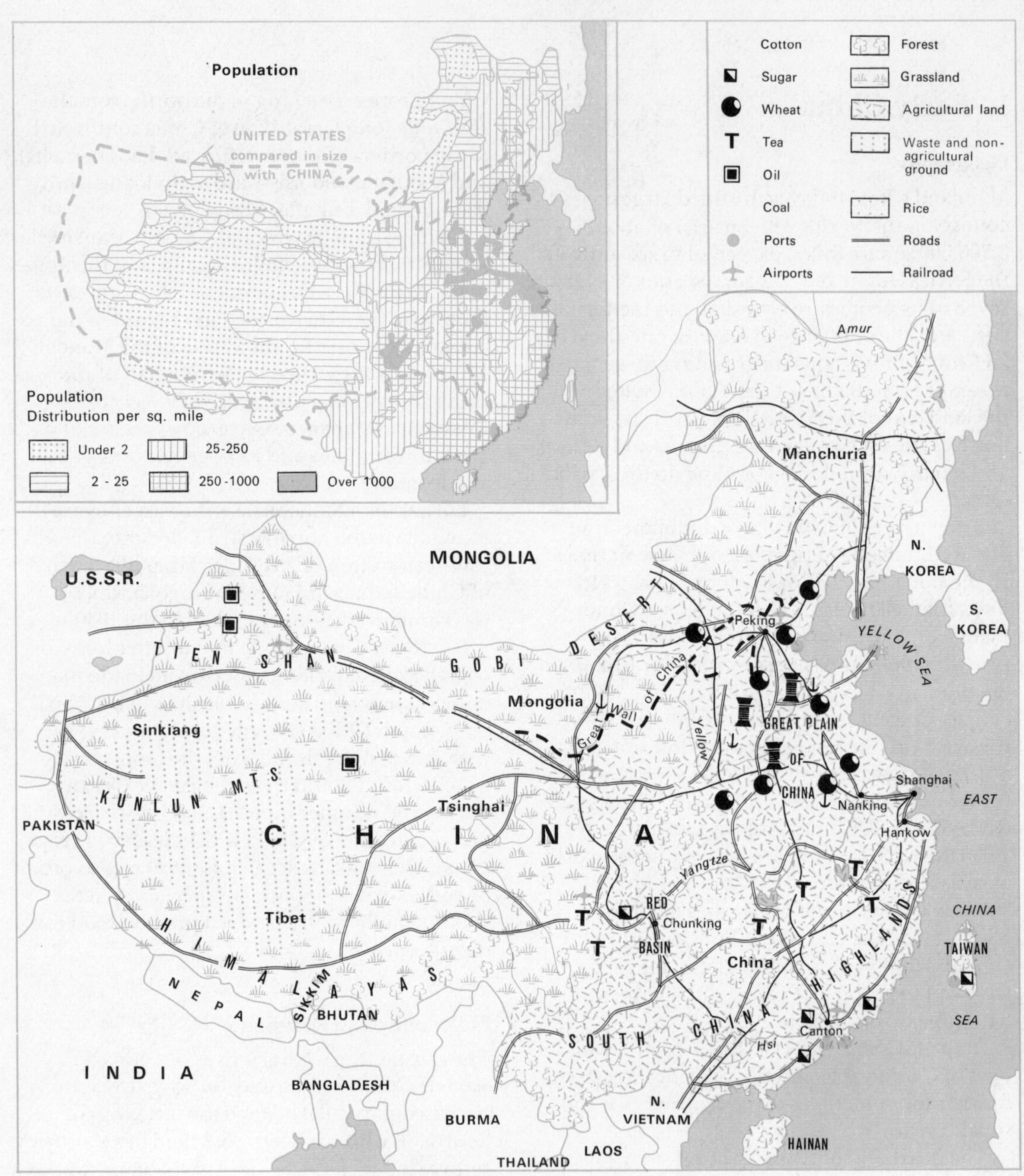

China. Land and resources. The population relates to modern figures.

from priests, Confucius received a good education, taught for some years, entered government service, and spent the last years of his life wandering and living with disciples and teaching his doctrine. He lived in an age of feudalism in which the country was constantly disturbed by struggles between local feudal princes, and he determined to try to improve conditions. He taught that people could prosper only if the ruler had their interests at heart, and if men lived together in harmony and good will. He hoped to persuade men to accept basic rules of behavior to accomplish this purpose, which is essentially what people and nations are still attempting to do 2,500 years later in the 20th century.

Confucianism was not a religion but a philosophy or belief about men's relationships with each other, and a code of ethics or behavior setting up rules of conduct. The early religion of China was a worship of the spirits of departed ancestors. Confucius did not oppose this practice. Good government was the primary concern of Confucius, who said that if the government was good, then the whole country would be secure and the people happy. A government which was good was one which kept the country safe, provided sufficient food for the people, and had the support of the people. The one central teaching of Confucius, the central problem of life, was the behavior of people toward one another, expressed simply as, "What you would not have done to you, do not do unto others." Confucius was not concerned with salvation, the soul, or afterlife, because he believed that man must first learn to behave fairly and properly in this life. These personal relationships between ruler and people, father and son, within the family, and between friends explain much of the history of China. Emperors and leaders have fallen because the Chinese people lost confidence in their rulers. A recent example is the career of Chiang Kai-shek (jee ahng kye shek), who was driven into exile on the island of Taiwan because he failed to give his people the leadership they expected from him. The very close relationship of the Chinese family, its responsibility for every member, and its ancestor worship, is Confucianism put into practice.

Confucianism, or rather its interpretations in later centuries, had certain weaknesses. It did not teach what is today called nationalism, the belief that a nation succeeds and benefits from common agreement and action by its people. The Confucian stress upon family life emphasized local interests rather than national ones. The history of China indicates that not until recent decades has a national feeling developed within the country, and that it was brought about essentially by the interference of foreigners in Chinese affairs.

According to Confucius, China could be administered only by able and therefore educated men. Not all men could learn the difficult Chinese writing system which contained over 300 signs; those who could learn to write and could most profit by education had the obligation and responsibility, not simply the choice, to govern and inspire others. To Confucius, a cultured person was one who not only had an education but who also knew how to conduct himself as a gentleman with good manners and consideration for others. Unfortunately for China and her later history, education became too aristocratic and narrow; it consisted of learning by rote the literature and culture of the past, rather than learning by experience or by thinking and asking questions. Education became stereotyped and formalized and tended to discourage new ideas. Nevertheless, the good characteristics of Confucianism obviously did a great deal to help people to live together harmoniously.

Taoism

Confucius had his critics and rivals who believed that he failed to suggest how to deal with economic and social problems. Poor people could not afford an education, and for centuries the great majority of people were poor peasants who were usually at the mercy of landlords and extortionate moneylenders.

One of these critics was Lao-tzu (low oh dzuh), perhaps a mythical character but credited with teachings which have greatly affected China down to modern times. Where Confucianism tried to teach that men had obligations and responsibilities toward each other, Lao-tzu's philosophy of Taoism, from Tao meaning the Way or the Road, taught that it was useless to attempt to change conditions. Taoism was a type of fatalism because it taught that man could change nothing by his own efforts. Man should accept his life without trying to change it. The best government was the least government; the universe went its own way unchanged by man; any effort to improve conditions was a waste of time and effort because they would be unsuccessful efforts to control the universe and the future. Actually, man should try to find harmony with the forces of the universe. Man therefore should be patient, humble, and uncomplaining. Taoism appealed to poor people because it taught them to accept a life which they were unable to improve.

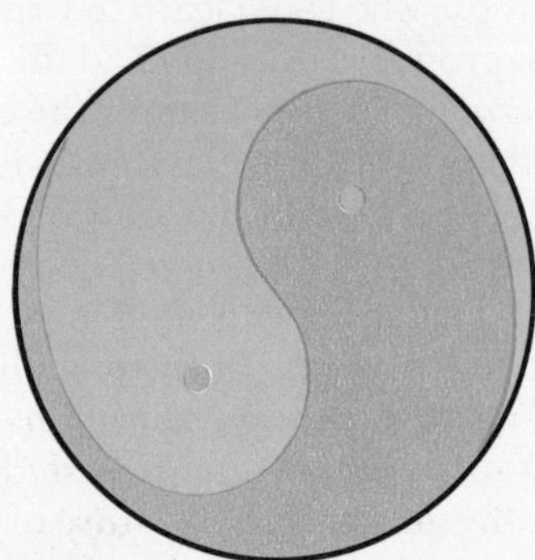

Chinese Symbolism. Taoism embraced the concept of the relativity of all values. Here is the graphic symbol of *yang* and *yin*—the summary of life's basic contrasts: good-evil, active-passive, male-female, light-dark, etc. The *yang* and the *yin* are always in tension yet they intermingle and are part of each other. Both are resolved by being within the circle which is *Tao*—the way of life.

Buddhism

At about the same time that Confucius and Lao-tzu were teaching their beliefs in China, philosophers in other parts of the world were also trying to understand man and his place in the universe. Greece, Israel, Persia, and India in the sixth century B.C. produced thinkers who tried to find answers to such problems. One of the great ones was Siddhartha Gautama, better known as Buddha, whose teachings came from India to China to influence Chinese religion down through the centuries.

Born into a royal family, young Siddhartha Gautama lived in great wealth and splendor. His father, fearful of the prophecy that his son would one day forego earthly pleasures and retire to a religious life, ordered him never to leave his palaces. Legend is that young Gautama knew nothing of illness, old age, and death until one day he rode out among the people and for the first time realized that life could be miserable and painful. At the age of twenty-nine he left the palace, changed his royal clothes for a coarse yellow robe, and set out to find an answer to the problem of salvation. For six years he became a disciple of several religions and beliefs, even practicing the strict discipline of the Yogas, who believed that the mind must have absolute control over the body. Buddha then came to the realization that such self-tortures were not preparing him to help ordinary people face their daily problems, so he searched for an answer that neither learning nor self-mortification had brought. With the knowledge that he finally found he became known as Buddha, the Enlightened One. His enlightenment was his realization and acceptance that life is misery and pain, that at death a man's soul is born into a new body, and that man is therefore condemned to endless misery. Man's unhappiness is the result of his constant desires for things he cannot get, for expectations that he can never realize. In order to find peace man must give up these desires and seek peace and satisfaction through proper behavior to others. The Middle Path between the extremes of self-mortification and self-indulgence will buy man peace of mind and wisdom. He will become free of worldly desires, no longer will his soul be born into another body, and he will reach Nirvana, the state of perfect peace.

Buddhism demanded self-control, and because ideally a Buddhist should be detached from the turmoil and demands of daily life he should live apart as a monk. The Buddhist accepts some of the beliefs of Hinduism, such as reincarnation and that of *karma*, that conduct is appropriately rewarded in future reincarnations. But a Buddhist does not accept the Hindu's belief in the caste system and the inequality of men.

The essence of Buddha's teachings is in his principles of the Four Noble Truths: (1) suffering is universal, (2) the reason for suffering is man's desire for earthly things, (3) suffering can

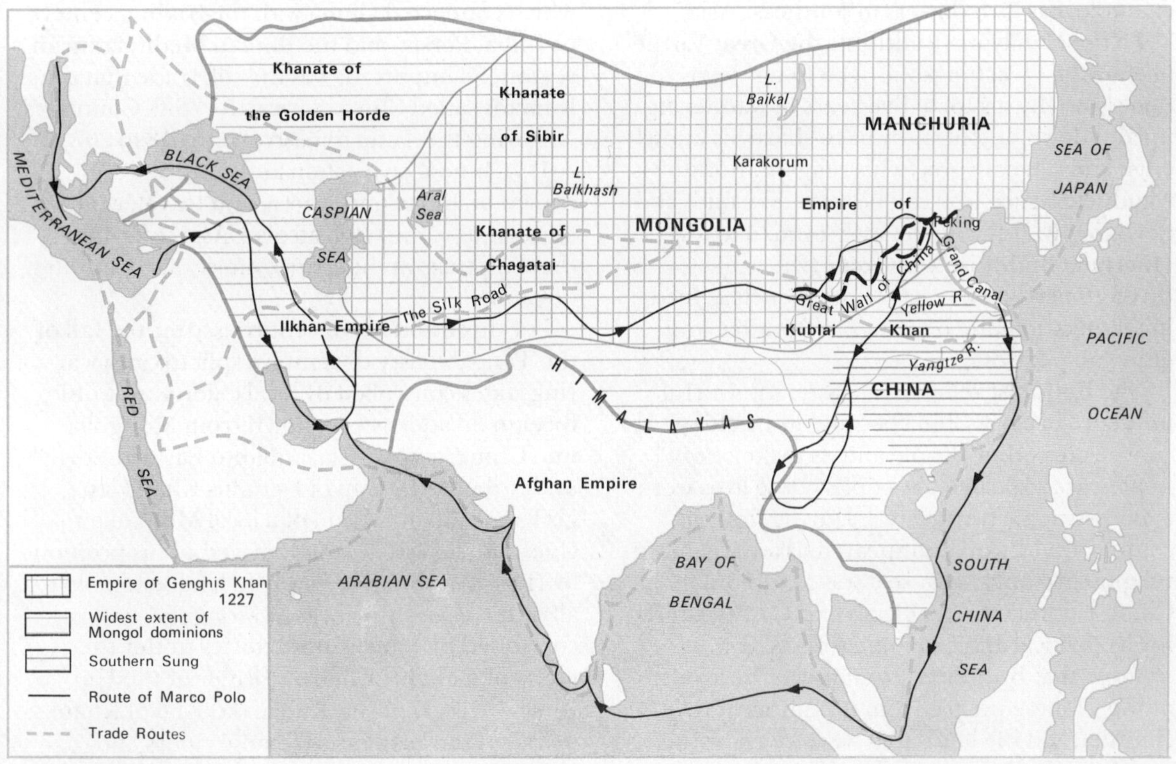

Early China

be cured by giving up these desires, and (4) the way to ged rid of desires is to follow the Noble Eightfold Path based on "right" action such as knowledge, intentions, conduct, effort, and concentration.

Buddhism changed during the twenty-five centuries since Buddha's time because different lands and cultures influenced it with local customs, but its basic characteristics remained and are to be found among the millions of people who accept its teachings.

Today there are two main schools or practices of Buddhist doctrine. Mahayana Buddhism, which is based on salvation by faith and good works, is followed in China, Tibet, Mongolia, Korea, and Japan. Hinayana Buddhism, based upon austerity and salvation by personal example, has its followers in southeast Asia.

To the Mahayana Buddhists the Great Virtue of Buddha's teachings was seen in his devotion shown by his forty-five years of wandering up and down northern India to share his knowledge and win converts to his religion. Buddha is a god-like figure who can be served by faith and devotion. Buddha is primarily human to the Hinayana Buddhist, who attains Nirvana through performing acts of merit such as feeding monks, making offerings to Buddha, and going on pilgrimages.

The Buddhist religion had a very powerful influence in early China because its teachings of concern for other people and its promise of final peace appealed to people whose lives were a daily struggle for survival. During the 9th century Buddhism disappeared as an organized religion in China because it was persecuted by Chinese government officials and Confucianists for its political and economic effects. It was thought that Buddhism would turn the loyalty of the Chinese people from the emperor to Buddha, and the lands that were given by the faithful to Buddhist monasteries were exempt from taxes that the government would otherwise collect. The Buddhist religion was not forbidden in China but its property was confiscated, and Buddhist monks and nuns were driven from their places of worship.

2. Brief History to Modern Times

The Ruling-Dynasties

Between 221 B.C. and 1912 A.D. ten dynasties or ruling families governed China. The first was the Ch'in dynasty which organized the Chinese Empire. The second was the Han dynasty which by 200 A.D. controlled the important Silk Road which connected China with the trading centers of India, Persia, and the Roman Mediterranean region. So important was the silk trade that the Romans called China, Serica, the "Silk Country."

During the Tang dynasty, from 618 to 907 A.D., Chinese civilization and culture were copied by Japan and Korea, and travelers and merchants came from all over Asia to admire the sculpture, architecture, music, and painting of China.

For three and a half centuries after the fall of the Tang dynasty the empire split up into warring states controlled by local chieftains, until foreign invaders swept down from Mongolia into China, across Asia, and into Eastern Europe under the leadership of Genghis Khan (jeng' gis kahn). Born the son of a local Mongolian chieftain, he was at first deprived of his position by rivals, but fought his way to leadership over all other *khans* or princes of Mongolia, and continued his whirlwind victories under the name of Genghis Khan or "Ruler of the Universe." His grandson Kublai (koo' blye) Khan defeated the last of the Chinese rulers and established a new dynasty called the Yuan or

Marco Polo and his brothers meeting Kublai Khan.

Mongol. Much of what became known of China under Kublai Khan was written by the Venetian merchant Marco Polo who arrived with his father at the Khan's court in 1275 and spent the next seventeen years in the imperial service and in traveling through China. So extraordinary were Marco Polo's descriptions of Peking with its 12,000 stone bridges spanning the canals that criss-crossed the city, the warm baths, the use of coal for heating purposes, and other unheard-of wonders that Polo was not believed when he finally returned to Venice.

The Mongol regime was nevertheless a brutal one for the peasants of China, who were dispossessed of their land, taxed almost beyond endurance, and forced to accept increasingly worthless paper money issued by the Mongol rulers. Seven successors of Kublai Khan lost power through their inability to control the country and their unwillingness to appoint Chinese scholars to positions in the government. Discontented peasants revolted in many parts of the country, particularly in the Yangtze valley and the south, until finally a Buddhist monk united them, defeated the Mongols, and established a new Chinese dynasty, the Ming, which lasted from 1368 to 1644; then the Manchus came in from Manchuria to assist the Chinese government against peasant rebels, and stayed to take over the Chinese Empire and rule it until they were forced to abdicate in 1912 A.D.

Traditional Daily Life in China

A great error made by modern Europeans, and Americans too, during the 19th century, was to judge China by Western standards. Because the emperor and the ruling class frequently seemed to be incompetent and corrupt, the West assumed that China really had no government. Because Westerners were living in an industrial age they did not put China's local agrarian economy into proper perspective. China until recent years was little more than a collection of agricultural villages that had only slight connection with each other. The people of one province might actually starve to death while another province enjoyed an abundance of food. There were no easy means of transporting food, and the people of one region did not feel responsible for those of another.

The Guild. Almost the only contact the average peasant had with the government of China was the tax collector, who acted also as lawmaker and judge on behalf of the emperor. Usually he left the people of his district alone to continue in ways which had been traditional for centuries. Government of the modern type was unknown in China. The two agencies that "managed" the affairs of each locality were the guild and the family.

Just as did the guild in the Middle Ages in Europe, the guild in China regulated the life of the local people. The representatives of the

The Great Wall

several guilds in the locality, the bakers, the fishermen, cooks, boatmen, and others formed the ruling group of the area. The emperor's tax collector conducted his business through the guild. If he proposed a tax or some other measure which the guild representatives regarded as too harsh or unfair, they could force the official to reconsider by threatening to boycott him, to ignore him as though he were not there, and to refuse to pay any tax whatever.

The local official would probably be charged with incompetence by his superiors, and they in turn by their superiors, as having broken the accepted code of conduct and proven themselves to be incompetent. Such a charge no official wanted to face; consequently he made every effort to act reasonably. The guild left the official alone if he did not interfere unfairly with the community, unfairly according to tradition and according to immediate conditions as judged by the guild.

Another important function of the guild was to regulate the economy of its own region, and to limit the actions of the individual in the interests of the community. The member of the locality could sell his product or services at as high a price as he could get. But he was strictly forbidden to sell below the minimum set by the guild, because he might "corner the market" by underselling his competitors. In this situation, other merchants would lose business and face starvation, or more picturesquely, their rice bowls would be empty, and they would have to be looked after by others. In an overpopulated society this could not be allowed to happen. The Chinese government was effective but it was basically local, and the allegiance of the Chinese was naturally to their local government.

The Family. Another important agency which looked after local affairs and the people of the community was the family, which was actually the foundation of Chinese society. In Western history, on the other hand, the individual increasingly became important as a person, partly because of the development of competition in European society, and partly because of Christianity which taught that salvation depended upon a man's own conscience and actions.

In China the family usually included all related people, much like a Scottish clan, so that a village might consist of one "family." It was ruled by its elders, its property was frequently held in common, and the group was responsible for every one of its members. The important fact to be appreciated is that no matter how old were the "younger" men of the family, they made no individual decisions. Judgments were made collectively, and collectively the family cared for all its members, whether they were ill, unemployed, or too old to look after themselves. In this sense the Chinese centuries ago accepted the idea that society as a group had responsibility for the welfare of all its members.

There were several important results of this traditional Chinese society. One was that a country of this type could not be easily defeated. Part of it could be invaded and overrun by an enemy, but this conquest had little, and sometimes no, effect upon other sections. There were no vital nerve centers, such as industrial cities or communications centers whose capture or destruction could paralyze a nation. Another important result was that China could not become a unified nation in the modern sense, because the loyalty of the citizen was a local one, to his family and his guild. He had no sense of belonging to a nation whose defense against attack by an enemy was his responsibility.

A third result which must be remembered in evaluating the rise of the Communist government in China was that the country has traditionally been a "communal" society, where the "community" or group regulated even the livelihood of its members. The Chinese did not have capitalism as the West knew it. Consequently, state ownership does not shock the Chinese as it does the democratic western nations, because the Chinese have had very little experience with the western type of free enterprise.

Relations with Foreign Nations

Diplomatically and economically China had no official relations with any foreign governments. She neither sent nor received diplomats, and she had no trade treaties with foreign nations. Any relationship which she might have had with the outside world was based upon the emperor's decision only. In the later 18th and the early 19th centuries, foreign trade was limited to the port of Canton, and upon conditions specifically laid down by the emperor.

The main export of China was tea, and because China had little need for European goods, she received payment in large quantities of silver bullion which she made into her own coins. This "favorable" balance of trade was reversed by the introduction of the opium business by the West, and China had to pay out her money for opium from India in increasing amounts. Partly for this reason and partly because of the bad effects of opium-smoking upon the people, the emperor attempted to prohibit further importation of opium. This resulted in the Opium War of 1840, and the repeated and increasing interference of other nations in Chinese affairs. (*See* III, 5.)

3. The Revolution of 1911

End of the The Manchu Dynasty

The causes of the Revolution of 1911, which led to the final end of imperial rule in 1912 and its replacement by a republic, were partly dissatisfaction with internal conditions, and partly the aggressions by foreign nations upon China.

The Treaty of Nanking of 1842 was only the beginning of foreign interference in China. By this treaty and the so-called Treaty Settlements of 1844 and 1860 foreign nations, including the United States, dictated tariff rates on goods taken into China and received "extraterritorial" rights of special courts of their own in China to handle cases involving their own citizens.

During the Taiping Rebellion in which the leader Hung proposed seizing land from the wealthy and setting up a fairer taxation system, foreign governments sent troops to Peking and obliged the Manchu government to open up more ports to foreigners, allow them to travel into the interior, and to grant more land concessions. Russia forced China to give her a large area of land north of the Amur River, known as the Maritime Provinces, where Russia built the port of Vladivostock. The Sino-Japanese

CHINA SAFE—FOR THE PRESENT

Imperialism. A comment on the treatment of China by European nations in the 19th Century.

War of 1894–1895 was a disaster for the Manchus because their large mainland empire was defeated by a small island nation, and because other nations were able to demand spheres of influence such as Germany's lease of Kiaochow (jih ow' joh) Bay for 99 years, Russia's lease of Port Arthur, and several others.

Some nations, Great Britain and the United States in particular, were more interested in actual trade than in securing Chinese territory, and they were afraid that Germany, Russia, and other nations might turn their spheres of influence into actual colonies and keep out all foreign trade. The British approached the United States, which also did not want to see China broken up into exclusive foreign colonies, and suggested that practical steps should be taken. In 1899 Secretary of State John Hay wrote identical official Notes to several governments suggesting that each nation should support the idea of "equal trading opportunities" for all in the various spheres of influence.

This was the Open Door policy, and was accepted by other nations, although rather vaguely, because no one nation trusted the others. A year later the Boxer Rebellion broke out and foreigners were besieged in their legations for 55 days in Peking until relieved by troops sent in by six nations. Russia took the opportunity to send the army into Manchuria, and the United States feared that other powers would take advantage of the situation to partition China.

In a Second Open Door Note Secretary Hay, calling upon the great powers to respect China's independent government and her territory, actually committed the United States to so doing. "The policy of the Government of the United States is to seek a solution which may bring about permanent safety and peace to China, preserve Chinese territorial and administrative integrity . . ."

Inside China disillusionment with the Manchu dynasty was already preparing the way for revolution. Intelligent Chinese had seen Japan westernize as the only way to avoid possible control by foreigners. Some Chinese administrators wanted to westernize too, but were opposed by other Chinese who enjoyed their own special privileges, and were opposed also by the Manchu ruler who refused to admit that Chinese ways were inferior to western.

Sun Yat-sen: Revolutionary Leader

The man who finally organized successful opposition to the imperial regime was Sun Yat-sen (soon' yaht sehn) who was born in Canton in 1866, went to Hawaii at the age of 13 where his

Sun Yat-sen. This photograph was taken about 1912.

older brother had settled, and studied at an English missionary school in Honolulu. There Sun Yat-sen learned about Western civilization, then went to Hong Kong to attend medical school, from which he graduated in 1894 and commenced his medical career. But the humiliating defeat of China by Japan in 1895 convinced Sun that he must devote his life to saving his country. In 1895 he attempted to lead a *coup* against the Manchus, but failed and was obliged to seek exile in Japan with a price on his head.

He visited Chinese communities in Japan, Hawaii, Southeast Asia, the United States, and Europe, and over the years was able to organize a revolutionary organization called the Kuomintang, the Nation-People Party or Nationalist Party.

The revolutionaries in China, assisted by funds collected by Sun in his travels, were forced to revolt prematurely. Home-made bombs accidentally burst in their secret headquarters in Hankow, and the revolutionaries decided to fight immediately rather than be quietly captured and executed. On October 10, 1911, the "double ten" of the tenth day of the tenth month, the revolution broke out and spread to other parts of China. Sun Yat-sen first knew about it as he read of it in an American newspaper while he was eating breakfast in a Denver restaurant.

Sun arrived in China in December 1911 to find that the troops of several garrisons had joined the revolutionaries in a series of local rebellions. Up to this point Sun had played only a minor part in the revolution, which at first was almost leaderless because nothing further had been planned other than the overthrow of the Manchus. Some leaders wanted a strong central government with a strong executive, while others wanted a representative parliamentary system and stronger local governments.

In desperation the Manchus turned to Yuan Shi-k'ai (yoo an shi kye), the retired general and organizer of the national army. In two weeks he defeated the rebels but entered into negotiations with them in order to gain power for himself. He made a bargain with Sun Yat-sen, who had been elected temporary President of the Republic by the rebels, and persuaded him to resign, by agreeing to support the republic and persuade the Manchu emperor to abdicate. In February 1912 the prince regent signed the abdication order of the five-year old emperor, and the reign of the Manchu dynasty ended after 248 years.

The revolutionaries supported Yuan only because they wanted a republic, although they

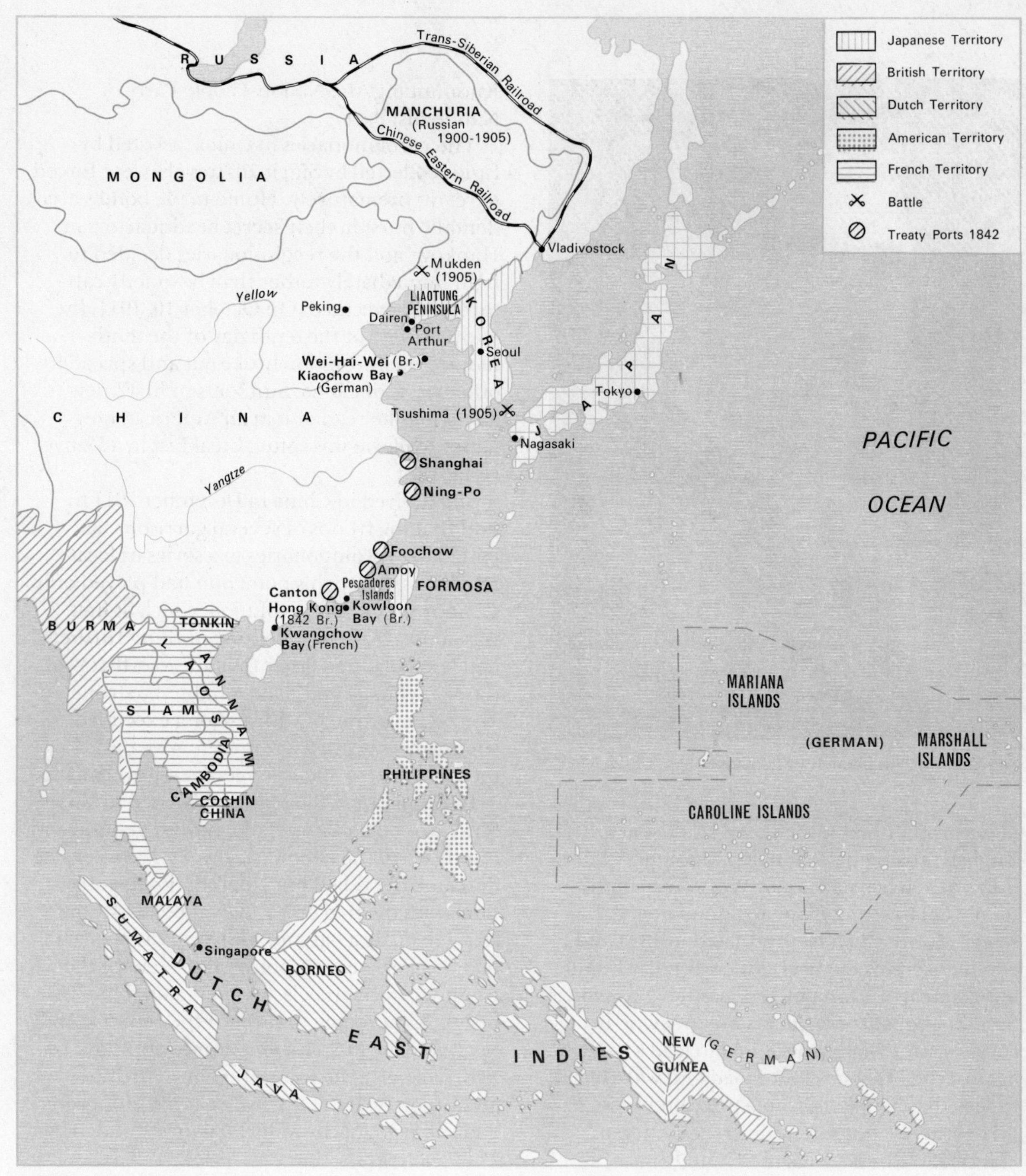

China and the Far East by 1914

did not trust him, suspecting his intention to take power for himself. Yuan began to assassinate political opponents, reduced parliament to a figurehead, forced Sun to flee to escape execution, and set himself up as dictator.

The Chinese understood almost nothing of a parliamentary system, elections, and political rights, and in 1915 Yuan skillfully organized a campaign "urging" himself to set up a new imperial dynasty with himself as the first of its emperors. Opposition to him was already starting when he died in 1916, but it was opposition by local warlords who were afraid of a strong central power, rather than by the revolutionaries. As a result, the country fell into the chaos of independent provinces under the selfish, brutal power of various warlords who preyed upon their people without restraint. The City of Peking became the target of several of the warlords because whoever controlled Peking was regarded by foreign nations as the official government of China.

The weakness of China provided foreign governments with the opportunity to squeeze more privileges from China, such as the right to station gunboats and troops in the interior to "protect" their citizens. Great Britain and Japan were most feared by China at this time because Great Britain's trade exceeded that of all the other foreign powers, and because Japan was steadily consolidating her position in China.

In 1905 she had received by the Treaty of Shimonoseki the island of Taiwan (Formosa) and the Pescadores Islands, and she was only prevented from taking over the strategic Liaotung (lyow doong) Peninsula by "advice" from Russia, France, and Germany to return it to China. In 1910 Japan had annexed Korea. Japan was the last of the major powers to recognize the Republic of China because she feared that in time the Chinese leaders would be able to organize their country and loosen the hold of the foreign powers.

Review Questions

Section 1

1. Why have rivers dominated the life of China?
2. In what respects is Confucianism a philosophy rather than a religion?
3. What weaknesses developed in the Confucian teachings in later centuries?
4. What was the Middle Path that Buddha taught?

Section 2

5. Why did the Mongol dynasty in China finally collapse?
6. What important functions did the guilds perform for the Chinese people?
7. What were the effects of the close family life upon China?
8. How was the "favorable" balance of trade for China made decidedly unfavorable?

Section 3

9. Was foreign influence advantageous or disadvantageous to the people of China?
10. Explain the causes of the Revolution of 1911?
11. Why did Sun Yat-sen's leadership prove to be ineffectual?
12. How did foreign nations benefit from the Revolution of 1911?

6

China: The People's Republic

Nationalism Develops in China

The Rivalry of Chiang Kai-shek and Mao Tse-tung

The Sino-Japanese War, 1937–1945

Establishment of the People's Republic of China

Foreign Policy of the People's Republic

Recognition of the People's Republic

Revolutionary Russia gave help after World War I to the Chinese leaders of the Rebellion of 1911, expecting to be able to further their own goal of world revolution. Chiang Kai-shek, who had been sent to Moscow for military training, returned to become commandant of the Whampoa Military Academy, China's West Point, and to become the leading opponent of Chinese Communists, led by Mao Tse-tung.

Chiang's successes against Mao alarmed Japan, whose expansionist ambitions in China could be seriously threatened by a united China under Chiang. Japan attacked China in 1937 but could not defeat Chiang Kai-shek, who led the resistance from Chungking. With Japan's defeat in 1945, civil war broke out again in China, and Chiang's failure to provide a much-needed reform program offered Mao the opportunity to win widespread peasant support.

In 1949 Chiang was driven off the mainland of China to Taiwan, and the People's Republic of China was proclaimed by Mao, who proceeded to attempt to increase agricultural production and to industrialize the nation. The People's Republic and the Soviet Union, despite their common belief in Communism, reverted to rivalry over frontier and land claims, and have become widely divergent over the ideology and methods of Communism, particularly in foreign affairs.

The initiation of a rapprochement between two major Pacific powers, China and the U.S., is a landmark in modern diplomatic history.

Terms

1. Twenty-one Demands
2. May Fourth Movement
3. Three Principles of the People
4. The Long March
5. The Chinese "Incident"
6. Marshall Mission
7. The "Great Leap Forward"
8. The "Great Proletarian Cultural Revolution"
9. Red Guards

People

10. Chiang Kai-shek
11. Mao Tse-tung
12. Chou En-lai
13. The Young Marshal
14. Joseph Stilwell
15. George Marshall
16. Lin Piao
17. Henry Kissinger

Places

18. Kiangsi Province
19. Hunan Province
20. Shensi Province
21. Yunan
22. Peiping
23. Hankow
24. Taiwan
25. Quemoy and Matsu

Events

1919	May Fourth Movement
1927	Purge of Communists
1934	The Long March
1937–1945	Sino-Japanese War
1949	People's Republic of China
1958	"Great Leap Forward"
1960	Sino-Soviet Breach
1966	"Great Proletarian Cultural Revolution"
1972	Peking Summit Meeting

1. Nationalism Develops in China

China and World War I

Almost as soon as World War I broke out in 1914, Japan captured Tsingtao (ching dow), the port of German Kiaochow Bay, and seized the German possessions. Because European nations were involved in the war in Europe, Japan saw a chance to put further pressure on China and presented her with the Twenty-one Demands. The basic terms were that Japanese citizens should be able to own land in China; Japan should have control of Manchurian railroads and have the right to build railroads in South China; China would not allow a third power to invest in industrial enterprises without Japan's consent; China must accept Japanese political, military, and financial advisers and place her police under joint Sino-Japanese control in specified areas. These terms would have made China simply a satellite of Japan, unable to operate as an independent country. The United States immediately notified Japan that she would recognize no demands on or agreements with China that contradicted the Open Door policy of China's independence. Japan gave way, temporarily.

Although China declared war on Germany and assisted the Allies, she was bitterly disappointed at the Paris Peace Conference, where secret agreements made between the Allies and Japan came to light. In 1917 Great Britain, France, and Italy had agreed that German possessions and rights in China would be transferred to Japan when the war ended. When China protested, the other members of the Conference agreed that China and Japan should settle the matter between themselves. The result was to be expected. Japan took what the other nations had no right to promise her in 1917. The Chinese delegation walked out of the Conference, refused to sign the Treaty of Versailles, and made a separate peace treaty with Germany later.

Reaction in China to the Peace Conference

The treatment of China by the Allies had a tremendous impact upon the Chinese people. On May 4, 1919, a series of demonstrations, later known as the May Fourth Movement, denounced the betrayal of China and organized a boycott of Japanese goods. The betrayal, as the Chinese regarded it, galvanized the Chinese into refusing to accept the humiliation in silence. In the following years demonstrations against foreigners increased, and a violent clash occurred between the Chinese and foreign governments in the International Settlement of Shanghai. At one point a general strike by Chinese workers paralyzed Shanghai for weeks. Trade in Hong Kong was brought to a standstill for more than a year over the shooting of Chinese by foreign police and troops.

The Chinese republican leaders launched a tremendous campaign against illiteracy. They wrote books and articles in the language spoken by the ordinary people, instead of in the classical Chinese. They explained to the people the purposes of the revolution and the aims of the nationalists. Those who could not read for themselves were read to.

Sun Yat-sen launched another revolutionary movement against the warlords and gained popular support for his Three Principles of the People: Nationalism; Democracy; People's Livelihood. By Nationalism he meant not only that China should be run by the Chinese but also that the people should get a sense of belonging to a nation, not just a locality. By Democracy he meant a government in which the people should take part. And by People's Livelihood he meant an improvement in the everyday life of the people, a fair distribution of land, and lower taxes for the peasants, and, if necessary, a limited socialist economy. He hoped to get assistance from the West, but when only a little was forthcoming he approached the Soviet Union. The Russians favored world revolution and were quite willing to help unite China, expecting that they would be able to organize and direct the Kuomintang Nationalist Party into a powerful revolutionary party. They sent in Michael Borodin as adviser, and helped to establish Whampoa Military Academy, the West Point of China, where eager Chinese republicans could be trained for the new Chinese army that would free China from dependence upon armies of the warlords.

Chiang Kai-shek

2. The Rivalry of Chiang Kai-shek and Mao Tse-tung

Campaigns against the Communists

Chiang Kai-shek (jee ahng kye shek) was born in 1887 in the Shanghai region, became a cadet in the old imperial army, and then a supporter of Sun Yat-sen. In 1923 he was sent by Sun to Moscow for military training and soon after his return was appointed Commandant of the Whampoa Military Academy. After Sun's death in 1925 Chiang began to emerge as a leading figure in the Kuomintang, which unfortunately was suffering from disputes over leadership and policies. One of the most serious problems for Chiang was the Communist group within the party because they had been ordered by the Soviet Union to become members of the Kuomintang in order to take over and seize the government of China at the opportune time.

Chiang became increasingly suspicious of the Communists but decided that his first task was to lead the Nationalist army against the warlords and capture the capital city of Peking. In 1926 he led his army out of Canton in southeast China on the Northern Expedition into Central China, seized Hankow, and continued down the Yangtze valley to Shanghai. Here he became convinced that the Communists were ready to seize control through a series of organized demonstrations and strikes. With the assistance of a secret society he seized the Chinese section of the city, hunted down Communists in a veritable reign of terror, and continued on to Nanking to eliminate the Communists there and make the city his capital for the moment. Early in 1928 he captured Peking and renamed it Peiping (bay ping), meaning "northern peace." Chiang had by no means brought all of China under the control of the Kuomintang government because the more powerful warlords still remained completely independent, especially in the north and west and the provinces of Manchuria and Sinkiang (shin ji ahng).

Mao Tse-tung and the Communist Party

The Communists who escaped Chiang's purge in 1927 fled south to the provinces of Kiangsi and Hunan in the mountains of southern China. By 1931 they had set up there a Chinese Soviet Republic, with a population of nearly 3,000,000.

One of the original members of the Chinese Communist Party, founded in 1921, was Mao Tse-tung (mah oh dzuh doong), born in 1893 to a poor peasant family. His father joined up with a local warlord, and after several years he was able to move up into the ranks of the landlord class, the group of landowners his son was one day to eliminate. Mao's early education was sketchy at best, largely because his temper and obstinacy led to his expulsion from a succession of schools. Excited by the Revolution of 1911, he decided that he needed military training in preparation for revolutionary activities.

He joined the regular army for a short while, went back to school after the abdication of the emperor in 1912, then spent six months of what he later called self-education by reading avidly in the Hunan provincial library such translations as Darwin's *The Origin of Species*, Herbert Spencer's *Study of Sociology*, and Adam Smith's *Wealth of Nations*. From 1912 to 1917, until he was 24 years old, he attended the Normal School in Changsha, where he later became an administrator. During 1920 he read the Chinese translation of *The Communist Manifesto*, the first Marxist book published in China.

In 1921 he attended a meeting in Shanghai organized by a Russian agent of the Comintern to form a Communist Party in China. Mao became a member of the Central Committee of the party, later disagreed with the official position that the urban workers would be the core of revolution in China, and was dismissed from the Politburo of the party. He was then sent off to organize the peasants of Hunan province, and was soon under constant danger of capture by the Kuomintang army. In 1928 the arrest and execution of his wife and sister by the Kuomintang drove Mao into bitter opposition against Chiang Kai-shek. Mao built up a peasant army, served as its commissar or political leader, and enforced rules which gained for the army wide peasant support.

"On the Road to Revolution." This poster appeared in the *Daily Worker* in 1927.

In the meantime China was facing another enemy, the Japanese. They had attacked

Manchuria in 1931 and made it their puppet state of Manchukuo, or Manchu Land, under the Emperor Pu Yi who, as a child, had abdicated in 1912 as Manchu Emperor of China.

In Hunan and Kiangsi provinces Mao Tse-tung then organized a Communist movement of peasants, in complete contradiction to the Marxist-Leninist concept that oppressed factory workers would spearhead a revolution. His early life on the farm gave him an insight into the minds of the peasants, who had very strong grievances against oppressive landlords and a government that seemed completely indifferent to their plight. Mao had no choice but to use peasants for his Communist revolution, since he was far away from any industrial center.

Chiang Kai-shek understood the threat from the Communists who were determined to overthrow the Kuomintang sooner or later. In 1931 he decided to eliminate them. Between 1931 and 1934 he launched five expeditions against them. Four of these expeditions, one of 300,000 men, were defeated by the Communists, but the fifth one, trained by a German general, finally succeeded in threatening the Communists with extinction.

China, 1914–1936

The Long March

With over 900,000 troops and 200 airplanes Chiang drove the Communists into an ever-closing circle. Some million people were said to have been killed or starved to death in the siege before Mao and his lieutenants finally managed to break out. Mao had requested help from the All China Soviet Congress in early 1934, to save his Soviet Republic, but his appeal had been rejected. Preparations for Mao's breakout were kept secret, and only one week's notice was given for mobilization of some 140,000 men, women, and children to set out on what became known as the Long March.

In October 1934 they set out on the journey that took them for 6,000 miles on foot westward to the border of Tibet then northward through

China's Communist Leaders, 1930. From the left are: Mao Tse-tung, Chou En-lai, Po Ku, and Chu Teh.

barren lands to Yunan in Shensi province. They suffered winter storms and constant harassment from Chiang's forces as they made their way across some of the highest mountains on the continent. One year later they arrived, but only 20,000 strong. These veterans of the Long March, including Chou En-lai (joh en lye), later Prime Minister in Red China, and Chu Teh (joo duh), the professional soldier, became the hard core of the Communist Party of China; this group then set up its own republic in northwest China and, ten years later, set out to take over all China and drive Chiang Kai-shek off the mainland to the island of Taiwan.

Chiang Kai-shek Kidnapped

Chiang Kai-shek continued his campaign against the Communists and ordered the Army of the Northeast under Chang Hsueh-liang (jahng shoo-eh lyahng), the Young Marshal, to attack Mao in his new base and wipe out the Red Army. The Young Marshal was the Manchurian warlord who had resisted the Japanese invasion of Manchuria in 1931 until he had been forced to withdraw. His Manchurian soldiers were much more concerned about recovering their homeland from the Japanese than in fighting Chinese troops, even if they were Communists.

In December 1936, Chiang flew up to the Young Marshal's base to put more energy into the campaign, but he and his staff were arrested by the Young Marshal's officers, who wanted Chiang to give up his fight against the Communists and to concentrate on the Japanese. Although a prisoner, Chiang ordered the Young Marshal to come before him, and made it perfectly clear that as Head of the State he refused to discuss any issue while a prisoner. Some of the Young Marshal's officers demanded that he execute Chiang, but this he refused to do and only continued to beg Chiang to attack the Japanese in Manchuria. Even Chou En-lai, the trusted lieutenant of Mao Tse-tung, came to the Young Marshal's headquarters to counsel Chiang's release for the sake of internal peace in China and a common front against the enemy.

On Christmas Day, twelve days after his arrest, Chiang was released. The Young Marshal went along with Chiang as his prisoner, willing to stand trial for his action. He was tried, convicted, and spent the war years from 1937 to 1945 in prison wherever the Kuomintang made its headquarters; and when Chiang was finally driven off the mainland to Taiwan, the Young Marshal was taken along.

The incident was another humiliation for the Chinese who looked ridiculous in the eyes of the world and who faced another civil war. Chiang's release was the signal for spontaneous demonstrations that were formerly unknown to the country, and Chiang made a triumphal entry into Nanking.

3. The Sino-Japanese War, 1937–1945

The "Chinese Incident"

The reaction in China to Chiang's release was not lost upon the Japanese, who realized that the Chinese still had the determination to fight. A few months later delegates of the Kuomintang and the Communists agreed to settle their differences and unite against Japan. Chiang agreed to call off the civil war against the Communists, and they in turn agreed not to attempt to overthrow the Kuomintang or carry out any other of their objectives.

Japan was now faced with a basic question. Should she give up her intention of conquering northern China, or should she strike before

Sino-Japanese War. Japanese troops storm a northern section of the Great Wall.

China became strong enough to wage a full-scale war? She decided to strike immediately, not only because China was not yet fully united but also because Japan judged the temper of the European nations and gambled that they would not intervene. Mussolini had already attacked and conquered Ethiopia, the Spanish Civil War was in full operation, and Hitler had successfully defied the Western nations by rearming and reoccupying the Rhineland in direct violation of the Treaty of Versailles.

On the night of July 7, 1937, Japanese troops, which had been stationed in Peiping since the Boxer Rebellion, clashed with Chinese troops in what the Japanese described as a local "incident." Evidence indicates that the Japanese militarists believed that two divisions of troops would be sufficient to defeat Chiang's forces and take Northern China. Peiping and Tientsin quickly fell, but the Chinese resisted fiercely for three months in Shanghai, and despite enormous losses showed their determination to keep Japan from complete victory. If they held out long enough, the Chinese hoped they would receive foreign assistance against Japan. But no foreign help came, and when Nanking surrendered and was turned over by Japan to her troops for two weeks of deliberate and indiscriminate slaughter, the Chinese refused even to consider peace with Japan. Nanking, the capital city of the Kuomintang, was looted and sacked, men, women, and children were shot and bayoneted, and young Chinese men were led out in batches to be cut down with machine-gun fire.

Chiang Kai-shek moved his capital city up the Yangtze river to Hankow, and when that fell to the advancing Japanese he moved 800 miles further up the Yangtze to Chungking in southwest China, and made that the capital until the end of the war. The Japanese soon captured all the Chinese seaports, and most of east central China; they then cut off China from all outside contact by a naval blockade.

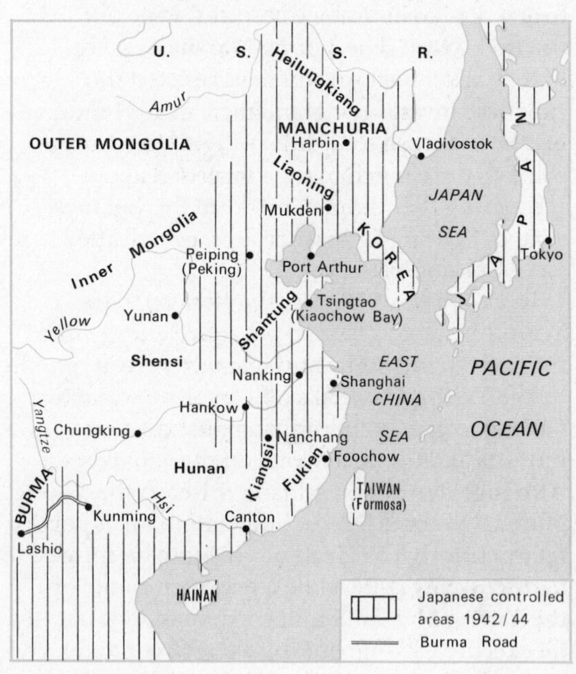

China, 1937–1946

The mass migration of Chinese officials, teachers, students, and people to Chungking was an incredible feat in that part of the country where there were no railroads. Everything—military equipment, machinery, libraries, hospital equipment, medical and laboratory supplies—had to be taken upriver in small boats or carried overland on the backs of volunteers. The Japanese repeatedly bombed Chungking in an attempt to drive the Chinese government into exile, but repeatedly the city was rebuilt and the war continued, a monument to sheer Chinese determination and indestructible will to survive. After 1939 the war was little more than sporadic fighting, with neither side taking an all-out offensive. Japan had won a technical victory, and expected the Chinese to realize the hopelessness of continuing the struggle.

During the years until European nations and the United States found themselves at war with Japan, the greatest problem for China was getting necessary civilian and wartime supplies. In 1937 the Chinese government, already realizing the probability of a Japanese blockade, had started to build what came to be known as the Burma Road, from Kunming in China to Lashio just inside the frontier of Burma, to link China with India and the western world. Although the two towns were only 360 miles apart by air, the road wound 700 miles over rugged mountain terrain. It was built by hundreds of thousands of men, women, and children, equipped only with picks, shovels, and baskets, for there was no road-making equipment whatever in the area.

Allied Assistance to China

Once the United States was in the war against Japan in December 1941, the American government moved in to keep the Chinese fighting and holding down Japanese troops in China. Supplies were sent along the Burma Road and by air-shuttle over "The Hump" of the rugged mountains along the Burma-China border. General Joseph Stilwell of the United States Army was sent out to train and equip Nationalist Chinese troops, and to attempt to co-ordinate Allied efforts in the China-Burma-India (CBI) theater.

However, the main allied effort against the Japanese was in the Western Pacific, where bases had to be won before Japan itself could be attacked. The Allies tried to boost Chinese morale in other ways. In 1943 the United States and Great Britain voluntarily gave up their special rights in China, and that same year they recognized China as an equal by inviting Chiang Kai-shek to meet with Churchill and Roosevelt at Cairo, where it was agreed that Manchuria, Formosa, and the Pescadores Islands should be restored to China at the end of the war.

Civil War Again in China

When World War II ended in 1945, Japan still controlled a great deal of Chinese territory, but she withdrew her forces after her surrender in August. The problem facing Chiang Kai-shek and the nation was now the danger of the revival of internal strife between the Kuomintang, or the Nationalists, and the Communists. Chiang's popularity was already slipping in 1945; the government had become corrupt and had lost touch with the people, and it had all the trappings of a dictatorship: secret police, imprisonment and punishment without trial, and repression of any opposition to Chiang Kai-shek.

Nationalist troops were not paid, medical and military supplies were sold by Kuomintang officers for personal profit, the black market flourished, and Chiang's government increasingly seemed to represent only the businessmen, landlords, and military men. These groups lost sight of the basic problems of the nation.

Despite their apparent agreement to form a united front against the Japanese, both the

Communists and the Kuomintang rightly distrusted each other. By 1941 the truce between them had actually ended when Chiang cut off all supplies to the Communists, and in fact blockaded them in the northwest corner of China. As the Japanese war came to an end, Chiang knew that Mao was determined to bring all China under Communist control. The Communists cleverly worked in favor of the peasants and won their support by forcing landlords to give up their land for redistribution to the peasants, and by putting the Red Army to work helping the peasants with local projects. The peasants believed that they would eventually own the land themselves. Later they were to be obliged to give up their land to the state, and work as collective farmers.

The Marshall Mission

The United States sent the former Chief of Staff, General George Marshall, out to China in late 1945 to try to persuade both sides to work together and set up a government for the Chinese people. The mission was hopeless from the start because neither side would trust the other, and collaboration between the Kuomintang and the Communists, each of whom meant to eliminate the other, was impossible. After thirteen months of frustrating and unsuccessful effort, General Marshall reported to the President of the United States.

"On the side of the National Government, which is in effect the Kuomintang, there is a dominant group of reactionaries . . . opposed, in my opinion, to almost every effort I have made to influence the formation of a genuine coalition government."

Of the Communists, General Marshall had nothing better to say. "The dyed-in-the-wool Communists do not hesitate at the most drastic measures to gain their end as, for example, the destruction of communications in order to wreck the economy."

4. Establishment of the People's Republic of China

With the end of the war in Asia in sight, the United States government wanted the Japanese troops in China to surrender to the Nationalist government of Chiang Kai-shek rather than to the Communist army. Because the Chinese Communists were nearer to strategic Manchuria than were the Nationalists, United States transport planes flew 100,000 Chinese Nationalist troops to Shanghai, Peiping, and Nanking, and subsequently ferried in another 400,000 by planes and ships.

Nationalists and Communists now renewed the civil war. The Nationalists advanced so rapidly that they seemed assured of success. Their army, nearly three times the size of Mao's forces, was much better equipped. But the Communists followed their earlier policy of retreating as the enemy advanced, and then waiting for him to overextend his lines and offer a weak spot for attack. During 1947 the Nationalists took city after city, thousands of square miles of territory, which included much of northern China and Manchuria, and most of southern China. But the Nationalists had one serious weakness. Their main forces were centered in large cities, and they did not effectively control the countryside.

Then the Communists struck. They moved rapidly, cut communications and supply lines, and simply waited until Nationalist garrisons in the cities were starved out. American advisers in Nanking tried to persuade Generalissimo Chiang Kai-shek to shorten his lines and pull out of exposed positions. He refused to do so, and by mid-summer of 1948 the Communists laid siege to them. By the end of the year cities in Manchuria were surrendering with hundreds of thousands of troops. In January 1949, the Red Army entered Peiping and Tientsin, and from then on the Nationalist government was doomed. In October 1949, Mao Tse-tung proclaimed the establishment of the People's Republic of China in Peiping, which once again became the capital of the country under its traditional name of Peking, meaning "northern capital."

Chiang Kai-shek and some 200,000 Nationalist troops fought their way to the coast and crossed the 150 miles of sea in small boats to Taiwan, which they claimed to be the government of the whole of China. This exile to Taiwan ended one of the world's great revolutions, for it brought nearly one-quarter of the world's people under Communist rule. The tragedy of Chiang Kai-shek was that although his indomitable will had saved China from Japan he was now driven out of the country. In 1945 he had represented not only victory over Japan but was the symbol of hope for a new China. But by 1949 the Communists had taken over China almost by default, because the Chinese people had simply refused to support Chiang Kai-shek, who had failed to carry out the Confucian principles that a government must serve the interests of its people. Chiang Kai-shek had forfeited the Mandate of Heaven.

Agriculture in the People's Republic

The primary and constant problem of Communist China has been that of increasing the food supply to meet the rapidly-expanding population. One of the early programs of the Communists was to win peasant support by confiscating land from its owners and turning it over to the peasants. Then the government organized the peasants into what they called co-operatives of 30 or 40 families.

These were enlarged into groups of 100 to 300 families called "collectives," in which land, machinery, and labor was collectively controlled and run by the central government. The purposes were simple. The land would be used more efficiently by removing wasteful paths and boundaries between little farms, labor could be conscripted and used on community projects such as roadbuilding and the construction of irrigation ditches, and new methods too expensive for the individual farmer could be introduced. The collectives were supervised by cadres or groups of reliable managers of trusted Communist Party members, to see that they functioned properly.

When in 1957 production declined despite, or perhaps because of, the collectives, the government allowed peasants to have small private plots of their own and sell these crops on the free market. Experience showed that peasants worked harder when they were allowed to keep part of their products for themselves. Nevertheless in 1958 the government stepped up the system of collective farms and organized

Nursery of an Agricultural Commune, 1958. This "day-care center" was typical of the arrangements made to enable mothers to work in the fields.

"communes" of between 4,000 and 5,000 families, who were allowed to own no private plots and were obliged to eat in community dining halls in order to free housewives for work in the fields. Within one year more than 20,000 communes were organized in a vast undertaking that involved more than 100,000,000 people.

Once again a sharp drop in production occurred, caused partly by drought in the north and floods in the south, but also through a slowdown of peasant workers. The communes quietly disappeared and agriculture returned to collectives of fewer than a hundred families each. The Chinese Communists learned, as had the Russians, that incentive in the form of reward for extra effort motivates people, whatever their political belief or form of government. Increasing population may make agricultural production a continuing problem for the People's Republic.

Industry: The "Great Leap Forward"

Lack of widespread industrialization was another problem inherited by the Communists, who were well aware that efficient industrial development and methods were necessary for the modernization of farms, for road-building and railroads, and the economic future of China. So they set out to copy Russian techniques by starting their First Five-year Plan in 1953 to build steel mills, tractors, railroad equipment, and electric power plants. Ordinary consumer goods were of secondary importance, but all necessities were strictly rationed so that everyone received a share of the goods available.

This concerted effort was so successful that a more ambitious scheme was undertaken. China was to take the "Great Leap Forward," as the Second Five-year Plan was called, and surpass other nations in the production of coal and iron. The entire nation was to participate, and people were urged to build small blast furnaces near their homes and turn out millions of tons of iron ore. The "backyard furnaces" proved to be a failure because the iron ore was so crude with impurities that it was worthless.

The tremendous impact upon Chinese people in all walks of life of the promise of the "Great Leap Forward" can be appreciated from an account by a Canadian businessman who has long observed the China scene.

"The situation, politically speaking, was aggravated by the fact that the government had

Modern Chinese Industrial Plant

not only published, but widely distributed among the people for study in their weekly discussion groups, industrial and agricultural figures for 1959 and 1960 which turned out to be wildly inaccurate and unbelievably inflated . . . These soaring production forecasts which were to be 'fulfilled and overfulfilled' were a source of pride and exhilaration to people in all walks of life. I recall how impressed I was in 1959 to observe that a peasant in a commune, a worker in a factory, a waiter in a hotel, or any high school girl or boy could reel off figures concerning China's steel, coal, cement, or electrical production with the accuracy of a lesson well learned.

Lin Piao and Mao Tse-tung, 1969

"When, toward the end of 1959 and throughout 1960, realistic production figures began to filter through to the public, when they saw plants closing down or operating on a part-time basis, when all building projects were halted and hundreds of thousands of city workers were returned to the communes, the disillusionment of the people was great indeed."*

The disappointment was tremendous but the government was realistic in wisely deciding that in future priority of materials and labor must be given to those industries that helped agriculture by supplying tractors, tools, and fertilizers. The goals for industrialization have not been changed, but the target date has been set later, for the leaders have realized that there is a limit to what people will endure without sufficient reward.

The "Great Proletarian Cultural Revolution," 1966

In August 1966 Peking announced a new meeting of the Central Committee of the Communist Party which launched a nationwide campaign aimed at invigorating the Communist system in China. That is what Mao claimed it to be. Among other objectives, it called for the reorganization of the educational system to encourage young people from deprived backgrounds. But "China Watchers," foreign experts who attempt to evaluate what goes on in China, gave it a broader interpretation. They suggested that the real goal was to insure Mao's supremacy as a leader, and the appointment to high positions in the party and the government

---

*James S. Duncan, "Red China's Economic Development Since 1949," from *Contemporary China*, edited by Ruth Adams, pp. 144–149. Copyright 1966 by Educational Foundation for Nuclear Science. Reprinted by permission of Pantheon Books, a Division of Random House, Inc.

of men whom Mao trusted. Further objectives, they believed, were to enforce Mao's principles of strict party control and to encourage "people's revolutions" in other parts of the world under the leadership of Communist China.

From this meeting a veteran of the Long March of 1934 emerged as Mao's choice of his own probable successor to leadership. He was Lin Piao (lin byow) a supporter of Mao's hard line policy. Lin had attended the Whampoa Military Academy where he studied under Chiang Kai-shek in company with Chou En-lai, later to be Premier of China, and with Ho Chi Minh, later the leader in North Vietnam. He changed his name to Piao, meaning Tiger Cat, became commander of the vanguard forces on the Long March, fought against the Japanese during the war, and in 1948 drove Chiang's Nationalist forces out of the Liaotung Peninsula and captured or killed over 400,000 of his troops.

In October 1966, the seventeenth anniversary of the founding of the People's Republic of China, Lin was officially recognized as "number two" man in China with the rank of Defense Minister, followed by Chou En-lai as "number three." Lin apparently spoke for Mao, who remained silent at this anniversary, when he spoke of "power coming out of the barrel of a gun." He also claimed that the world situation was favorable for revolution and he denounced the United States and the Soviet Union as conspirators "plotting swindles for stamping out the Vietnamese people's revolutionary struggle."

It was evident in 1966 that Mao felt that some of his programs had not succeeded during the seventeen years of his regime. There were indications that the Chinese might be tired of a struggle that over the years had not brought them the material benefits they had hoped for. Mao was probably afraid of "revisionism," demands for changes or revisions in the Communist system which could undermine his personal power. There was apparently a split, as there had been earlier in the Soviet Union, between the "hard line" Communists who wished to control and dictate all policies according to Communist doctrine, and the "revisionists," the practical men who were concerned with industrializing the country and improving the condition of the people by various methods.

During the fall of 1966 "Red Guards" began to appear throughout China. Hundreds of thousands of young people, eager disciples of Mao carrying copies of his sayings, traveled

Red Guards enact an anti-U.S. propagandist representation of the fight against "imperialism."

across the country to Peking and held huge rallies to carry out Mao's slogans of "Down with capitalism!", "Down with the Old World!" and "Down with evidences of the past!" They loudly criticized some of China's leaders who questioned Mao's policies, interfered with businesses, broke into stores and factories, and generally antagonized, and probably frightened, earnest Communists who resented this interference. Mao may have succeeded in crushing opposition, but he later restricted the Red Guards probably because they had served their purpose, and in part because their enthusiasm got out of hand and interfered with China's economic development. The use of the Red Guard movement by Mao indicated to many that Mao's policy was at that time too rigid, and that his theory was out of step with China's practical needs.

5. Foreign Policy of the People's Republic

Much of China's traditional policy must remain unchanged. China has its long northern land frontier and its long seacoast, and it pursues the same ancient objective of wanting to dominate in Southeast Asia. This is not necessarily simply a desire to control more territory, but rather to forestall any adversary's plan to occupy Southeast Asia. The United States had replaced Japan as the traditional enemy of China for several reasons, at least as Mao saw them. Mao feared that the United States meant to overthrow him and restore Chiang Kai-shek to the mainland. This motivated his visit to the Soviet Union in 1949–1950, where he received a promise of economic aid and a defensive treaty.

In 1950 the Korean War became another threat when South Korean and United States troops drove up through North Korea to the Yalu River border between Korea and China. Was the United States planning to establish military bases on China's border? Did the United States intend to invade China? Did the United States plan to take over Manchuria and deny its vital resources to China? These questions were undoubtedly behind Mao's decisions to send in thousands of Chinese "volunteers" against the United States forces.

The Korean War also interfered with Mao's probable plans for Taiwan. While Chiang Kai-shek ruled over the island, Mao could not consider his victory complete. As soon as the Korean War broke out in 1950, the United States Seventh Fleet was sent to patrol the Formosa Straits separating Taiwan from mainland China; this action put Taiwan under the protection of the United States and beyond the reach of Communist China. This protection, together with a defensive treaty between the United States and Chiang, have provided Mao with the excuse to charge the United States with "imperialist" designs on Southeast Asia, and to make "Liberate Taiwan" a slogan for rallying support against the United States.

Invasion of Tibet

Like other dictators in history, Mao felt the need to defend his country by expanding his frontiers. Tibet had been associated with China since the 17th century but had been virtually independent under hereditary priest-rulers, the Buddhist lamas. When Mao proclaimed the People's Republic as the new nation of China, he also claimed that Tibet was a part of China, despite the fact that it had acted as an independent nation since the Revolution of 1911.

In 1959 the Chinese invaded Tibet, deposed the supreme ruler called the Dalai Lama and subsequently made Tibet a part of China.

Clashes on the Indian Frontier

During the years of the Cold War Prime Minister Jawaharlal Nehru of India had been a neutralist, refusing to take sides with either the United States or the Soviet Union, and accepting Communist China's friendship. In fact, Nehru and Chou En-lai signed an agreement pledging the "Five Principles of Peaceful Co-existence" of non-interference with each other's boundaries and government. Nehru's confidence in China's friendship was abruptly broken in 1962 when Chinese forces in Tibet attacked Indian troops on the Tibet-India border. Today the Chinese hold several thousand square miles of territory which both nations claim as historically their land.

The Sino-Soviet Breach

It is impossible to point to any one incident or occasion when tension began to develop between Communist China and the Soviet Union, but indications are that 1957 was the year. The death of Stalin in 1953 brought out disagreements in policies within the Communist Party in Russia, and it appeared that the idea of peaceful co-existence between the Soviet Union and the West was gaining ground. In 1957 Chinese leaders seemed determined to "liberate" Taiwan; the first step would be the occupation of the offshore islands of Quemoy and Matsu, held by the Nationalist Chinese on Taiwan. Communist China could not do this, however, unless the Soviet Union indicated her willingness to help her, for she knew that the United States was committed to the support of Chiang Kai-shek.

Sino-Soviet Breach. Chinese forces at the Soviet-Manchurian border, 1969.

China criticized the Soviet Union for its failure to promise aid, and the Soviet Union then proceeded to withhold further economic assistance and to withdraw nuclear and other technicians from China. By 1960 the breach between the two nations was serious, with Mao and Khrushchev denouncing each other in bitter terms.

Issues of Conflict between China and the Soviet Union

The main charge against the Soviet Union by Communist China has been that the Soviet Union is no longer the leader of Communism because it has abandoned the Marxist-Leninist belief that war between the "imperialists" and Communists is inevitable and necessary. The Soviet Union has replied that the Chinese Communists are willing to start a world war that would result in nuclear devastation.

Another Chinese charge is that the Soviet Union is abandoning the dictatorship of the proletariat and is permitting capitalism to reappear in Russia. To this the Soviet Union has answered that there is no need for continued dictatorship, since no classes now exist in Russia.

The Cuban missile crisis of 1962 was another reason for charges and counter charges. The Soviet Union was guilty of a "Russian Munich," said China, because it capitulated to the United States by withdrawing atomic missiles from Cuba. Khrushchev replied that since the United States had agreed not to invade Cuba, he was responsible for preventing a nuclear war by withdrawing the missiles.

Communist China accused the Soviet Union of "racism" by not actively fomenting "national wars of liberation" in Africa, Asia, and Latin America. The Soviet Union charged Communist China with deliberately pursuing a racist anti-white policy which has nothing to do with Russia's policy of supporting revolutions in favor of underprivileged people throughout the world.

It is not likely that Communist China is actually prepared to attack the Soviet Union, but she may be using this technique as a means to head off any expansionist moves by Russia. Under the leadership of Mao the relations between Communist China and the Soviet Union will probably not improve. New leadership in China may be more conciliatory and lessen the tension. Actual conflict between the two nations could scarcely be to the advantage of the United States, since a general war might result, with devastating consequences to the world.

Korea: Relations with China

Korea's strategic position in Northeast Asia has made it over the centuries a battleground for ambitious nations. A peninsula jutting out from the Asian mainland into the Yellow Sea and the Sea of Japan, it is hemmed in by Russia, Japan, and China. For centuries China had considered Korea a vital outpost of her empire, but in the late 19th century Russia showed great interest in its warm-water ports, and Japan regarded Korea as a threat to her own security if it should fall into the hands of a powerful adversary. Japan also saw Korea as a gateway for her own expansion on to the Asian mainland. Korea is about 85,000 square miles in area, about half the size of California, with a population of some 40,000,000 people, of whom more than two-thirds live in today's South Korea.

The Koreans are a mixture of people from Manchuria, Siberia, and China, who regard the 7th to 10th centuries as their Golden Age, when they absorbed much of the Chinese culture into their own life and transmitted it to Japan. In the 13th century Korea was conquered by the Mongols, and later on was invaded first by the Japanese and then by the Manchus on their way to conquer China. Korea was allowed to rule herself as a tributary state of China, and for 250 years adopted a policy of isolation which kept all foreigners outside its boundaries.

It could not escape the imperialism of foreign nations in the 19th century, and found itself the target of demands for special trading privileges. Fearing that Russia would take Korea and perhaps threaten her own security, Japan fought China in 1894–1895 and forced China to recognize the "independence" of Korea, after the Sino-Japanese War in 1895; ten years later Korea became the object of Russian-Japanese rivalry. Although both nations agreed in the Treaty of Portsmouth after the Russo-Japanese War, to respect the independence of Korea, the Japanese made it a protectorate in 1907, and then annexed it in 1910 as Japanese territory under the name of Chosen.

For the next 35 years the Japanese developed Korea with railroads, highways, coal mines, and steel industries, but it also exploited the land for their own benefit. Not only were the Koreans deprived of proper educational opportunities, but they were deliberately subjected to a campaign designed to wipe out their culture and their language. Japanese was made a compulsory language in schools, and newspapers were printed in Japanese and were under strict censorship. Sygnman Rhee, who was to become South Korea's first president in 1949, opposed Japan's activities before 1910, and when Japan annexed Korea in 1910 he went into exile in Hawaii, and from there waged a campaign for

Korea's independence. A Korean uprising of 1919 was crushed, and throughout the years Korea, or Chosen, was completely integrated into Japan's economy and was used as a base for Japan's attack on Manchuria in 1931.

When Japan surrendered to the United States in 1945, the agreement of the Cairo Conference of Allied leaders in 1943 was supposed to go into effect. Korea was promised independence "in due course," which was officially interpreted to mean a period of trusteeship up to five years to prepare it for independence. Events turned out very differently.

On August 8, 1945, two days after the United States dropped the atomic bomb, the Soviet Union declared war on Japan, and two days later Russian troops entered Korea, and a few days later accepted the surrender of Japanese troops there. Not until September 8, nearly a month after Russian troops entered the country, did United States forces land there. An agreement on the division of occupied areas had previously been decided upon, and temporarily the 38th parallel was made the dividing line between Russian occupation troops in the north and American occupation troops in the south.

In December 1945, the Foreign Ministers of the United States, Great Britain, and the Soviet Union met in Moscow and agreed to set up a provisional or temporary government in Korea on democratic principles. Two difficulties immediately became evident. The Korean leaders refused to consider any solution except immediate independence, even though the Korean people had never had any political rights in the past. The other difficulty was that already the governments of the United States and the Soviet Union were eyeing each other with deepening distrust.

The Russians made the military demarcation line at 38° latitude a political barrier behind which they set up an administration of Communists, and trained a Korean "police" force armed with planes, tanks, and artillery. All negotiations became deadlocked, and after fruitless meetings of the joint American-Russian Commission, the United States saw no alternative but to set up a separate government for South Korea. Unlike the Russians, the Americans organized a South Korean army unit only lightly equipped as a police force.

In November 1947 the United Nations Assembly decided that all the Korean people should form a government chosen by free and secret-ballot elections in both sections of Korea, to be supervised by a United Nations Temporary Commission on Korea. The Commission arrived in Korea in January 1948, but could make no headway with the Russians in North Korea. The United States consequently decided to hold elections in South Korea, which turned out to be "free" elections in a limited sense only and were a victory for the rich landowners. North Korea had its own elections carefully arranged by the Russian puppet leaders, and Korea was from then on divided between the southern Republic of Korea and the northern Democratic People's Republic, each claiming to be the official government for all Korea.

In June 1950 North Korean troops crossed the thirty-eight parallel and attacked South Korea (*see* Volume IV, Ch. 6).

Nationalist China and the People's Republic

Since the establishment of the People's Republic of China in 1949, the term Nationalist China has been used for the island of Taiwan, the offshore islands of Quemoy and Matsu, and the Pescadores or Pengho Islands, all governed by the Kuomintang under the leadership of Chiang Kai-shek. Until October 1971, this government represented China as a permanent member of the Security Council of the United Nations.

Taiwan has a population of 15,000,000, consisting of 12,000,000 Taiwanese and 3,000,000 Chinese. Representation in the legislature is entirely out of proportion because the 85 percent native Taiwanese are allowed only 3 percent of the seats in the Assembly. Until October 1971, when the United Nations General Assembly voted to replace Nationalist China with the People's Republic of China in the Security Council and in the United Nations, the 700,000,000 mainland Chinese were officially unrecognized and had no representation in the United Nations.

Taiwan, called by the Portuguese Formosa, the Beautiful, came under Chinese control during the Manchu dynasty, and was ceded in 1895 to the Japanese who modernized its economy by developing its natural resources and building highways, railroads, hydroelectric plants, and oil refineries. At the Cairo Conference of 1943 the Allied leaders agreed that after the war Taiwan would be restored to China. With the surrender of Japan, the Nationalist forces landed on Taiwan and were at first received as liberators. But disillusion soon set in, as officials representing the Kuomintang proved to be inefficient and corrupt. Riots broke out against the Kuomintang in 1947 but were ruthlessly crushed at the cost of several thousand Taiwanese, including many leaders.

With the defeat of Chiang on mainland China, more than 500,000 Nationalist troops and officials eventually came to Taiwan, and the 11,000,000 Taiwanese found themselves under the domination of Chiang Kai-shek, officially President of the Republic of China, leader of the ruling Kuomintang political party, and Commander-in-Chief of the Chinese Nationalist forces. The Nationalists held most of the important government offices, and allowed no serious political opposition.

The United States has played a dual role in the foreign policy of Nationalist China. When the Korean War broke out in June 1950, President Truman sent the 7th United States Fleet to prevent invasion from mainland China and in effect to serve notice on Mao Tse-tung that the United States would defend Taiwan if necessary. At the same time, the United States made it clear to Chiang Kai-shek that it would not support him in any attempt to invade the mainland and that it might intervene to prevent any such attempt. The United States did not intend to be forced by Chiang Kai-shek into a war against the People's Republic of China.

The two little islands of Quemoy and Matsu, just off the mainland coast, are part of Nationalist China, but are claimed by the People's Republic as an integral part of its territory. Garrisons on the islands have fired upon the mainland, and are in turn fired back upon.

6. Recognition of the People's Republic

For more than twenty years United States policy resulted in the problem of "Two Chinas" and raised the controversial issue of recognition or non-recognition of the People's Republic of China. A second issue was whether Communist China should replace Nationalist China in the United Nations, and whether it might be invited in as an additional new member of that organization. A potential problem raised by United States support of Nationalist China was confrontation by Communist China's claim that Taiwan belonged to mainland China.

The refusal of the United States to recognize officially the People's Republic of China contradicted traditional American policy, which has been consistent since the days of President

Jefferson, with one exception in the 20th century.

Traditional policy has been that once a foreign government has the power to exercise authority over its people and to operate as an independent nation, then it is a government which the United States automatically recognizes and deals with officially, regardless of how that government came to power.

President Wilson departed from that policy in 1913 when he refused to recognize the revolutionary government of Victoriano Huerta in Mexico. A more recent example is the refusal of the United States to recognize East Germany, the German Democratic Republic, on the grounds that East Germany is a creature of the Soviet Union and is not an independent nation.

Why did the United States refuse to recognize the People's Republic of China for more than twenty years? One reason was that Americans believed that the United States had been partly responsible for Chiang Kai-shek's defeat in 1949, despite clear indications that his government was corrupt, was without a constructive program for China, and had forfeited the support of the Chinese people.

Another reason was that when Chiang was defeated by the Chinese Communists in 1949, the United States was experiencing the pressure of the Cold War in Europe. Communist Russia was attempting to expand her influence and her political and economic ideas wherever she could. Containment of Soviet influence was the counter-policy of the United States.

The victory of Mao Tse-tung was, in the view of many Americans, one more success for international Communism. Politicians were in general unwilling to support such a widely unpopular issue as recognition of the People's Republic of China.

Some Arguments against Recognition

For more than twenty years several arguments were offered against recognition. The United States has traditionally been dedicated to the concept of government by free choice of the people. Recognition of a government which comes to power by force encourages dictatorship and tyranny.

The United States should never have recognized the Soviet Union in 1933, claimed opponents of the Soviet Union, because that recognition gave official approval of a government dedicated to forcible world revolution. The Soviet repression of revolts in East Germany and Hungary in the 1950's, and the invasion and occupation of Czechoslovakia in 1968 gave further support to such an argument. Furthermore, the United States should not recognize a government which retained American prisoners from the Korean War and refused to return them.

Some Arguments for Recognition

Those who supported recognition of the People's Republic of China had a forceful argument in the fact that the United States came into existence through revolution against Great Britain. Jefferson wrote, "We cannot deny to any nation that right whereon our own was founded." Every nation, he said, "may govern itself according to whatever form it pleases."

The rule of recognition is not concerned with the morality or legitimacy of a government, but is only a formal way of accepting political facts; it does not indicate approval or disapproval. Recognition of the Soviet Union by the United States in 1933 was simply acceptance of the fact that the Communists were in political power in the Soviet Union. If recognition should be based on whether a government was "good" or "bad," who would determine what is a "good government" or a "bad government," and on

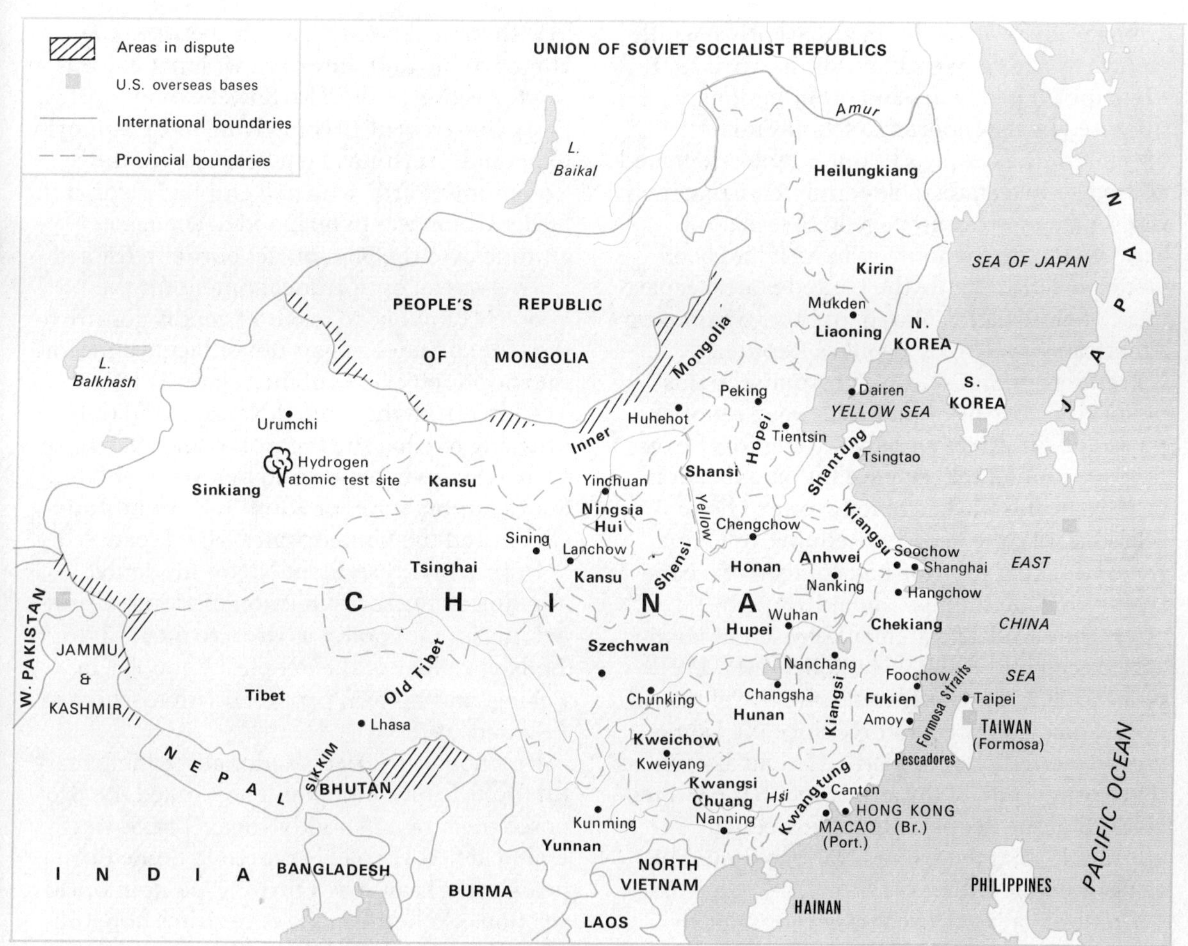

Modern China. This map shows each province and its capital city.

the basis of what conditions? Furthermore, has one nation the right to impose its ideas upon another?

The supporters of recognition argued that whether or not the United States liked the situation, the fact was that the Communists were in power in China. The United States was unrealistic in its refusal to recognize the existence of a nation comprising one quarter of the world's population, and one obviously developing its own nuclear power. If limitations on the restriction and use of nuclear weapons is ever to be effective, then all atomic nations, including the People's Republic of China, must work together.

1971: A New China Policy

The year 1971 proved to be a turning-point in United States relations with the People's Republic of China. The issue of recognition was dramatically reversed by an apparently friendly gesture by the People's Republic in April 1971, when the United States and other nations were surprised by the report that Chou En-lai, premier of the People's Republic, told an invited visiting United States table-tennis team that their visit "opened up a new page in the relations between the two nations." The visit had been made possible because the United States Department of State had in March lifted restrictions on American travel in the People's Republic.

President Nixon's prompt response to this political gesture of Chou En-lai was a set of prepackaged proposals already waiting for the opportune moment. Ever since his inauguration in 1969, he has worked quietly toward better relations with the People's Republic of China, reiterating that the time had come to "face the reality" of Communist China. In April 1971, after Chou En-lai's statement, President Nixon announced his "New China Policy" of a five-point program relaxing trade and travel restrictions which had been in force since the Communists seized power in 1949. He had also stated that the question of the admission to the United Nations of the People's Republic needed "reappraisal," that the United Nations should be realistic on the issue.

Chou En-lai's gesture was perhaps not so sudden as it appeared to be. He, too, had probably been waiting for the appropriate occasion to narrow the gap between the two nations. Mao Tse-tung and other Chinese leaders are shrewd practical politicians who are aware that improved political relationships between the United States and the People's Republic of China could have a far-reaching impact upon world politics and the world balance of power.

The People's Republic of China, whose relations with the Soviet Union have been acrimonious for nearly a decade, would have good reason to wish to weaken the relations between the United States and the Soviet Union. One reason was the action of the 24th Soviet Communist Party Congress of 1971 in giving more authority to Leonid Brezhnev, First Secretary of the Communist Party, who had emphasized that the Soviet Union was in no mood to change its attitude over the Sino-Soviet border tensions.

This was an opportune moment for the People's Republic to make a friendly gesture to the United States as part of her tactics aimed at the specific objectives of the removal of Nationalist China from the United Nations, and the breaking of what she regards as an iron ring of United States bases around her, the United States puppet states of South Korea and Indo-China, and the United States' ally, Japan.

In July 1971, President Nixon suddenly announced the secret mission of Henry Kissinger, his foreign policy advisor, to meet Chou En-lai, premier of the People's Republic, in Peking, and his own proposed visit to China in February 1972.

Reaction was varied. Nationalist China, fearful for its future independence, called the proposed meeting a "shoddy" deal. The Soviet Union at first virtually ignored it. Some European leaders saw it as a turning-point in world relations. At home many Americans hopefully expected a quick end to the Vietnam War.

Chou En-lai, in well-publicized interviews with western visitors, made it very clear that bargaining would be hard, and that the People's Republic would never enter the United Nations while Nationalist China was a member. This was obviously directed at the "Two Chinas" policy of the United States. Chou En-lai quickly replied to those who expected a quick solution to the Vietnam War by stating that the People's Republic would continue to give aid to the Viet Cong and the North Vietnamese "until the complete withdrawal of the United States forces."

Although the Soviet Union indicated that relations between it and the United States could deteriorate, it is not unlikely that the Soviet Union will become more conciliatory than in the past. An indication of this was a tentative agreement in August 1971 granting West Berliners freer access to East Berlin.

Chou En-lai's insistence that the People's Republic would not accept an invitation to become a member of the United Nations while Nationalist China remained a member was not put to the test. On October 25, 1971, the United States lost its motion in the General Assembly of the United Nations to make the expulsion of Nationalist China an "important question" requiring a two-thirds' majority vote. The motion was defeated by 59 to 55, and action on the two Chinas was then to be decided by a simple majority. The delegates of Nationalist China immediately left the Assembly before their expulsion could become official.

Later that same day the General Assembly voted to admit the People's Republic of China and to expel Nationalist China, by a vote of 78 to 35, with 17 members abstaining. The official delegation to the United Nations from the People's Republic of China arrived in New York on November 11, 1971.

Significance of the Peking Meeting

The Presidential visit marks the end of the Two Chinas Policy, and recognizes that the People's Republic is the government of China. It ends the United States policy of more than twenty years of refusing to recognize the government which has ruled 750,000,000 people for the past two decades. The claims of Chiang Kai-shek to be the ruler of China are no longer tenable. "The United States acknowledges that all Chinese on either side of the Taiwan Straits maintain there is but one China and that Taiwan is part of China. The United States does not challenge that position."

Historic Handshake between Mao Tse-tung and Richard Nixon, February 22, 1972, in Peking.

The physical accomplishments of the meeting were virtually negligible, but politically the results are of increasing significance in international affairs. Both nations agreed to conduct their relations on the principle of respect for each other's sovereign rights "regardless of their social systems," and to open their frontiers for scientific, artistic, and people-to-people contacts.

To emphasize the new relationship between the two nations, Nixon and Chou En-lai repeatedly returned to the basic theme that despite their conflicting ideological beliefs, beliefs in no way changed by the meeting, the two nations have common interests. This is a realistic approach in a world where time-distance constantly decreases, and marks a mature appreciation of the right of a nation to determine its own form of government.

The initiation of a rapprochement between two major Pacific powers is a landmark in modern diplomatic history, and should contribute to the lessening of international tensions.

Review Questions

Section 1

1. In what respects could the Twenty-one Demands have made China a satellite of Japan?
2. Why were the terms of the Paris Peace Conference a great disappointment to China?
3. What was the objective of Sun Yat-sen's "second revolution," and why did Russia give aid to China?

Section 2

4. Why did Mao Tse-tung rely for support upon the peasants rather than upon industrial workers?
5. What was the Long March, and why do the Chinese Communists regard it as a great victory?

Section 3

6. Why did Japan strike against China in 1937? Were conditions particularly favorable to Japan then?
7. In what respects did Chungking, the wartime capital of China, become a symbol of Chinese resistance?
8. Why did civil war break out in China in 1945? Why was the Marshall Mission doomed to failure from the beginning?

Section 4

9. Why were the Communists able to be successful against Chiang Kai-shek, even though he had American military aid?
10. In what ways were "collectives" and "communes" a contradiction to traditional family life in China?
11. What was the "Great Leap Forward," and what seem to have been the reasons for its failure?

Section 5

12. In what ways is the foreign policy of Communist China a continuation of the policy of the Chinese Empire?
13. Why should there be a breach between the two strong Communist nations, the People's Republic of China and the U.S.S.R.? What are the issues between them?
14. What seemed to be the reasons for the "Great Proletarian Cultural Revolution"? What was the nature of this "revolution"?
15. What conditions in Korea caused the people to wish to be free of Japan? Why is Korea today divided into two parts?

Section 6

16. Was the question of recognition of the People's Republic of China in any way affected by Chou En-lai's remark about "a new page in relations"? How did it affect the "Two Chinas" policy?
17. Why did China continue to support the North Vietnamese and at the same time develop friendly relations with the United States?

7

Japan: Westernization of an Asian Nation

For more than two hundred years before the American, Commodore Matthew Perry, appeared with his ships off the coast of Japan, that country had been closed to all contacts with foreigners, except for the tiny Dutch settlement at Nagasaki, where the traders were virtually prisoners of the Japanese.

In 1853 the Japanese were a feudal people accepting the authoritarian rule of the military. In the 1860's Japan decided that the only way to avoid the fate of China was to westernize and also to expand as quickly as she could. By 1895 Japan had forced China to recognize the independence of her semi-satellite Korea, and to surrender to Japan the Pescadores Islands, Formosa, and the strategic Liaotung Peninsula on the China mainland. By 1905 Japan had defeated Russia and forced her to surrender half the islands of Sakhalin and rights in the strategic Manchurian railroad. In 1932 Japan acquired complete control of Manchuria, and then embarked upon an expansion program in Southeast Asia and challenged the United States at Pearl Harbor in December 1941. At the height of her power during World War II, Japan had brought nearly one billion Asians under her control. By September 1945, Japan was beaten at home and abroad, and for the first time in her recorded history became an occupied nation.

Twenty-five years later Japan had become the most vigorous of all Asian countries, and was one of the great industrial powers of the world, with by far the highest standard of living in Asia and with a parliamentary democratic form of government.

Terms

1. Shintoism
2. Kami Way
3. Torii
4. Buddhism
5. Zen Buddhism
6. Samurai
7. Confucianism
8. Yamato
9. Kamakura System
10. Shogun
11. Daimyo
12. Kamikaze
13. Tokugawa Shogunate
14. Treaty of Kanagawa
15. Meiji Restoration
16. Imperial Diet
17. Genro
18. Treaty of Shimonoseki
19. Zaibatsu
20. Supreme Commander of the Allied Powers (SCAP)
21. Article 9
22. Soka Gakkai
23. Security Treaty
24. Tengakuren

People

25. Ainu
26. Yoritomo
27. Hideyoshi
28. Tokugawa
29. St. Francis Xavier
30. Matthew Perry
31. General Douglas MacArthur
32. Kishi

Places

33. Hokkaido
34. Honshu
35. Kyushu
36. Shikoku
37. Tokyo
38. Yokahama
39. Osaka
40. Kobe
41. Kyoto
42. Nagoya
43. Yalu River
44. Edo
45. Ryukyu Islands
46. Korea
47. Pescadores Islands
48. Formosa
49. Liaotung Peninsula
50. Tsingtao
51. Kiaochow Bay
52. Kwangchow
53. Wei-Hai-Wei
54. Hong Kong
55. Mukden
56. Shantung
57. Okinawa

Events

1274–1281	Mongol Attacks on Japan
1603–1868	Tokugawa Shogunate
1854	Treaty of Kanagawa
1881	Acquisition of Ryukyu Islands
1894–1895	Sino-Japanese War
1895	Treaty of Shimonoseki
1904–1905	Russo-Japanese War
1905	Treaty of Portsmouth
1910	Annexation of Korea
1931	Manchurian Incident
1937–1945	War against China
1941, Dec. 7	Pearl Harbor
1945, September	Surrender of Japan on board *U.S.S. Missouri*
1945–1952	Occupation Forces in Japan
1952	Independence of Japan
1971	Hirohito and Nixon meet in Alaska
1972	Reversion of Okinawa to Japan

1. Geography, People, and Religion

Geography

Contemporary Japan consists of four main islands that stretch over 1,200 miles in an arc along the coast of East Asia, covering the same latitude and the same general range of climate as that of North America from Montreal to Florida. The total area of the islands is 142,700 square miles, slightly smaller than California. The four main islands are peaks of mountain ranges that cover most of Japan, some rising to 10,000 feet. These mountains have pushed the Japanese people on to the narrow plains along the seacoast, and have helped to make them one of the greatest seafaring people in Asia. Their fishing catch approximates one-half of that of the entire world.

The most northerly of the four islands is Hokkaido, the Northern Seaway; it is so cold that it is covered with snow for several months of the year, and is relatively sparsely inhabited. Honshu, the Main Provinces, is the largest; it has the most and the largest plains, and the majority of the population of Japan. Along its coast are three plains, Kanto, Kunia, and Nobi on which are the six largest cities of the nation: Tokyo, Yokohama, Osaka, Kobe, Kyoto, and Nagoya. The island of Kyushu, the Nine Provinces, is the most southerly of the four; it is closest to the Asian mainland, and was the first part of Japan to be affected by Chinese cultural influences. The great port and shipbuilding center of Nagasaki is located here. Shikoku, the Four Provinces, is the smallest of the four islands; it has no large plains and no rich material resources.

Although coal is found in abundance, there are few other mineral resources, and Japan has become increasingly dependent upon other nations for the vital raw materials necessary for its processed exports. Its mountains and heavy rainfalls of between 40 and 100 inches a year give it vast water resources for its rice crops and hydro-electric power. The dense vegetation which covers Japan is fed by the summer monsoons from the south and southwest, and the winter monsoons from the west and northwest which bring the heavy spring and summer rains and the deep snow to Hokkaido. One severe handicap for Japan is that only one-seventh of its land is arable. Consequently, Japan must import increasing amounts of food as her population grows. In 1965 the population was over 98,000,000 and in 1971 it was well over 104,000,000.

Japan's geographical position, one hundred miles from Korea, and five hundred miles from the coast of China, kept her isolated in the days of primitive shipping, when such sea distances were barriers to communication. Japan was consequently one of the most isolated of the older countries, and as a result she developed her own distinctive culture and customs.

People

The original inhabitants of the islands were probably ancestors of the Ainu, a group which split off from the white race far back in prehistoric times. They were apparently inferior in culture to the Mongoloid invaders of the islands, and they were gradually pushed into the more remote sections of the island of Hokkaido. They may have given to the Japanese the thicker and heavier hair that distinguishes them from other Mongoloid people.

According to archaeological evidence, the main group of the early Japanese came by way of Korea from the mainland, perhaps from the more distant regions of northeastern Asia. Others came from the south, possibly from what is now modern Indonesia and from the Philippines and Polynesia. The Japanese are a Mongoloid people closely related to the Koreans and Chinese.

Religions

Shintoism. The early religion of Japan was a simple nature worship called *Shinto*, the Kami Way or Way of the Gods. It was based on respect

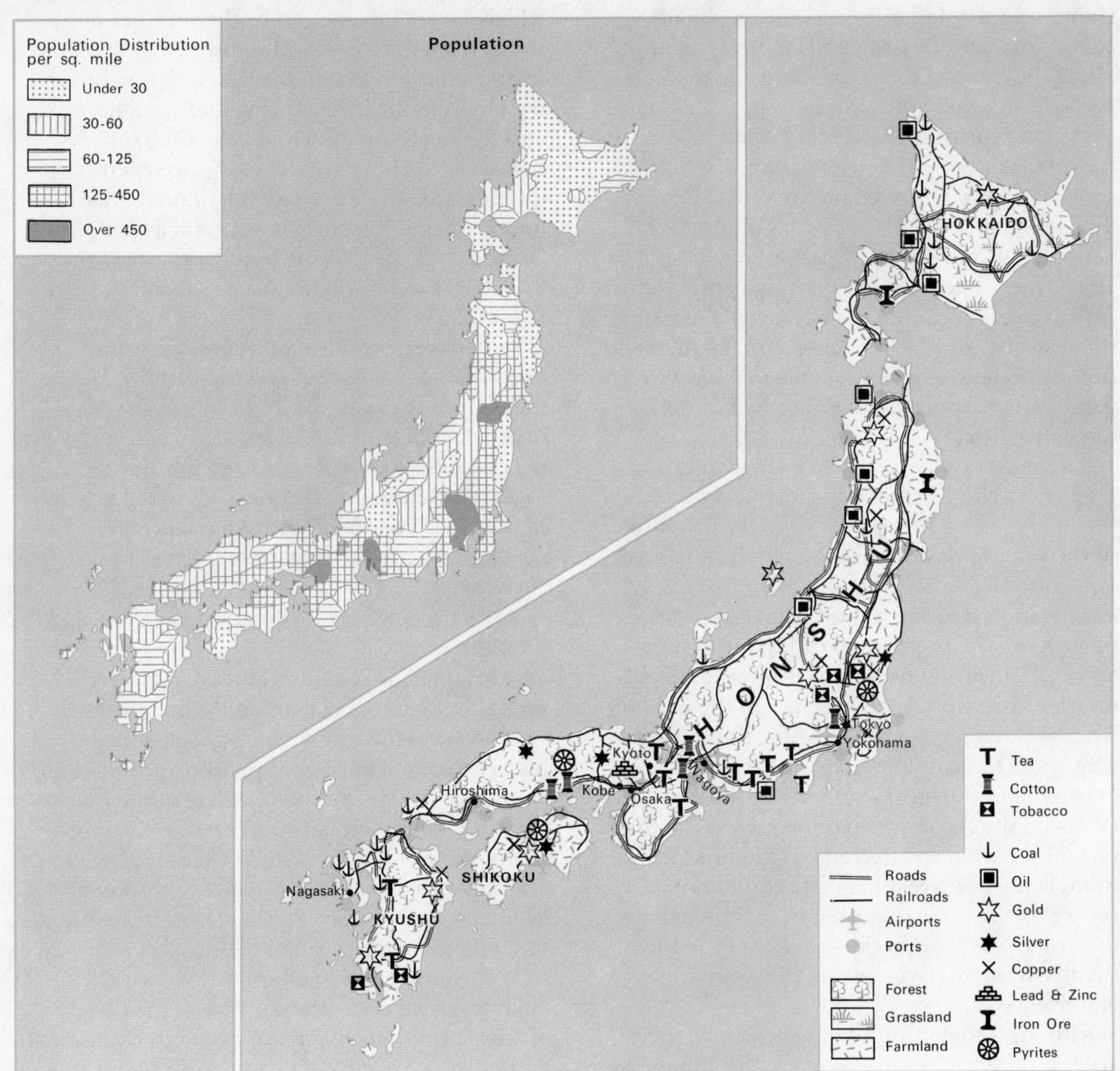

Modern Japan

and a feeling of awe for natural objects or places, such as a mountain peak, a waterfall, a special tree. A Kami is a mysterious invisible being or god that resides in the special object or person that the community worships. A Kami is believed to have supernatural power to produce and prolong life in plants, animals, and people, and to assist people in special times of need. Since Kamis move around, special Shinto festivals include portable shrines in which the Kami is carried from one place of residence to another. A permanent Kami shrine always has a *torii*, or gate, consisting of two horizontal beams placed on two vertical posts. Emperors conducted official Kami ceremonies and had their own guardian Kamis. The simplicity of the Shinto faith explains why Japanese emperors could be credited with special powers, and could be deified by their people.

Buddhism. Buddhism came from China into Japan in the 6th century A.D., when the Japanese became aware of the superior civilization of China, which had been a great military empire between 200 B.C. and 200 A.D. It suffered decline, civil wars, and invasions, until in the 6th century when it began to emerge again; during the T'ang Period of the 7th and 8th centuries China was one of the wealthiest countries in the world, with outstanding cultural achievements.

The Buddhist faith, brought to Japan by missionaries from Korea or China, became the means of introducing Chinese culture to Japan. Embassies sent to China by Japan during the T'ang Period included carefully chosen young scholars who came back to Japan skilled in Chinese history, literature, Buddhist theology, and the arts of music, painting, and poetry.

Buddhism, which originated in India, had changed from its early concept when it came to Japan. Buddha in China and Japan was regarded as a godlike figure who could give salvation to a faithful and devoted follower.

In Japan the Buddhist faith took on three principal forms. Holy Way Buddhism included complex teaching and such long study that only aristocrats could afford it. The simplest form was Pure Land Buddhism which appealed to the common man because he needed only to repeat the sacred name of the particular divine being named Amida Buddha to be admitted to paradise, the Pure Land. The most significant of the Buddhist beliefs in Japan was Zen Buddhism which was brought to the country in the 13th century by monks returning from study in China. The word Zen means meditation, and it stresses physical discipline and mental concentration as a means to a person's understanding of the universe. A Zen follower did not depend upon scriptures or teachings of religion, but waited for a sudden inspired understanding of himself. Because of Zen Buddhism's stress upon individualism it became the philosophy of the warrior class of *samurai* of feudal Japan; its strict discipline appealed to the simple yet tough-fibered warrior. Zen Buddhism played an important role in the development of the officer caste of modern Japan.

Confucianism. The philosophy of Confucius, although practiced in China for several centuries before Christ, was not given official standing in Japan until the 17th century, when an important feudal family called the Tokugawa, who were the actual rulers behind the throne of Japan, decided to use it for their purposes. The Tokugawa, who were to retain their powerful position for more than 250 years, between 1603 and 1868, needed skilled administrators to carry out their orders throughout the country. The teachings of Confucius suited the Tokugawa regime because they not only insisted upon high educational standards for administrators, and divided the people into four social classes, but they also taught that Heaven controlled the universe and that Heaven appointed rulers. Confucianism therefore conveniently supported the Tokugawa regime by encouraging the *samurai* warrior class to obey their superiors.

Confucianism became a very strong force in Japan, particularly for the unwritten code of the samurai called *Bushido*, the Way of the Warrior. Bushido was not unlike the feudal code of European chivalry, a set of principles which the warrior or knight was supposed to follow, stressing courage, benevolence, politeness, honor, and self-control. Bushido was the guide which the samurai were supposed to follow, although it was not necessarily what they actually did.

2. Feudal Society

Origin of the Imperial Family

The Mongoloid invaders of Japan, who came in about the beginning of the Christian era, brought with them a more advanced civilization based on bronze and iron, and in central Japan they set up their original state, Yamato. At first Yamato was only one of many clan states, but as it grew stronger it extended its authority over other clans. Yamato allowed these clan states to run their own affairs but demanded allegiance of all clan chiefs. The Yamato clan claimed the Sun Goddess as its ancestress, and became the founder of the Japanese imperial family.

The Kamakura System: Military Dictatorship, 1185–1338

The prominent victor in later struggles between rival groups was Yoritomo, who set up his government in the seacoast village of Kamakura, and not at Kyoto where the emperor and his court lived. This set up a dual government, and Yoritomo, who held the real power in Japan, proclaimed that the emperor ruled the country, and that he himself was given by the emperor the title of *Shogun*, or generalissimo, indicating that he commanded the emperor's army. Actually there was no central army but only an association of feudal knights who owed allegiance to their superiors, and they in turn to the shogun. This system of feudalism continued in Japan for more than six centuries, with the professional samurai warriors running the country.

Mongol Attacks

The most serious threat to Japan came from the Mongols, who rode out of the steppe lands north of China and swept westward all the way to the Adriatic. In the 1270's after taking all of China and Korea, they then planned to include Japan in their domains. The Mongol emperor Kublai Khan sent emissaries to Japan demanding capitulation, but was answered with the beheading of some of those emissaries. In retaliation a strong force of Mongol warriors set out in Korean ships in 1274 and landed in northern Kyushu, but withdrew because of storms that threatened the fleet. In 1281 a second expedition set out with 150,000 men – the greatest overseas invasion fleet and force in history up to that time – and landed at Hakata Bay in Kyushu.

The Mongols, with incomparable cavalry and fire bombs hurled by catapults, would have easily overcome the handful of Japanese knights who were trained only to single combat. The Mongol fleet was held up briefly by the more mobile Japanese vessels, and then it was almost completely destroyed by a providential typhoon, the *kamikaze*, or Divine Wind, protecting the land of the gods from foreign invaders.

Establishing National Unity

While Europe was experiencing the results of the Age of Exploration and was establishing trade routes and settlements across the world, Japan began closing her doors to outsiders, while setting up a stable and dictatorial government. She was entering upon a period known as the Tokugawa Shogunate, which was to last from 1603 to 1868.

Japan's trade had grown steadily in the 14th and 15th centuries, until by the 16th century it was an important factor in the life of the country. Japan imported silks, paintings, books, and coin money which began to replace rice and cloth as mediums of exchange. Her exports were at first limited to raw products such as lumber, mercury, pearls, and sulphur, but by the 16th century they included folding screens and the magnificent laminated swords that were unequaled even by Toledo or Damascus.

By 1590 Japan had become unified under the *daimyo* Hideyoshi, who decided to conquer China. He may have been afflicted with an expansionist complex, or he may have decided that there were too many unemployed warriors in Japan who had better be put to use. His invasion of Korea in 1592 was successful, but when he moved northward to the Yalu River, the boundary between Korea and China, he was defeated by Chinese troops who came to the assistance of their Korean satellite. Hideyoshi was killed, and the Japanese abandoned their first unsuccessful attempt at expansion.

Early Tokyo. The street of silk merchants.

Up to this time the family of the shogun had changed as rival leaders gained power. A new victor now decided that he would set up a system so strong that power could be kept in one family.

The Tokugawa Shogunate, 1603–1868

Tokugawa Ieyasu succeeded Hideyoshi, and between 1603 and 1615 defeated all rivals, including the powerful Hideyoshi family. By 1650 the Tokugawas had set up their system which gave peace to Japan for nearly 250 years but was based upon an authoritarian form of government which ruthlessly suppressed individual rights, thoughts, and creative abilities. The regime remained for two and a half centuries a centralized military feudalism.

Tokugawa reverted to Yoritomo's plan of two capitals, the emperor's court at Kyoto, and the shogun's headquarters at Edo, sometimes spelled Yedo. Here each successive shogun of the Tokugawa family conducted the military, economic, and actual political affairs of Japan.

The Tokugawas allowed individual daimyos almost absolute rights over their own estates but they organized a clever set of controls that prevented any threat to the central authority of the shogun. Each daimyo was obliged to maintain a permanent residence in Edo (today's Tokyo), live there part of the year, and leave members of his immediate family as hostages in Edo. Road controls were set up on all roads leading to Edo, to prevent the smuggling in of arms or the smuggling out of hostages. Either action would be a preliminary to revolt. The Tokugawas were responsible for instituting a secret police, the Metsuke, who were to play an increasingly important role in Japan.

A class system had existed in Japan long before the Tokugawas, but they elaborated and crystallized it into a form which lasted more than two centuries. They wanted to reduce unnecessary large military forces in the country, and to draw a sharp line between the aristocratic warrior class and the rest of the people.

At the top of the social system was the emperor and his immediate court nobles. The emperor performed the ceremonial functions, bestowed honors, appointed the shogun, exercised very little political power but enjoyed enormous prestige as the divinely appointed head of the nation. No shogun attempted to remove the emperor, for the very sound reason that he ruled in the name of the emperor and therefore enjoyed great prestige in that position.

Second in the social scale, but great in power and prestige, were the privileged men, the samurai. This was the ruling class in the military-feudal dictatorship of Japan. At the head of the samurai class were the daimyo, or great lords with their feudal estates, who were served by the baishin or lesser samurai. This hereditary class of warriors alone, of all the people, had the right to bear arms, and were distinguished by the two swords which they wore as the mark of their social standing. They were not permitted to engage in trade or other enterprises which were regarded as below their dignified rank.

The next class was the peasantry, who were vitally important as growers of food, and were divided into gradations according to ownership of land. At about the same social rank as the peasants were the artisans who made articles for daily use, and the superb samurai swords. Peasants and artisans fed and equipped the samurai and were therefore useful members of society. The lowest social class of all was the merchant group which, according to Confucian theory, performed no worthwhile function, and were therefore parasites deserving the lowest social standing in the Tokugawa military-feudal society. Far down at the bottom of the social barrel, and regarded as outcasts of society, were the *senmin,* who were the professional entertainers, executioners, beggars, animal slaughterers, and those who processed leather. They were obliged to live alone, could not even be servants to commoners, and were not even counted in a census.

Samurai, 17th Century. Note the two swords.

Isolation of Tokugawa Japan

One of the first nations to trade in the Far East was Portugal, and by the 1540's the Portuguese were trading with the Japanese on an island off the southern tip of Kyushu. Traders were followed in 1549 by the missionary St. Francis Xavier, who spent two years introducing Christianity to Japan. Buddhist priests soon saw Christianity as a serious rival and bitterly opposed it. But Japanese merchants encouraged missionaries because foreign traders preferred to come where Jesuit missionaries were permitted to preach and convert. The Tokugawas, however, sensed that Christians owed allegiance to a foreign European "ruler," and therefore they considered that Japanese Christians were a threat to the unity of Japan. In 1587 all Christian missionaries were officially banned from the islands, although little was done to follow up the edict. Thirty years later European missionaries and thousands of native Christians were either executed or obliged to renounce their faith.

In 1637 some 40,000 Japanese Christian peasantry, resentful of economic and religious oppression, rebelled and held out for several months in a castle near Nagasaki. They were eventually overcome, slaughtered almost to a man, and Christianity as an organized religion in Japan ceased to exist. To prevent further threats from foreigners, the Tokugawas issued the Edo Decrees of the late 1630's forbidding Japanese to go abroad, denying the right of any Japanese living abroad to return to Japan, and forbidding the building of Japanese ships for overseas trade. Only one contact with the outside world was permitted, and that was a trading post for the Dutch, who were no threat as missionaries, at Nagasaki under strict control that kept them as virtual prisoners.

The effects of these decrees were to isolate Japan from developments in the world, prevent industrialization and the rise of a middle class, and to keep Japan a military-feudal society until well into the 19th century.

The Opening of Japan

The visit of Commodore Matthew Perry and his "black ships" whose guns and speed amazed the Japanese, suddenly confronted a nation which had an antiquated political system and a relatively limited economic society, with vigorous Europeans. The Edo government was caught in a dilemma by Perry's return in 1854, because it knew of China's defeat at the hands of Europeans in 1842, and it realized that it was certainly unable to expel the foreigners. So it signed the Treaty of Kanagawa opening the ports of Shimoda and Hakodate to American ships, and granting most-favored-nation treatment. Three years later, the British, Russians, and French negotiated treaties which gave them, with the Americans, (1) most-favored-nation rights, (2) the right to obtain supplies at Nagasaki, Shimoda, and Hakodate, (3) permission to trade in these ports under official Japanese supervision, (4) the right to have resident consuls in Japan, and (5) limited extra-territorial rights. (*See* Vol. III, Ch. 5.) When the Japanese attacked European merchantmen in 1863, warships from Great Britain, the United States, France, and Holland bombarded Shimonoseki.

Some time before 1853 the Tokugawa regime was already declining, because new forces were at work in Japan. The merchant class, in spite of its officially despised position, had steadily increased in economic importance. The use of currency since 1700 had encouraged trade, and by the middle of the 19th century such merchant families as the Mitsui were enjoying large fortunes. They felt that they were entitled to a more important place in society and government. Other Japanese believed they were being denied rightful participation in the expanding economy, and the peasants, who were bound by law to the soil, were dissatisfied with conditions that compared unfavorably with wages to be earned in towns.

3. The Meiji Restoration

Japan Westernizes

The events of mid-nineteenth century convinced younger Japanese that their country needed

Mutsohito and Family, c. 1900

decided change in methods and objectives. The shogunate system and its military feudalism could not serve Japanese interests in the modern world. The leaders of a movement for change were actually some of the samurai who were able to strip the Tokugawa clan of its power, persuade landowners to turn their estates over to the emperor, abolish the feudal system, restore the emperor to a position of greater importance, and introduce a completely centralized and constitutional government.

These objectives were not all unselfish; they were motivated in part by dislike of the Tokugawas and by personal desires for power. The Tokugawas resisted the changes but were defeated. The shogunate and the dual government were abolished, and the boy-emperor Mutsohito, fourteen years of age, was in theory restored to full power under the reign-name of Meiji, Enlightened Government, and ruled from 1867 to 1912.

Under the immediate reforms the daimyo received as compensation for their lands an annual pension equal to one-tenth of the nominal income of their estates. Since most of them had mortgaged their lands, they were better off under the new arrangements. Furthermore, they were no longer responsible for the debts of the samurai, and most of them acquired status by a new system of such titles as baron, count, marquis, and prince. The samurai, more than 2,000,000 strong, were not so well taken care of. They lost their privileged position, and while some went into commerce and industry, many chose the new army, the navy, and the police force. The peasants became free men able to own land and move around as they saw fit.

A new constitution was granted by the emperor as a gracious gesture in 1889. Revealed to a carefully-chosen few, it was not allowed to be criticized because it was a gift of the emperor, and most certainly not an expression of the will of the people. The date 1889 was claimed to be the 2,549th anniversary of the founding of the Japanese nation, and was therefore an auspicious occasion for proclaiming a new constitution. It was actually a set of rules which established an oligarchy, the rule of a few self-appointed men, who could rule the country in the name of an emperor whose position was "sacred and inviolable," who was officially supreme commander of the armed forces, with the power to declare war and make peace treaties; the emperor appointed and controlled all government officials, and made laws with the consent of the Imperial Diet, or legislative body, but laws were not operative without the emperor's sanction.

He became an object of national worship and was accepted by the nation as an absolute ruler who could do no wrong. His ministers, ruling in his name, were accorded great respect, but could be severely criticized if they were thought to be acting against the emperor's wishes.

The Diet consisted of two houses with equal powers. The House of Peers was partly appointed and partly elected by the lower nobility and the highest taxpayers in the country. The House of Representatives was elected by a very limited group of voters, only about one percent of the total population. The Diet could initiate a measure, but only the emperor could make it law; the Diet had no power to remove a cabinet because cabinet members were responsible or answerable for their actions to the emperor only. The new Japanese government was a constitutional one but certainly not a democratic one because the people of Japan had virtually no say in its daily functioning. One unwritten political tradition was that older statesmen who had served an active political life became members of a group called the *genro*, the highest advisors of the emperor, forming an inner ring of great political power. Although the constitution did not state so, the Ministers of War and Navy were always active members of the armed services and were therefore under the authority of the Supreme Command and their chiefs of staff. Their superiors could force them to resign at any time, or refuse to permit them to serve. These two ministries could not be controlled by the Diet, and no cabinet could be formed without the approval of the chiefs of staff of the armed services. This was obviously a very significant negative control on government and on official policy-making.

The new leaders sent young men to foreign countries to learn modern methods; to Great Britain for the merchant marine and navy; to Germany for the army and medicine; and to the United States for business methods. In 1871 a Ministry of Education was established to inaugurate an ambitious scheme of universal education, not only to develop the necessary skills for an industrializing nation, but to educate young Japanese in emperor-worship and in belief in their descent from the Sun Goddess.

4. The Expansion of Japan

Japan's perceptive new leaders had seen the necessity of westernizing Japan if it was to survive in the modern world. They also saw that their poor and small country needed sources of raw materials if Japan was to gain the ranks of the great powers. Expansion into adjacent territories could supply these needs, and since Korea and China were evidently disintegrating, they became objects of Japanese expansion.

The Ryukyus

The Ryukyu (or Liu-chiu) Islands had been an island-kingdom for centuries past, sending tribute to China since the 14th century but also to Japan because the royal family of Ryukyu was said to be related to the Japanese Yoritomo clan. In 1874 Japan sent an expedition against Formosa and the Ryukyus, and in 1881 the islands were incorporated into Japan as the administrative district of Okinawa.

Korea

The relationship of Korea to China was uncertain during the 19th century. China disclaimed responsibility for Korea's actions but at the same time let foreign nations know that Korea was a dependency of China. Britain and France secured protectorate rights over the former Chinese areas of Burma, Sikkim, and Annam, and when five European nations negotiated treaties with Korea, the Chinese feared for the loss of that territory. In Korea itself an organization advocating a program that was anti-Japanese, anti-Christian, and generally anti-foreign, rebelled against the Korean government. Korean government troops were defeated, and China decided to send troops to assist her "tributary state." The Japanese, claiming a threat to their interests, also sent in troops and stated that Japan had never regarded Korea as a tributary state of China. As the two hostile armies, Japanese and Chinese, faced each other, the Japanese proposed joint administration of Korea. China refused, so Japan removed the Korean king and set up a new government which requested Japan to expel the Chinese. In the ensuing Sino-Japanese War of 1894–95 China was obliged to sign the Treaty of Shimonoseki and (1) recognize the full independence of Korea, (2) cede to Japan the Pescadores Islands and Formosa, and the strategic Liaotung Peninsula, and (3) open seven Chinese ports to Japan on the most-favored-nation basis.

By this successful engagement, Japan had shown herself to be a modern military power, and had taken the first step in what was to be a policy of expansion on the Asian mainland. Not unexpectedly, some European nations* resented sharing the "Chinese melon" with another power. Germany, Russia, and France then forced Japan to return to China the Liaotung Peninsula, and three years later proceeded to take pieces of China for themselves. Germany took the city of Tsingtao and Kiaochow Bay; France took Kwangchow Bay in South China; Britain took the port of Wei-Hai-Wei in the north, and increased her foothold in Hong Kong in the south; while Russia cynically took the very territory which she had forced Japan to give up, the Liaotung Peninsula.

The Russo-Japanese War, 1904–1905

Japan knew that Russia, with her influence in Manchuria and her increasing attempts to control independent Korea, could be a major threat to Japanese expansion on the Asian mainland. Japan negotiated the Anglo-Japanese Alliance of 1902 by which each nation agreed to come to the aid of the other if it was attacked by a third power while at war with one nation. This served Britain's interests by obliging her adversary Russia to tread warily, and it also gave Japan a virtual free hand against Russia. Japan attacked the Russian fleet in the Far East in February 1904, and then officially declared war. Russia was the stronger nation but it was hampered by revolutionary outbreaks at home and by the tremendous handicap of fighting a war at the end of the single-track Trans-Siberian Railroad several thousand miles long. The Japanese captured Russian forts in the Liaotung Peninsula and drove Russian armies back across Manchuria. Theodore Roosevelt, the American President, offered to negotiate a peace because he did not wish to see the balance of power drastically altered. By the Treaty of Portsmouth, 1905, Japan became a world power through its acquisition of paramount rights in Korea, possession of the Liaotung Peninsula, and the southern half of the Russian island of Sakhalin, north of the island of Hokkaido. In 1910 Japan annexed Korea and proceeded to exploit it for the material benefit of herself.

In 1919, only fifty years after the Meiji Restoration, Japan came to the Versailles Peace Conference as a great military and industrial power, and was confirmed in her occupation and possession of former German islands in the Pacific and possessions on the mainland of China.

Rise of Militant Sentiment

During the later years of the 19th century and the early 20th century great business empires, called *zaibatsu*, played an increasingly significant role in Japanese politics. Western-style party government began effectively in 1918 but ended in 1932; during this period there was a series of parties backed by various business interests, and sometimes by the army and navy. In general,

---

*Great Britain, Germany, Italy, Russia, and France.

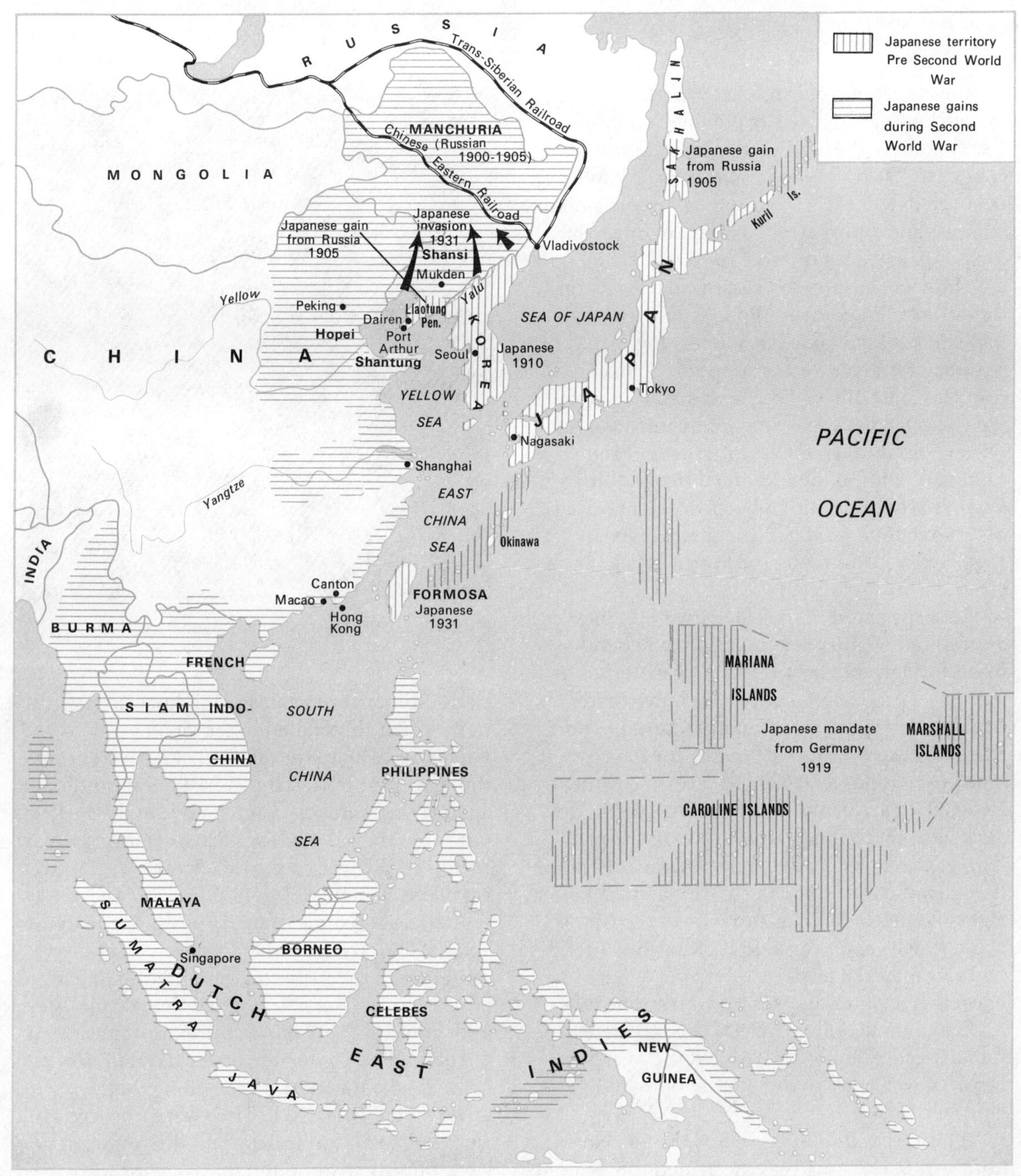

Japan, 1900–1945

the businessmen believed that economic trade expansion was far more profitable and much less expensive than expansion by war and conquest. The militarists, on the other hand, believed in colonial expansion by force, gained increasing support after 1925 when universal male suffrage gave the vote to 14,000,000 men. The bulk of these were peasants in the several thousand villages throughout Japan, and they had been indoctrinated as soldiers to accept authoritarian rule and to support expansion overseas. The officer caste consisted largely of men with similar ideas, and many were sons of officers or landowners. As inheritors of the samurai tradition they resented the wealth and the economic and political domination of "merchants" who had for centuries been regarded as comprising the lowest social class.

Militarism, 1905. Japanese schoolboys with dummy rifles.

The depression of the early 1930's further discredited the businessmen. Japan depended upon foreign sources for vital raw materials to support a processing nation. Such raw materials could only be paid for in manufactured exports, whose market was now closed by the depression. The population of 60,000,000, growing by nearly 1,000,000 yearly, could not be supported by an agricultural economy. And to add to the problem, as the Republic of China became organized it determined to eliminate all special trading rights from China. This threatened the China trade which Japan regarded as vital. So, if food and raw material imports were vital to her existence, Japan was prepared to resume her earlier colonial policy. In 1931 the Japanese militarists deliberately provoked the Mukden incident which led to the domination of Manchuria by Japan.

At home the militarists defied the civilian authorities, claiming that the armed forces alone represented the true imperial will, whose views were being misrepresented by corrupt politicians. Militarists encouraged political assassinations which culminated in the violence of February 1936. In the election of early February the voters supported the more liberal candidates against the reactionary militarists, and clearly indicated their desire for parliamentary government. A group of young officers from a Tokyo regiment, fearful of loss of power for the militarists, led some of their fully-armed troops against liberal government leaders. They slaughtered the inspector general of military education, and an able and old finance minister, and Admiral Saito, one of the emperor's closest advisors. The young officers held out in downtown Tokyo for some days, hoping that the government would fall. They were unsuccessful, were obliged to capitulate, and the ringleaders were punished, although the assassins were portrayed as patriotic young men who wished to restore the "national spirit."

Japan Moves into Southeast Asia

The military leaders used their new puppet state of Manchukuo as the base for further expansion into China. One objective was the establishment of an independent state in North China, consisting of the five northern Chinese provinces of Hopei, Chahar, Suiyan, Shansi, and Shantung. Other Japanese army units attempted to set up an independent Mongolia under the slogan, "Mongolia for the Mongols."

In 1937 the attack by the Japanese at the Marco Polo Bridge near Peiping triggered the "police action," as the Japanese called it, which expanded into the war with China that ended only in 1945.

Japan's position in Asia was one of waiting for China to collapse. In that expectation Japan was disappointed, but when Holland and France were defeated in 1940 by the German armies, then Japan was able to take advantage of the situation. In June 1940 the Japanese foreign minister announced that the countries of Southeast Asia and the South Seas were historically, geographically, racially, and economically closely related. They would, therefore, under Japan's leadership organize the Greater East Asia Co-Prosperity Sphere.

Convinced that the United States would be opposed to her expansion, Japan opened the war with its successful attack on Pearl Harbor in December 1941, as a necessary preliminary to the conquest of Southeast Asia. But the Americans stopped Japan's eastward expansion at Midway in the summer of 1942, and in 1943 started the offensive which ended with the defeat of Japan in August of 1945. (*See* IV, 5 for World War II.)

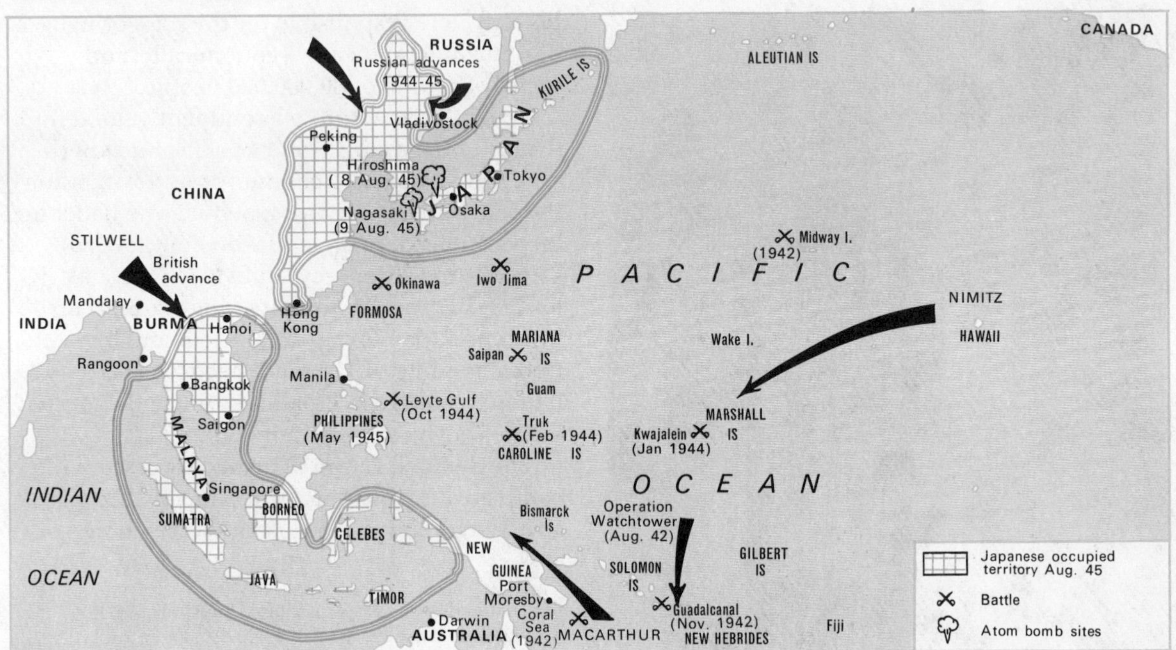

Allied Victory in the Pacific, 1942–1945

5. Japan under United States Occupation

Occupied Japan

On September 2, 1945, on board *U.S.S. Missouri* the representatives of Japan signed the surrender terms which included (1) the elimination of Japan's overseas empire, (2) the elimination of her armed forces, (3) the payment of reparations to the nations she had despoiled, and (4) occupation by the Allied forces until a peace treaty formally went into operation.

The Allied policy of occupation was to be carried out by the Supreme Commander of the Allied Powers, SCAP. The Russians wanted joint commanders in Japan, one to be a Russian, but finally agreed to the appointment of General Douglas MacArthur as Supreme Commander. The eleven countries* at war with Japan set up the Far Eastern Commission "to formulate policies . . . under the terms of surrender." The decisions of the Commission were then to be put into the form of directives for SCAP by the United States. The only official link between the Far Eastern Commission and SCAP was the United States.

Japanese Surrender, 1945

Immediate Occupation Force Actions

The basic purpose of the American government was to use the occupation forces as the "instruments of policy" to remove Japan as a threat to future peace, and to encourage a democratic government which would be responsible to the wishes of the Japanese people. In practical terms, this meant that MacArthur and his staff were responsible for the staggering task of remaking politically, economically, and socially a nation of 80,000,000 people.

General MacArthur was eminently fitted for the task. An administrator of skill and experience, he came in as a conqueror understanding the role he must play for a people who had long respected leadership, and who now needed someone to whom they could give personal loyalty. Because of his autocratic manner, his insistence upon loyalty to himself, and his keen understanding of Japanese needs, he became a national idol to the Japanese, who had expected severe reprisals from their conquerors.

The demobilization of armed forces and the complete disarmament of Japan, and the destruction of her war industries were carried out

---

*The United States, Great Britain, China, France, the Netherlands, Canada, Australia, New Zealand, India, the Phillipines, and the Soviet Union, Burma and Pakistan were added in 1949.

promptly. War criminals were prosecuted, held responsible for the nation's war crimes, and were punished with imprisonment or execution. The United States intended to break up the monopolistic *zaibatsu*, believing they were, with the military, in great measure responsible for war. However, economic needs of Japan obliged the United States to limit such action to the largest of the zaibatsu. The Japanese Ministries of War and Navy, and the Imperial General Staff were abolished.

Political Reforms

The Japanese constitution was completely revised at the insistence of and under the supervision of the Occupation authorities. On May 3, 1947, it was proclaimed by the Emperor, with the approval of SCAP.

The emperor had already officially denied the "false concept of the emperor as divine," and the new constitution clearly placed political power in the hands of the people.

"We, the Japanese people, acting through our duly elected representatives in the National Diet . . . do proclaim that sovereign power resides with the people. Government is a sacred trust of the people, the authority for which is derived from the people."

The emperor became the official and ceremonial head of state, the symbol of the nation "deriving his power from the will of the people."

The Diet, consisting of two elected houses, was "the highest organ of state power," and the only branch of government authorized to enact laws. The House of Councillors was the upper house elected for six years; the House of Representatives was elected for four years, and since it could override a veto of the upper house, had final legislative power. The prime minister and cabinet were responsible only to the Diet, no longer to the emperor. The judiciary was headed by a supreme court which was independent of the legislature and could determine the constitutionality of any law.

A significant clause of the Japanese constitution is Article 9, which is in part the cause of present political disturbances in Japan, because it provides that Japan should renounce war and *never* have armed forces other than for self-defense. Japanese political parties differ today over the interpretation of this clause.

Preparations for Japan's Independence

One complication for the Occupation authorities was the success of the Communists in China in 1949, and orders from the Cominform to the Japanese Communist Party required that it participate in the international revolutionary movement. The Japanese Communist Party then assumed as its immediate task the preparation of a "democratic" revolution to get rid of American interference in Japanese affairs.

The Soviet Union took this as the opportunity to demand that the United States take punitive measures against the Communists, in the hopes that such an action would result in a slowing down of Japanese economy.

General MacArthur had originally advised that the Occupation should end as quickly as possible so that the Japanese could assume their own responsibility for government, and be free to improve their economic conditions.

A peace treaty could not be signed without the consent of other nations. On September 8, 1951, forty-nine nations, not including the U.S.S.R. or the other members of the Soviet bloc, signed the peace treaty and ended the state of war with Japan. On the same day the United States signed a Security Pact with Japan, providing for American troops to remain in Japan indefinitely. This meant that the United States was assuming responsibility for Japan's security and defense.

Japan did not officially become independent until April 28, 1952, when the necessary number of ratifications of the peace treaty were registered.

Economic and Social Change

The war had left Japan physically devastated and in a state of economic collapse. Nearly 2,500,000 buildings were destroyed throughout Japan, and two-thirds of its industrial gains since 1930 were wiped out. In Tokyo alone, where 100,000 lives were lost in the fire bomb raids of 1945, over 700,000 buildings were destroyed. Japan's vital overseas markets and her merchant marine were gone, city people were homeless and destitute, and food was scarce. The disillusion of the Japanese people with their militarist leaders, whose promises had turned to ashes, prepared them to accept defeat at the emperor's request, although they had been told that defeat would mean pillage and slaughter by their enemies. The remarkable achievement of the American Occupation authorities and the Japanese people is the result of the skill and great sense of responsibility of the victors, and the willingness of the Japanese to face adversity with the determination to succeed.

One of the first major economic changes was the extensive land reform developed by the Japanese at the insistence of SCAP. The objective was to increase the number of peasant-owners and provide them with enough economic independence so that they would take an active part in Japanese politics. Absentee landlords were allowed to keep only two and a half acres, and were forced to sell the rest; farmers who cultivated their lands could keep seven and a half acres and rent out another two and a half. Land was available at relatively low cost, and peasants who rented land did so at around 4 percent of the annual crop yield, not at the pre-war average of 40 percent.

Within less than twenty years Japan recovered her economic impetus to a degree that was not thought possible. The per capita income was three times the average income of any Asian country, and above that of the Soviet Union. Farm output increased as farm population dropped. Japan had become once again one of the leading industrial nations of the world, and it led the world in ship production. The initial impetus of recovery was partly American aid of $2,000,000,000 during the early years of occupation, and some $4,000,000,000 in purchases for the Korean War. A generous American tariff policy encouraged Japanese exports, which paid for the necessary imports into Japan.

These developments in agriculture and in-

Osaka—Expo City

dustry affected family life and politics. In traditional Japanese society, the family was the foundation upon which all authority was built. Decisions were made by family consensus, not by majority vote; the individual gave way to group decision; politics inevitably reflected this traditional non-democratic concept.

Former traditional restriction and authority broke down in Occupied Japan. Landlords could no longer dictate to peasant-tenants; the growth of industrialism broke down family ties of respect and dependency; women gained legal, economic, and political equality with men; and the break-up of large estates sent younger sons into city businesses. Labor was for the first time allowed to organize, and it became an increasingly important factor in politics. These great freedoms were not without their disadvantages. A people unaccustomed to them are apt to be irresponsible and extreme at first.

Political Parties

Despite the social and economic upheaval since 1945, Japan has remained conservative in its politics, and in the first twenty years the conservative party remained in power except for a brief period. Certain characteristics of Japan's political parties must be appreciated because they are not necessarily counterparts of western political parties. Each party is a combination of groups and factions, and because the conservative party has been in power during most of the years since the end of the war the other parties have had no experience of government and therefore little appreciation of the responsibilities of power.

There have been four main political parties, two of them conservative, and two which have been liberal to radical. The chief rivalry has been between the conservative Liberal-Democratic Party and the liberal Japan Socialist Party.

The Liberal-Democratic Party. This party is the conservative one; despite its name has carried out the reform of the early post-war years and kept some traditions and continuity of the past. The conservatives accepted land reform, put into operation the new kind of government based upon popular elections, and also had considerable influence in helping the industrialists and the nation to rebuild the economy. In 1955 the Liberal-Democratic Party started to build a national organization that was able from then on to keep the Japan Socialist Party out of power. Their main support comes from businessmen, and also from most of the farmers and government employees. The party is accused by its opponents of being unwilling to accept further necessary changes.

The Fair and Bright (Clean Government) Association. Military defeat and economic devastation, and the great social changes of recent years have influenced a number of Japanese to turn to religion. Half a dozen new "religions" or movements in recent years have appeared. Some observers regard them as cults which will soon disappear, while others regard them as already influencing Japanese life. The most publicized group, reportedly with 10,000,000 members, and the fourth largest party in the House of Representatives is the Fair and Bright Association, supported by the religious sect called the Soka Gakkai, or Value Creating Association. It advocates world peace, lower taxes, and honest politics, and generally is conservative. Some critics accuse it of strong-arm methods to win converts, and of extreme nationalism.

The Japan Socialist Party. The Japan Socialist Party is the larger of the two so-called liberal parties, and is in fact the right wing group of socialists. Its platform opposes the Security Treaty which still retains American troops in Japan, advocates government ownership of basic industries, opposes the restoration of Japanese forces, and favored recognition of the People's Republic of China. Its greatest support comes from the trade unionists, but by 1972 it had not succeeded in winning control of the Diet. It has split into two parties.

The Japanese Communist Party. This party has not been able up through 1972 to elect to the Diet more than 38 members, its greatest number since 1949. Its platform includes closer relationship with Communist countries, opposition to American troops in Japan and to the Vietnam War. Its traditional tactics have been to attack the Liberal-Democratic Party as imperial puppets, fascists, and traitors who are selling out to foreign capital. Another tactic has been to encourage strikes, attempt deliberately to paralyze the nation's economy, compel the government to take strong measures, and then accuse it of "undemocratic" methods.

6. Japan since Independence

Domestic Problems

One of the basic problems facing Japan is her large population, about 98,000,000 in 1965, which had risen to 104,000,000 by 1971. Although Japan's birth-rate has decreased in recent years, its death-rate has markedly declined, with an increased life-expectancy for the people. Japan's food production and natural resources cannot possibly meet her needs, and she is becoming increasingly dependent upon foreign markets for her livelihood.

Japan may face increasing violence at home as minority parties refuse to accept their role, and use disruptive measures to gain power. If the Great Powers should, through events which they cannot control, be forced into a war, the pressures for Japan's support could result in violence among Japan's political parties.

The Revised Security Treaty

A significant factor in modern Japanese politics is the young generation which knew little of the war except resentment for leaders who had brought disaster to their country. They are opposed to war, are strongly in support of the constitution, and intensely in favor of Article 9 of the constitution prohibiting the re-arming of Japan.

The original Security Treaty was signed in 1951, before Japan was independent. Since that time Japan built up its own defense forces, and in 1958 the United States and Japanese governments revised the treaty and signed the completed document in January 1960. American ground troops were entirely withdrawn before 1960, but the United States retained numerous air bases and two naval repair depots. Even before the new treaty was signed, popular Japanese opinion criticized the continued presence of any American troops and bases, which provided instances of disputes through accidents, personal incidents, conflict with Japanese labor hired by the troops, but particularly resentment over the loss of scarce farmland to American runways.

Because Japan agreed never to maintain "land, sea, and air forces," she accepted a succession of mutual security treaties in which the United States guaranteed Japan's safety. However, Japan needed her own internal security forces, and in 1950 she organized a 75,000 National Police Reserve to assist local police forces. In 1952 the Reserve was renamed the National Security Force and included a small naval force. By the early 1960's this was enlarged into the Self-Defense Force, with 200,000 men, more than 1,000 planes, and a naval force of destroyer size.

The most important concession by the United States in the 1960 Security Treaty was that it must consult Japan if it wishes to move substantial forces into or out of Japan. This would prevent Japan from being used as a United States base in the event of war, and also getting involved in such a war. Because Japan does not wish to re-arm herself, she must depend upon United States defense, and as China develops its own nuclear weapons, Japan may be reluctant to terminate the Security Treaty. American commitments in Southeast Asia give Japanese bases increased importance in international affairs.

Opposition to the Revised Treaty

Prime Minister Kishi of the Liberal-Democratic Party tried to force through a vote on the 1960 treaty, after ordering the police to remove Socialist deputies who were staging a sit-in strike in the Diet. The student organization, the *Tengakuren*, played a significant part in organizing mass demonstrations to urge the resignation of the Kishi government. Organized labor held a brief strike of over 5,000,000 workers; over 12,000,000 people signed petitions demanding new elections for the Diet; the United States ambassador, and others preparing for the visit of President Eisenhower, were threatened at Tokyo airport; and Prime Minister Kishi felt obliged to ask the president to postpone his visit. Although the treaty was finally ratified, Kishi was obliged to resign.

Foreign Policy and the U.S.A.

Much of the opposition to the treaty was based upon memories of Hiroshima and Nagasaki, and the fear of nuclear war. The widespread demonstrations were evidence of the conviction that the treaty could involve Japan in war again. The issue is becoming very important because the treaty can be terminated after one year's notice by either party, at any time after June 23, 1970. The Liberal-Democratic

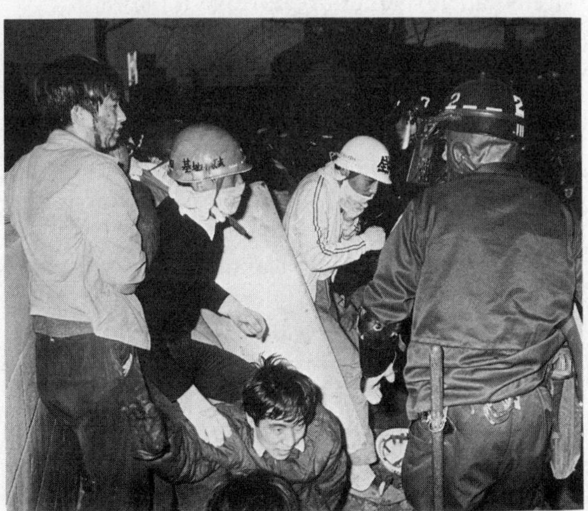

Anti-U.S. Riots. By the 1960's the students in Japan had become vociferous and the rioting violent.

Emperor Hirohito and President Nixon meet in Alaska, 1971. This was the first time a Japanese emperor had set foot outside Japan as Emperor.

Party received support for the treaty in elections for the House of Councillors in 1967, but the Socialists and Communists oppose the treaty and favor unarmed neutrality, and use the term "nuclear allergy" to emphasize their disapproval of any possible involvement in war. Many Japanese realize that America guarantees the security of Japan with nuclear forces, bringing Japan in under the "nuclear umbrella," and that Japan has no obligation to assist in the defense of the United States.

Some Japanese object to being associated in any way in foreign policy with the United States because this automatically labels Japan as anti-Communist China and anti-Soviet Union.

Okinawa

On Easter Day, April 1, 1945, one of the bloodiest Pacific battles of World War II started when United States troops landed on the beaches of Okinawa, a strategic East China Sea island fortified by the Japanese. Not until eighty-two days later was this craggy island, later to be used as a staging base for the invasion of Japan, in the hands of the invaders, and only after the deaths of 12,000 Americans, 100,000 Japanese troops, and 62,000 Okinawans caught between the fighting armies.

The occupation of Okinawa and another hundred and forty islands in the Ryukyu chain became one of the more difficult problems for the United States after the war. The nearly one million inhabitants preferred to be part of Japan, but as the Cold War escalated in Europe and spread to Asia, Okinawa became increasingly important.

The United States built a vast complex of military bases and nuclear installations capable of retaliation in the event of an attack upon Japan or the United States. American use of Okinawa as a base for B-52 bombing raids on North Vietnam drew increasing protests from Japan.

As the years passed, the Okinawans resented the United States military everywhere across the island, and the evident belief of the local United States command that Okinawa was a permanent United States base in Asia. Some of the best farmland was appropriated for bases, airfields, schools, and housing programs for United States personnel; six-lane highways with hamburger stands and used-car lots crossed the island; legal cases involving American troops and Okinawans were tried in United States military courts in which Okinawans were convinced they received less than justice.

Resentment grew, and in 1968 the Okinawans elected as their Chief Executive in their 32-seat Assembly a man who campaigned for the office on the platform demanding reversion of Okinawa to Japan. In 1971 opposition to continued United States occupation became so insistent that the United States withdrew all its B-52's and chemical-warfare weapons.

In June 1971, the United States and Japan signed an agreement restoring Okinawa to Japan, an agreement finally ratified by the United States Senate and the Japanese Diet. In May 1972 the ceremony of the reversion of Okinawa occurred in Imperial Palace in Tokyo. There Vice-president Spiro Agnew read the proclamation signed by President Nixon, ending the United States military occupation of Okinawa and the other islands of the Ryukyu chain, resolving what Agnew described as "the last major issue of the war."

Despite this ceremony, the Okinawans are troubled by the continued American presence, and the fear that they may find themselves being used by Japan for her own interests. The United States bases will remain virtually intact, although their use is restricted by the agreement, and it is not expected that they will be removed. During the years since 1945 the United States has spent vast sums in the island, with one result that native wages have risen to nearly $2,000 per capita, second in Asia only to Japan.

Older Okinawans who remember pre-war days recall that Okinawa was one of the poorest prefectures in Japan, and that its citizens were treated as second-class citizens by Japanese. Businessmen on the island fear higher taxes and competition from Japanese firms. So, some Okinawans are not altogether enthusiastic about the island's return to Japan.

Like the British in the African colonies, the Americans in Okinawa inevitably introduced the natives to the idea of self-government. As one Okinawan said, "By teaching us democracy you strengthened our resolve to be free of foreign rule – your own."

Japan and Southeast Asia

Japan's invasion of much of Southeast Asia during World War II has left memories of exploitation which some nations still resent. Nevertheless, the need for markets has reduced this antagonism, and in recent years Japan has established a better relationship with her Asian neighbors.

As part of the price of winning her post-war independence, Japan recognized the regime of Chiang Kai-shek, and did not establish diplomatic ties with Communist China. One factor which still affects Japanese thinking today is that before 1940 hundreds of thousands of Japanese lived on the China mainland. Consequently, some Japanese people objected to the isolation of Communist China by the United States; they thought that America greatly exaggerated the threat of Chinese Communism, and did not agree with a close alliance of Japan with the United States at the expense of closer relationships between Japan and mainland China. Nevertheless, increasing criticism by Communist China of the United States tends to work to the benefit of the United States because Japan still appears to believe that her best interests are served by support of the United States.

The former Greater East Asia Co-Prosperity Sphere is being revived, but on the basis of economic co-operation between Japan and her Asian neighbors. It is to the advantage of Japan to raise the standard of living of its neighbors, who can become valued customers.

On Vietnam the Japanese government formally gave the United States its support, but it believed that the problem of Vietnam could be resolved by economic and social means rather than by military. In the minds of many Japanese the ideological conflict between the United States, Communist China, and North Vietnam interfered with the economic development of Japan and Southeast Asia.

Japan's prime minister, Kakuei Tanaka, after the China-U.S. summit meeting in 1972, met with the Chinese in Peking, starting a new page in Japan-China relations.

Review Questions

Section 1

1. How has geography affected the living conditions and occupations of the people of Japan?
2. Can Shinto be regarded as a form of religion?
3. Why was the Japanese warrior class attracted to Zen Buddhism?

Sections 2 and 3

4. How did the Tokugawa Shogunate maintain its hold upon the Japanese people?
5. What did the Tokugawas expect to gain from the isolation of Japan? How did they carry out their policy?
6. What conditions and ideas led to the fall of the Tokugawa system?
7. Why did the people of Japan have little to do with the governing of their country, even after the constitution of 1889?
8. In what way did the armed services exercise a great deal of power in the government of Japan?

Section 4

9. How did the Sino-Japanese War of 1894–1895 and the Russo-Japanese War of 1904–1905 indicate that Japan had wide expansionist ambitions?
10. Why were the militarists able to get increasing support from the Japanese people?

Sections 5 and 6

11. Why was General Douglas MacArthur so effective during the occupation period in Japan?
12. How did the new constitution differ from the earlier constitution of the Meiji Restoration period?
13. In what ways is each of the following a problem for Japan: Population; the Security Treaty; Okinawa; Vietnam; the United States' New China Policy?

8

Nations of Southeast Asia

The name Southeast Asia is given to a vast area of land that stretches in a horseshoe around the South China Sea, 4,000 miles east to west, 2,000 miles north to south, and the home of 245,000,000 people. Today it includes the nine independent nations of Burma, Thailand, Laos, Cambodia, Indonesia, the Philippines, and North and South Vietnam, and the recently-independent island-state of Singapore. All these nations except Thailand, which has long been independent, were colonies which received their independence after World War II. During the war these former colonies quickly fell to the Japanese invaders. The speed with which the white rulers were overcome by Asiatics thoroughly undermined the prestige of the white man. As a result, the colonial peoples began to prepare themselves for independence.

Underground movements in opposition to the "invader" Japan continued after the war as nationalist groups dedicated to complete independence from French, Dutch, and British colonial masters. French opposition to independence led to eight years of fighting, the loss of her Indo-China empire, and that in turn to the tragic guerrilla war in Vietnam which devastated South Vietnam.

Several Southeast Asia nations are economically backward, industrially underdeveloped, and too fiercely independent to unite against the common danger of Communism.

Terms

1. Huks
2. Maphilindo
3. Vietminh
4. Geneva Agreement
5. Malaya
6. Malaysia
7. Pathet Lao
8. Ho Chi Minh Trail
9. Domino Theory
10. Tonkin Gulf Resolution
11. National Liberation Front (NLF)
12. Viet Cong
13. Tet Offensive
14. Vietnamization

People

15. Sukarno
16. Suharto
17. Souvanna Phouma
18. Ngo Dinh Diem
19. Ho Chi Minh
20. George Ball
21. Robert McNamara
22. General Westmoreland
23. Souvanouphong
24. Sihanouk
25. Lon Nol
26. Lee Yew
27. Nguyen Van Thieu

Places

28. Southeast Asia
29. Philippine Republic
30. Republic of Indonesia
31. Java
32. Djakarta
33. Celebes
34. West Irian
35. Australia
36. New Guinea
37. Indo-China
38. Laos
39. Cambodia
40. North Vietnam
41. Hanoi
42. Haiphong
43. South Vietnam
44. Dienbienphu
45. Saigon
46. Thailand
47. Burma
48. Malaysia
49. Sarawak
50. Sabah
51. Singapore
52. Brunei
53. North Korea
54. South Korea
55. Taiwan
56. Quemoy and Matsu

Events

1946 Philippine Republic
War in Indo-China
1950 Republic of Indonesia
Korean War
1954 French Defeat at Dienbienphu
Geneva Agreement
1957 Federation of Malaya
1963 Federation of Malaysia
1964 U.S. at War in Vietnam
Tonkin Gulf Resolution
1965 Independence of Singapore
1968 Tet Offensive
Paris Peace Talks begin
1970 Invasion of Cambodia
1971 Incursion into Laos
1973 Cease-fire signed: USA and North Vietnam

1. The Philippine Republic

The first of these colonies to attain independence was the Philippine people in 1946, as earlier promised by the United States. The Philippine Islands were discovered by Magellan in 1521 and named in honor of the Spanish king Philip II. Manila, founded in 1571, is the oldest permanent European settlement in any Far East country. The Spanish remained in the Philippines until the Spanish-American War of 1898, when Admiral Dewey's fleet sank the Spanish squadron in Manila Harbor. This situation led to the rather lukewarm annexation by the United States, over the bitter opposition of the natives under Aguinaldo, who led his people in a fight for independence.

In 1898 the Americans promised eventual freedom to the Filipinos when they had shown their ability to govern themselves. In 1934 the United States Congress finally passed an act promising freedom in ten years, a promise which was postponed until 1946 because of Japanese occupation. In that year the constitution of the Philippine Republic set up a government very similar to that of the United States, with a legislature of two popularly-elected houses, and a president elected for four years by all the people.

Domestic Problems

In domestic affairs the Philippine Republic faced the problems of being primarily a producer of raw materials, and of needing capital to rebuild the industries and public utilities that were largely destroyed during the war. As an independent nation it no longer enjoys the special trading rights it previously had in American markets, and it must now compete with other nations in selling its products on the American market.

During the Japanese occupation the guerrilla forces led by the Communist-dominated Huks, from Hukbalahaps, the Anti-Japanese People's Liberation Army, organized peasant resistance which continued long after the end of the war because the peasantry felt that its needs were being ignored. Not until 1950 was Huk resistance broken, although its influence still exists among peasants resentful of domination by the landlord class.

Some reforms were undertaken in 1954 when interest rates on loans were limited to 8 percent, and some land was redistributed to the peasants. But several economic weaknesses still remain. The population is growing too fast, unemployment is rising, the standard of living is low, and the country desperately needs a great deal of money in order to industrialize.

Foreign Policy

In foreign policy the Philippine Republic is a member of the South East Asia Treaty Organization, SEATO, and in general follows the United States policy. The Republic participated in the Korean War by sending troops in support of the United Nations action, and it recognized Nationalist China on Taiwan. It has a Mutual Defense Pact with the United States and provides its partner with naval and air bases. For its general policy of alignment with the United States it is greatly criticized by other Asian nations.

Another cause of friction in the international field is the Republic's quarrel with the Federation of Malaysia, which includes Sabah in the northeast corner of the island of Borneo. The Philippine Republic claimed Sabah as an integral part of its territory in 1962, as did Indonesia before the overthrow of its president Sukarno. The Philippine claim was based on the recent appeal to the Manila government by the heirs of the late North Borneo Sultan of Sulu, who, said the heirs, had "leased" but not sold the territory to the British North Borneo Company in 1878. The British insisted that its claim was established in 1885 when Spain, which then ruled the Philippines, gave up any claim to North Borneo. The Philippine claim was flatly rejected by the leaders of North Borneo's three political parties.

The Philippine Republic agreed to let the people of Sabah decide whom they wanted to rule their land. When a United Nations report showed that a majority of the people of Sabah wished to be a part of Malaysia, the Philippine Republic rejected the United Nations report. During the summer of 1968 the Philippine ambassador to the Federation of Malaysia was recalled to Manila after Malaysia announced that the Philippine claim to Sabah had no basis whatever and would not be the subject of further discussion. One Malaysia military leader claimed in 1968 that the people of Sabah fear that Philippine extremists intend to raid their coastal towns and infiltrate throughout the country.

This is another example of the frictions among the nations of Southeast Asia which wrecked the 1963 attempt to form a loose association called Maphilindo, consisting of Malaysia, the Philippine Republic, and Indonesia, for the purpose of closer economic and social cooperation.

2. The Republic of Indonesia

Indonesia today, officially the Republic of Indonesia, is the world's largest archipelago or group of islands, stretching between Asia and Australia over 4,000 miles east to west in the Indian and Pacific Oceans. It consists of more than 3,000 islands, the largest of which are Java, Sumatra, West Borneo, and Celebes, and has a population of nearly 100,000,000. Half of these live on the island of Java, one of the most densely populated areas of the world but no larger than Alabama, about 50,000 square miles.

Dutch Colony

Indonesia was once part of the great 14th century Majapaht Empire that included people from Southeast Asia, China, and India. In the 16th century Arab traders reached there and left behind the Moslem religion, which today includes some 90,000,000 Indonesians. In the 17th century Indonesia became the center of a great Dutch empire, which was then known as the Netherlands East Indies. The Dutch were paternalistic rulers who brought some improvement to the islands but paid little attention to the people and gave them no training in self-government until the 20th century.

In 1918 the Dutch felt obliged to meet rising demands for political rights, and gradually they increased them over the years, although when World War II broke out the Netherlands East Indies were far from self-governing. During the Japanese occupation from 1943 on, a nationalist named Sukarno worked with the Japanese, not to help the invaders but primarily to lay the groundwork for later independence.

Meanwhile, in Europe the Netherlands, overrun and occupied by the Germans, could do nothing about their East Indies possessions. At the end of the war when the Japanese surrendered, they did so to British troops acting on behalf of the Netherlands government. When the Dutch were ready to take over from the British, Sukarno had already declared the Dutch colonies to be an independent republic, had set up a government and had organized an army.

The Dutch hoped that the wealth of the Indies could be used to help their own recovery in post-war Europe. But by this time there was no possible compromise between complete independence and Dutch colonial rule. Desperate fighting between the Dutch and the Indo-

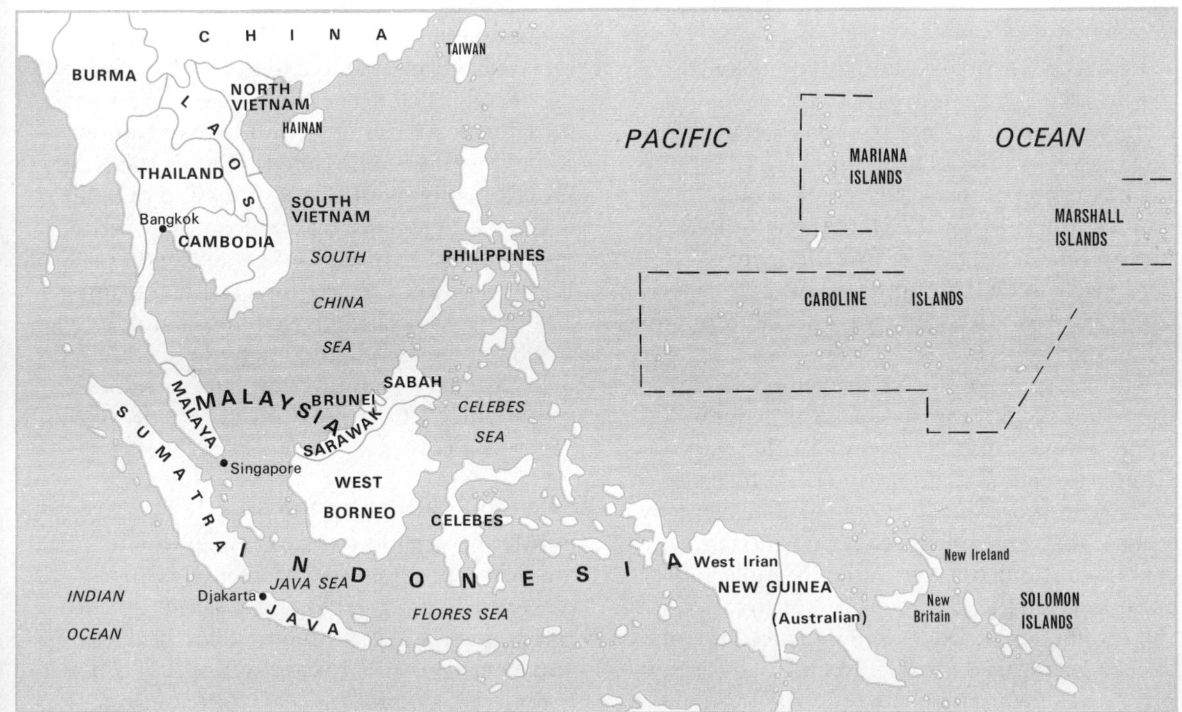

Southeast Asia

nesians raged for five years. The Dutch were embittered by the fact that the Indonesian nationalists refused to release Dutch women and children from the prisons in which they had been confined for three years by the Japanese.

Establishment of the Republic of Indonesia

In 1950 the Dutch government recognized their former colony as the United States of Indonesia, an equal partner with Holland under the Dutch queen. This did not suit Sukarno who then proclaimed his country to be the Republic of Indonesia under his presidency. In 1954 he declared that all official ties with the Netherlands were ended.

Potentially one of the richest nations in Southeast Asia, with resources of rubber, tin, petroleum, tobacco, and bauxite, Indonesia needs vast amounts of money to develop them. But a further problem is that these primary commodities are very sensitive to world price fluctuations, and when prices fall, the raw materials bring in insufficient money to pay for necessary imports.

Sukarno, who was largely responsible for his country's independence, and earned its gratitude, was not only unable to solve his country's economic problems but also drove away possible foreign capital by denouncing the United States with such statements as, "The hell with aid," and encouraging the Communist Party in Indonesia. In 1959 he dissolved parliament, postponed scheduled elections, appointed a rubber-stamp "mutual help" legislature, announced a "guided democracy" for the nation, and had himself named president for life.

Claims on West New Guinea

President Sukarno's regime could not solve the problems of a nation whose per capita income was only $55 a year, and this was perhaps one reason for his political campaigns demanding possession of the western half of New Guinea, still ruled by the Dutch. His "mission" was successful because in 1962 the United Nations decreed that this territory, now called West Irian, was to become part of the Republic of Indonesia.

Rather typical of the intense nationalism of the nations of Southeast Asia is the claim by some Indonesians that Australia-ruled East New Guinea is really East Irian, and therefore also belongs to Indonesia. A more extreme claim by some is that Australia is really South Irian, and that it too should be part of the Republic of Indonesia! In the same vein, Sukarno called the Indian Ocean the Indonesian Ocean. Sometimes a leader uses a "red herring" of a foreign threat, as a means to distract the attention of the people from poor living standards and other internal problems.

In 1963 four British colonial areas, Malaya, Singapore, Sarawak, and Sabah, formed the independent Federation of Malaysia, a large crescent of land 1,600 miles long around the South China Sea. Sukarno saw this federation as a threat to Indonesian plans of expansion in that area, and more seriously as an "imperialist" move by Great Britain who concluded a pact with Malaysia making British, Australian, and New Zealand troops responsible for its defense. In 1964 Sukarno sent guerrillas into Malaysia by plane, by small boats, and across the border from Indonesian Borneo. The British rushed warships to Malaysia, and by mid-1965 it had 50,000 troops ready for any attack by Indonesia, which had a large army, Soviet-built fighter-planes, and a Soviet-supplied navy.

In 1965 Sukarno pulled the Republic of Indonesia out of the United Nations when Malaysia was elected as a temporary member of the Security Council. He even went so far as to threaten to sponsor a second United Nations consisting of what he called NEFOS, the Newly Emerging Forces of new nations and of older nations with socialist or Communist governments, as a rival to the Old Established Forces of Western powers, or so-called colonialist-imperialist powers which exercised dominance in world affairs. He planned to build in Indonesia the headquarters of this new United Nations group called CONEFO, Conference of Newly Emerging Forces.

Sukarno Replaced by Suharto

Before the situation became much worse, Sukarno's position was threatened by army officers who opposed Sukarno's domestic incompetence and his foreign policy, and his apparent sympathy for and support of the Indonesian Communist Party, PKI, Partai Kommunis Indonesia.

In September 1965 three Chinese physicians came from Peking to attend Sukarno for a kidney ailment. A report that he was incurably ill apparently convinced the Communist party that this was the time to take over. They now had a membership of 3,000,000, and several million supporters in the youth and labor fronts. Sukarno had given them encouragement and had even allowed them to form a large People's Militia of their own, which they expected to use against their only real rival, the Indonesian army leaders.

On the morning of October 1, 1965, mobile police and some army units led by the commander of Sukarno's palace guards, who was a Communist sympathizer, seized radio and telephone facilities, and executed six leading anti-Communist regular army generals. Two important generals, Nasution and Suharto, escaped and within twenty-four hours had regained control of Djakarta, the capital; six weeks later they had utterly crushed the uprising. For eight months the army and the people of Indonesia literally slaughtered known and suspected Communists. Estimated dead were a minimum of 400,000. In some places rivers were choked with dead bodies massacred in the outburst. Not only was the third largest Communist Party in the world completely broken, but Sukarno was stripped of his titles and powers, and General Suharto replaced him. The army leaders left Sukarno politically powerless, but free, because to millions of Indonesians he was still the man who had won their independence from the Dutch.

Indonesian Independence. The Monument of Liberty in Djakarta.

General Suharto has ended agitation against Malaysia, and has gained re-admission of Indonesia to the United Nations. But he faces many problems in his poverty-stricken country; he is hoping to find foreign nations and private individuals willing to invest in his country's future. However, Indonesia is intensely nationalistic and apt to be suspicious that foreign investments are a prelude to domination by foreign powers. This is the major dilemma of many newly-independent countries in the second half of the 20th century. The gap between the older industrialized and younger underdeveloped nations of the world is growing wider instead of smaller.

3. The Vietnams

Indo-China: Colony of France

Indo-China was the name given to what are today the countries of Laos, Cambodia, North Vietnam, and South Vietnam. For centuries they were tributary states of China but semi-independent and able to depend upon China for assistance if they were attacked. Later they became a part of the Chinese Empire.

After the opening of China in the 1840's, European nations looked with great interest on this region, and when a foreign missionary was murdered in 1857 the French sent in a punitive expedition, secured a foothold in the southern part, and by 1885 were in possession of what was then called French Indo-China. In 1940, after the defeat of France, the French Vichy government permitted Japan to use the French facilities in French Indo-China, and agreed to joint control of the area.

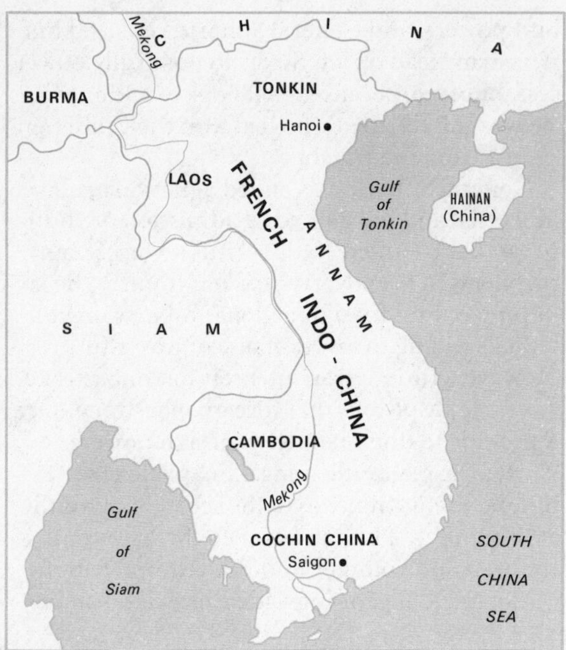

Indo-China, 19th Century. Under French domination.

Ho Chi Minh

This was the opportune moment for Ho Chi Minh to take over the leadership of the Vietnamese people in their fight for complete independence. Ho Chi Minh, whose name literally means He Who Shines, or The Successful One, had already devoted many years to the cause of Communism and to training in revolutionary tactics. He was born in a central province of Vietnam in 1889, the youngest of three children, and at the age of 19 was expelled from the Lycée Quoc Hoc, the French secondary school, for revolutionary ideas and opposition to French colonialism. In 1912 he was forced to flee from Vietnam, worked his way over to Europe on a French ship, and lived for a time in London. Here he worked at odd jobs, and then became a pastrycook under the famous chef Escoffier who, according to legend, unsuccessfully tried to persuade Ho Chi Minh to give up revolutionary activities and devote himself to his profession and become a great chef.

In 1918 Ho Chi Minh went to Paris, worked as a photographer and a truck driver, and sent in a petition to the Paris Peace Conference requesting independence for Indo-China. The petition was disregarded. When the French Socialist Party split over policy, Ho Chi Minh helped to organize the French Communist Party, and was appointed by the party as an expert on colonial questions. He traveled all over Europe in this capacity, and was sent as a delegate to the Communist International Conference in Moscow in 1922. Here he stayed to learn revolutionary tactics, became a Russian subject, and was sent to Canton as an interpreter in the Soviet Consulate. When Chiang Kai-shek purged the Communists in 1927, Ho Chi Minh fled back to Moscow, and then returned later to Shanghai as chief of the Communist International Asiatic bureau.

During the 1930's he traveled widely in Southern Asia in various disguises, as a Buddhist monk, a beggar, a salesman, all the while organizing revolutionary groups. In 1941 he organized a revolutionary army in China, called Vietnam Doc Lap Dong Minh Hoi, or Vietminh for short, committed to the creation of an independent Vietnam Republic. Late in 1944 Ho Chi Minh slipped quietly into Vietnam for the first time in thirty years, fought against the Japanese occupation troops, saved many United States fliers forced down in French Indo-China, and gave information to the United States army in exchange for American equipment. As soon as the Japanese surrender took place, Ho Chi Minh formed a provisional government for Vietnam, and on September 2, 1945, he proclaimed the independent Republic of Vietnam, including in the proclamation quotations from the American Declaration of Indepen-

Ho Chi Minh in 1950

dence and the French Declaration of the Rights of Man.

President Roosevelt, who disliked colonialism, authorized the dropping of arms to Ho Chi Minh to help him to resist the French in their determined effort to retain Indo-China as a colony.

Aid for Independence Requested

Immediately after World War II Ho Chi Minh repeatedly asked the United States for aid for the "same status as the Philippines." By this he meant a period of United States "protection" leading toward independence. After his request had been rejected several times by the United States, Ho Chi Minh agreed to a return of French power for five years, preferring the French to possible Chinese intervention. Although the United States disliked the return of French colonialism to Indo-China, it disliked Ho Chi Minh's Communism more, despite the fact that it was not possible to prove any connection between Ho Chi Minh and Moscow.

The growing success of the Communists in China apparently persuaded United States officials that Communism anywhere was Soviet Communism and the extension of Soviet influence. But the American attitude on Communism was by no means the same as that in Southeast Asia. To Europeans, freedom meant freedom of speech and freedom from the authority of a dictatorial government. In Southeast Asia freedom meant independence and the end of colonial rule.

The people of Southeast Asia did not consider that the Soviet Union was any of their concern, nor did they see Communism as a conspiracy to enslave them. To them, Communism suggested "anti-imperialism," freedom from the overbearing presence of the colonial overlord. In the eyes of the people of Southeast Asia the intruders were not Russians but the French, English, and Dutch, and now Americans.

The deciding factor against Ho Chi Minh was the success of Mao Tse-tung on mainland China and the establishment of the People's Republic of China.

The United States National Security Council reported,

"The extension of Communist authority in China represents a grievous political defeat for us. If Southeast Asia is also swept by Communism we shall have suffered a major political rout, the repercussions of which will be felt throughout the rest of the world, especially in the

Middle East and in a critically exposed Australia."

Two years later the National Security Council warned that the "domino" theory could lead to the loss to Communism of all Southeast Asia countries and even threaten the "stability and security of Europe."

France Loses French Indo-China

When France returned to Indo-China after the defeat of the Japanese, it recognized Ho Chi Minh's self-proclaimed Republic as a "free state within the Indo-China Federation and French Union." But Ho Chi Minh and the French soon clashed over the question of the control of the rest of Vietnam, and on December 19, 1946 Ho Chi Minh ordered General Vo Nguyen Giap to open artillery fire on Hanoi.

This attack was the beginning of an offensive to drive the French out of Indo-China, an offensive that lasted for seven and a half years. The French asked for American assistance, but the United States was caught in the difficult dilemma of not wishing to help either colonialism or Communism. The final tragedy for the French army, which annually suffered in Indo-China the loss of almost each graduating class of officers from St. Cyr, the French West Point, was played out at Dienbienphu in northern Vietnam in 1954. Here the French dug in, convinced that the Vietnamese could not dislodge them. But the Vietnamese literally man-handled artillery down from China, emplaced it in the hills surrounding Dienbienphu, and there broke French power in Indo-China. After 55

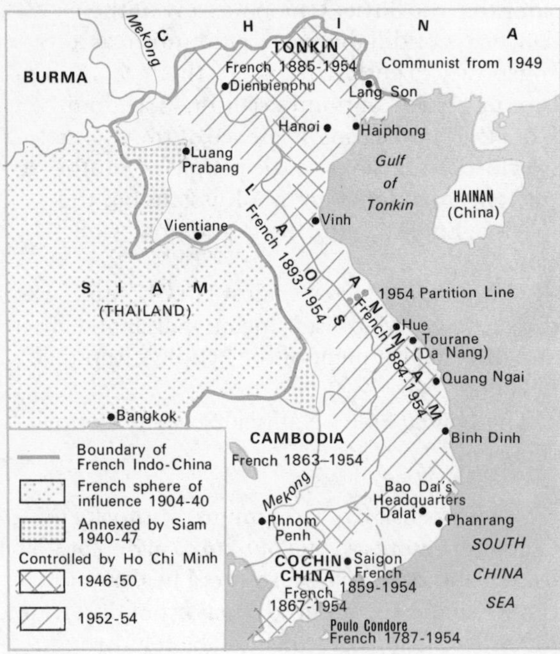

Vietnam

Dienbienphu. This picture of a wounded French officer at the battle is a symbol of the hopelessness of the French cause.

days of continuous siege, Dienbienphu fell to Ho Chi Minh's forces on May 7, 1954, but fighting continued in other parts of French Indo-China for several more weeks. Ho Chi Minh's victory would probably have been impossible without the existence of the People's Republic of China, which contributed not only guns and food but also training facilities for Ho's troops.

The Geneva Agreement, 1954

Meanwhile, at Geneva, Switzerland, representatives of nine participants met to arrange truce terms between Ho Chi Minh and the French. Truce arrangements were drafted by France, Great Britain, and the Soviet Union; the United States was represented by Undersecretary of State General Walter Bedell Smith, but he avoided any participation in drafting the terms. On July 21, 1954, the truce terms were signed by the representative of the French Commander in Indo-China, and by the Vietminh Defense Minister, and by no one else.

The main terms agreed upon were: (1) French forces were to evacuate North Vietnam within 10 months, (2) Vietminh forces were to evacuate South Vietnam within 10 months, (3) within two years an election would be held throughout all Vietnam to set up a unified government for North and South Vietnam, (4) the Vietminh were to respect the political and territorial integrity of independent Laos and Cambodia, which were to be demilitarized, (5) civilians were allowed to move voluntarily from either North or South Vietnam to the other section, (6) a commission consisting of Poland, Canada, and India was set up to supervise the actual operation of the truce terms.

South Vietnam Rejects Election

After the Geneva Agreement was signed by the two groups, over 1,000,000 refugees went from North to South Vietnam, and thus presented South Vietnam with the serious economic problem of feeding and housing them. In South Vietnam, Ngo Dinh Diem became the leader for the immediate present, declared Vietnam to be a Republic with himself as its first president, and retained power after the elections of March 1956. The new Assembly officially denounced the Geneva Agreement, declaring, "We do not consider ourselves bound by the Geneva Agreement, which has been signed against the will and in contempt of the interests of the Vietnamese people."

Diem refused to permit the elections provided for in the Geneva Agreement because, he said, free elections would not be possible in Communist North Vietnam.

In 1958 the International Commission for the Supervision of the Truce, feeling itself to be handicapped by the un-co-operative attitude of the North Vietnamese, moved from Hanoi to Saigon. In October of that same year, the Republic of South Vietnam was established, thus intimating that unification of the whole country was not possible.

But by 1960 opposition was building up in South Vietnam against Diem and his family, which was practically running South Vietnam as a family affair. Ngo Dinh Diem was president of the country; brother Ngo Dinh Nhu was the president's chief advisor; an older brother, Ngo Dinh Can, was governor of Central Vietnam; another brother, Ngo Dinh Thuc, was the Catholic Bishop of Hué, the ancient capital city; and a fourth, Ngo Dinh Luzen, was the South Vietnam Ambassador in London.

4. The Vietnam War

During the late 1950's fighting broke out between the two Vietnams, and the Eisenhower Administration decided to rescue the young South

Vietnamese country from a Communist take-over, an action which gave the United States "a direct role" in the ultimate breakdown of the Geneva Settlement made in 1954. At this stage, United States involvement was a "limited-risk gamble" with 600 United States military advisors helping to train South Vietnamese troops.

In December 1960 North Vietnam announced the formation of the National Liberation Front, NLF, in both Vietnams dedicated to the "liberation" of South Vietnam from Diem and the United States. Members and supporters of the NLF were known as Viet Cong, or VC, an abbreviation of Viet Nam Cong Sam, or Vietnamese Communist.

A year later President Kennedy announced that the United States was ready to help South Vietnam "preserve its independence," and by December 1962 there were 4,000 United States forces training the South Vietnamese forces. Kennedy's action may have been influenced by a report from his vice-president, Lyndon Johnson, in May 1961.

The vice-president saw the situation in Southeast Asia as crucial for the United States, and urged support for the South Vietnamese, warning that failure to achieve success there would mean that:

"The United States inevitably must surrender the Pacific and take up our defenses on our own shores. . . . We must decide whether to help these countries to the best of our ability or throw in the towel in the area and pull back our defenses to San Francisco and a 'Fortress America' concept."*

By November 1963 more than 17,000 troops were in South Vietnam, and combat casualties

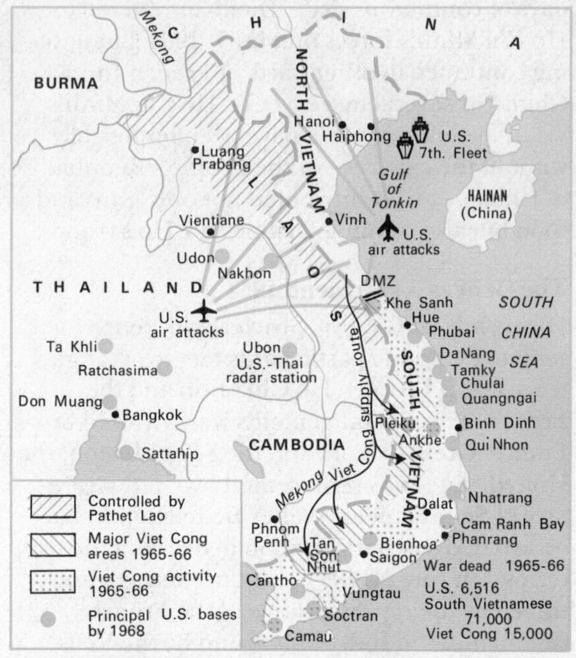

Vietnam, 1965–1968

U.S. Military Advisors, 1962

---

*Senator Gravel edition of the *Pentagon Papers*, Beacon Press, Boston, 1971. Vol. II, pp. 57–8.

were mounting. American "advisors" accompanied Vietnamese troops in anti-guerrilla patrols, American helicopter crews transported South Vietnamese troops to combat areas, American pilots flew bombing missions, and American technicians handled communications equipment in actual combat. The "limited-risk gamble" of the 1950's had now become a "broad commitment" to save South Vietnam.

During the year 1963 political tensions inside South Vietnam seriously increased. Demonstration by 9,000 Buddhists against the Diem regime resulted in several deaths. The Buddhists protests were directed against the orders of the Diem government, most of whose officials were Roman Catholics, forbidding the display of religious flags and the organization of parades to commemorate Buddha's birthday on May 8.

That date was politically explosive because it was the anniversary of the defeat of the French army at Dienbienphu by the Vietminh forces under Ho Chi Minh, and was celebrated as a major Communist holiday. The Buddhists, who were 70 percent of the population of South Vietnam, demanded equal rights with the Roman Catholics and the guaranteed right to practice their religion freely.

Although the situation inside South Vietnam was not publicized, the Diem regime had become increasingly autocratic since 1956. Promised land reform had not taken place, so-called democratic elections were a fraud, opposition leaders were imprisoned without trial, and discontent was wide-spread. In November 1963, Diem was assassinated.

The Tonkin Gulf Resolution

When Lyndon Johnson took office in November 1963 he had to make a choice between war and withdrawal, because the situation in South Vietnam had worsened, and escalation of United States troops was inevitable if South Vietnam was to be supported. Events decided for the President and Congress. Two United States destroyers were reported to have been attacked by North Vietnamese torpedo boats in the Gulf of Tonkin. By Joint Resolution, the United States Congress declared that "Congress approves and supports the determination of the President, as Commander in Chief, to take all necessary measures to repel any armed attack against the forces of the United States and to prevent further aggression." The Joint Resolution was voted unanimously by the House of Representatives, and by an 88 to 2 majority in the Senate, in August, 1964.

By 1973 there was still no official declaration of a war which was the longest in the country's history.

In the early months of 1964, before the passage of the Tonkin Gulf Resolution, the Pentagon drew up contingency plans for a full-scale bombing campaign of North Vietnam and

Napalm. The density of the jungle brought on the use of controversial bombing techniques: one was the use of petroleum jelly that caused instant fires and terrible burns. Other techniques included chemical defoliation and heat sensitive rockets to "home in" on hidden Viet Cong.

for the use of United States combat troops to protect their airbases. Also, prepared at this time, but not made public until 1966, were arguments to justify United States intervention in the war.

Arguments Justifying Intervention

The official American case for intervention in South Vietnam included the argument that South Vietnam was defending itself against "armed attack from the Communist North" and had requested American assistance.

The United States reported its interventionist action to the United Nations Security Council, and on several occasions requested that the Council consider the problem of the war in Vietnam.

"At no time has the (Security) Council taken any action to restore peace and security in Southeast Asia . . . the Council has not seen fit to act."*

The South Vietnam Republic was not a member of the United Nations because its admission was vetoed by the Soviet Union, but it is, said the United States, a separate "international entity" recognized by "approximately 60 governments."

The Australians, who contributed more than 8,000 troops for advisory and combat duty, besides several millions of dollars for rehabilitation projects in South Vietnam, regarded intervention as justified. Paul Hasluck, Minister for External Affairs, stated in 1965 that the conflict in South Vietnam was "not a local rebellion caused by internal discontent, but the application of methods and doctrines of guerrilla warfare." In his opinion the South Vietnamese were dealing with a "large-scale directed campaign of assassination and terrorism" with the direction of the campaign coming from outside.†

*U.S Department of State *Bulletin*, Vol. LIV, No. 1396, March 1966.

Australians in Vietnam. A major contribution of the Australians was the provision of health services and food programs.

Escalation of U.S. Troops

By late 1964 there were 23,000 United States troops in South Vietnam; in July 1965 the President authorized an increase to 125,000, then to 525,000 by June 1967, with a ceiling of 549,000 in April 1968.

Some members of the Administration were not in favor of sharp escalation, and in July 1965 Undersecretary of State George Ball sent a memorandum to President Johnson warning of the danger of invasion.

"No one can assure you that we can beat the Viet Cong or even force them to the conference table on our terms, no matter how many hundred thousand white, foreign (United States) troops we deploy . . . The decision you face now,

†Quoted from statement to the Australian House of Representatives on March 23, 1965. Alan Watt, *Vietnam: An Australian Analysis*, Cheshire, Melbourne, 1968, p. 131.

therefore, is crucial. Once large numbers of United States troops are committed to direct combat, they will begin to take heavy casualties in a war they are ill-equipped to fight in a non-co-operative if not downright hostile countryside. Once we suffer large casualties we will have started a well-nigh irreversible process. Our involvement will be so great that we cannot – without national humiliation – stop short of achieving our complete objectives. *Of the two possibilities I think humiliation would be more likely than the achievement of our objectives – even after we have paid terrible costs.*"*

In 1966 the Central Intelligence Agency reported on the bombing campaign:

"As of July 1966 the United States bombing of North Vietnam has had no measurable direct effect on Hanoi's ability to mount and support military operations in the South at the current level."†

This report contradicted the expectations of McGeorge Bundy, Presidential Assistant for National Security, in a recommendation in favor of a full-scale bombing campaign against North Vietnam. "Measured against the costs of defeat in Vietnam, this program seems cheap."

In October 1966 Secretary of Defense Robert McNamara tried to persuade President Johnson to cut back the bombing in North Vietnam and seek a political settlement, but not until seventeen months later did Lyndon Johnson make such a move, in March 1968.

McNamara, once optimistic about victory in Vietnam, began to be disillusioned and made every effort to persuade the President to change United States objectives in Vietnam. In May 1967 he advocated that the Administration end its efforts to guarantee a non-Communist South Vietnam and be willing instead to accept a coalition government in Saigon that included elements of the Viet Cong.

This proposal split the Johnson Administration. The McNamara group tried to get limits set on the war with the objective of reducing it. The military faction, led by the Joint Chiefs of Staff and General Westmoreland, Commander-in-Chief in Vietnam, urged that the war be widened and more United States troops sent in. President Johnson and several senior civilian officials at the White House and in the Department took a middle position, but the military finally persuaded the President to increase troops commitments to 549,000.

The Tet Offensive, 1968

The policy of gradual escalation changed drastically after the North Vietnamese swept out of the jungles on January 30, 1968 in a relentless attack on military installations and major cities in South Vietnam. They timed the attacks for the celebration of Tet, the Vietnam Lunar New Year, and caught the South Vietnamese forces completely off guard . The Saigon government suffered a severe "psychological blow," and there was doubt whether the South Vietnamese would "bear up under sustained pressure."

General Westmoreland was advised by the Joint Chiefs that the United States Government was not prepared to accept defeat, and therefore, if he needed troops, to "ask for them." He did, requesting a new ceiling of 730,000 men, but a few weeks later he was removed as Commander-in-Chief in Vietnam and appointed Army Chief of Staff. The Central Intelligence Agency had reported in February that no matter how much the United States stepped up the war, the Communists would continue the war in a prolonged stalemate.

**The Pentagon Papers*, Bantam Books, New York, 1971, p. 450.
†*Ibid*, p. 523.

Public opinion so bitterly denounced the President's policy of escalation and the rapidly-mounting United States casualties, that he ordered the bombing to be limited to the area south of the 20th parallel, and renewed his offer to negotiate with Hanoi, hoping for "prompt, productive, serious, and intensive negotiations in an atmosphere that is conducive to progress."

No effective negotiations resulted, and on March 31 the President announced his decision not to run for re-election in November.

Withdrawal and Vietnamization

In his presidential campaign speeches Richard Nixon announced that he would find a way to end the war within four years. During his first year in office he announced his intention to withdraw 25,000 troops by August 1969, with further reductions planned for the future.

South Vietnamese troops were to be trained to use American equipment and to take over the task of ground combat in Vietnam, a process called Vietnamization. To assist South Vietnam, President Nixon decided that the North Vietnamese must be deprived of their sanctuary and their depots in Cambodia.

The Invasion of Cambodia

President Nixon's decision to send United States troops into Cambodia at the beginning of May 1970 provoked vehement criticism in Congress, and loud and sometimes violent protests on college campuses. According to official sources, the United States intervention was undertaken in order to eliminate sanctuaries and supply depots inside Cambodia being used by North Vietnamese troops against South Vietnam.

The Senate Foreign Relations Committee asked President Nixon for an urgent conference on the subject, the first time since 1919 that such a meeting had been requested. Senators Goodell and Hatfield denounced the intervention as "ghastly" and "unbelievable," but Senator Scott, leader of the Republican senators, praised it as "a courageous and remarkable decision." Barry Goldwater said that his policy would be to give the North Vietnamese "fifteen days to make a peace or make Haiphong harbor a mud puddle."

Immediately, a protest movement began with a strike on the Princeton campus, followed by similar action on other college campuses. The most serious incident occurred on the Kent State University campus in Ohio, where clashes between students and police led the governor to send in the National Guard to keep order. Tragically, the confrontation led to the shooting of several students of whom four died. Strikes on 400 campuses protested the action, and many prominent Americans expressed deep anxiety at the Administration's apparent isolation from the younger generation, an isolation which they feared might divide the country.

The withdrawal of American forces from Cambodia a few weeks later left the Cambodians with the task of maintaining the war, with the assistance of limited American air support.

Student Protest. University of Massachusetts students at Commencement.

Critics of the Nixon Administration claimed that American intervention resulted in war throughout the whole of Cambodia, but General Lon Nol, who overthrew the regime of Prince Sihanouk and officially set up a republic, disagreed. He claimed that before the Americans intervened, the Communists had already moved westward out of their sanctuaries near the South Vietnam border, and were already attacking various areas of Cambodia. Both Lon Nol and Sihanouk predicted a protracted war.

Sihanouk, who professed not to be a Communist, has claimed that the United States intervention and the Lon Nol government have plunged his former country into the worst catastrophe of its history; he expressed the hope that the Communist revolution would succeed and thereby bring peace to Cambodia.

The New Cavalry. A helicopter gunship equipped with rocket firing capacity in Vietnam, 1971.

Sihanouk has also claimed that by their support of Lon Nol, the Americans have backed a regime that is no more popular in Cambodia than is the Thieu government in South Vietnam. Sihanouk has stated that in his opinion such United States action could drive more Asians into the Communist camp. Critics of Sihanouk claim that without United States assistance, Cambodia would have been taken over by the Communists, and that other Southeast Asia nations would have been forced to give in to Communist pressure.

Nixon's Five-point Peace Plan

Despite the reduction of United States troops to 396,000, not counting 23,000 Navy and Coast Guard personnel on off-shore duty, and 45,000 airmen stationed in Thailand and directly involved in the Vietnam War, American casualties were 43,700 killed, and more than 290,000 wounded and listed as missing. Public criticism mounted, and President Nixon attempted once again to negotiate with Hanoi.

In October 1970, President Nixon proposed a 5-point peace plan to North Vietnam: (a) a "cease-fire in place," (b) efforts by both sides to "search for a political settlement that truly meets the needs of all South Vietnamese," (c) United States readiness to "negotiate an agreed timetable" for the total withdrawal of United States troops "as part of the overall settlement," (d) an extended peace conference that would seek to end the fighting in Laos and Cambodia as well as in Vietnam, and, (e) the immediate and unconditional release of all prisoners.

The first two points were new proposals that it was hoped could be the basis for negotiations, but the peace plan was denounced by North

Vietnam, the Soviet Union, and Communist China. North Vietnam countered with its demands for (a) an unconditional and total withdrawal of United States troops, and (b) the overthrow of the South Vietnam "puppet" regime.

North Vietnam critized President Nixon for what it called his "unreasonable demand for mutual withdrawal," and claimed that by mid-1971 there would still be some 360,000 United States and allied forces in Vietnam.

Incursion into Laos, 1971

On February 8, 1971, more than 5,000 South Vietnamese troops crossed the border into the northeast corner of Laos, with United States troops committed to provide air, artillery, and logistical support.

President Thieu of South Vietnam claimed that the operation was justified as a "necessary act of legitimate self-defense of South Vietnam against the Communist North Vietnam aggressors," an action taken to end the war sooner.

The United States Department of State explained that the purpose was to protect "the security and safety of American forces in South Vietnam" and to make "the enemy less able to mount offensives and to strengthen South Vietnam's ability to defend itself as United States forces are withdrawn from South Vietnam." The United States Administration added, "the limited engagement is not an enlargement of the war," and claimed that the operation would ensure the success of Vietnamization, the taking over of the responsibility for the war in Indo-China by South Vietnam.

Prince Souvanna Phouma, the prime minister of Laos, said there was "no justification" for the operation, although he admitted that the North Vietnamese had used southeast Laos as a supply network for several years.

The Soviet Union, Peking, and U Thant of the United Nations all condemned the action. The Soviet Union regarded it as "a new front of war," Peking called it "a grave provocation," and U Thant condemned it as "one more deplorable episode in the long history of the barbarous war in Indo-China."

The British government regarded the operation as "fully understandable" in view of North Vietnam's continued violation of Laotian territory in defiance of the 1962 Geneva Agreement.

The military action, named Operation Lam Son, ended officially on April 19, 1971, according to a Saigon military official.

American pilots reported that North Vietnamese supplies were once again moving freely along the Ho Chi Minh Trail despite allied claims that this traffic had been disrupted by the South Vietnamese campaign.

Vietnamization Challenged

The responsibility for ground combat had been taken over by South Vietnam, and the reduction of troops continued as planned by President Nixon to 37,500 by mid-1972. Then in April North Vietnam challenged Saigon's ability and troop morale by suddenly attacking with Soviet heavy guns and tanks and smashing through South Vietnamese defenses in the north, in the central highlands, and toward Saigon. Their intention was to rebuild the Viet Cong in the South, damage the pacification program by re-taking villages and hamlets supposedly safe from Communist attack, and show up the weakness of the South Vietnamese troops.

The Nixon Administration felt obliged to give support to South Vietnam and also to safeguard the continued withdrawal of United States troops. Nixon took the calculated risk of offending the Soviet Union by renewing the bombing of North Vietnam on a saturation scale, and by mining the harbor of Haiphong to prevent supplies, many of them from the Soviet Union, from coming in by water. Technically, the mining was a "quarantine" permitted by international law.

By September the initial successes of the North Vietnamese appeared to be halted, although they controlled substantial areas of territory from the north down to the Mekong delta, and could commence another offensive later.

Henry Kissinger, the presidential assistant, made several trips to Paris and to Vietnam in the hopes of negotiating an end to the war. Hanoi publicly insisted that any post-war government must include representatives of the National Liberation Front, but in early October 1972 the official North Vietnamese newspaper *Nhan Dan* indicated that Hanoi might be willing to agree to terms that would give neither side political predominance in South Vietnam, at least for a transitional period.

Hanoi's attitude came close to President Nixon's proposal of a cease-fire followed in four months by a total withdrawal of United States troops, if American prisoners of war were also released.

While attempts to negotiate continued, Americans were actively engaged in the air war waged from United States airbases in Thailand and Guam and as crews of naval vessels shelling North Vietnamese positions.

Unfortunately American casualties continued, although on a much reduced scale. Since January 1961 the United States had suffered over 45,880 killed, more than 14,000 in the four years since 1967, and over 300,000 wounded and missing. During most of 1972 the rate of casualties in combat was 5 or fewer per week, occasionally more.

"Vietnam has been at blazing war for 27 years. There is hardly a person anywhere in Indo-China who has not been touched directly, in one way or another, by the fighting. . . . Farms, homes, towns, cities have been destroyed. . . . Wives have lost husbands, brothers have lost brothers, lovers have lost lovers.

"Yet it does not end, and does not show signs of ending. A map of Indo-China in 1954 with shaded map area marking Communist control, is so remarkably similar to a map of Indo-China today that one is overwhelmed by the futility of it, the unspeakable inhumanity of it on both sides. . . . North Vietnam will not give up, Nixon will not give up, Thieu will not give up, the Russians will not give up. . . .

"Such tragedy is part of all wars, of course. But this conflict has lasted so long and Viet Nam is after all such a tiny place, such an insignificant place in any grand scale of things. . . .

"The Vietnamese are Asians, and they accept their fate. . . . They want the war to end – now. They think it would if the powers, great and small, who keep pushing them into it, would at long, long last just let them be."*

Cease-fire

Preliminary cease-fire negotiations of October 1972 broke down within a few days, partly because of controversial details and partly because President Nguyen Van Thieu of South Vietnam objected to the continued presence of 145,000 North Vietnamese troops in his country. In early January 1973, negotiations were renewed and resulted in a signed cease-fire agreement on January 27, 1973.

The agreement consisted of nine main points, similar to the October proposals, in which both sides made a major concession. North Vietnam agreed to a cease-fire prior to a political settlement, and the United States accepted the

---

*From a personal assessment of the war by Stanley Cloud, Bureau Chief in Saigon. Reprinted by permission from TIME, The Weekly News magazine, May 1, 1972. Copyright Time Inc.

presence of the 145,000 North Vietnamese troops.

The basic points briefly stated are:

1. The independence of all Vietnam is recognized, as in the 1954 Geneva agreements.
2. Disputes over control of territory to be resolved by a joint Saigon-Viet Cong military commission; U.S. troops to be withdrawn within 60 days, U.S. military bases dismantled; no re-entry into South Vietnam of military forces and increases in materials.
3. All military prisoners to be released within 60 days.
4. The South Vietnamese people to determine their own political future. Internationally supervised elections to set up a National Council for National Reconciliation and Concord, consisting of representatives of the Saigon government, the Viet Cong, and South Vietnamese "neutralists."
5. The Demilitarized Zone, the DMZ, is the provisional military demarcation line between North and South Vietnam, which are expected to become united through peaceful negotiations.
6. Several groups, including the International Control Commission of Canada, Poland, Hungary, and Indonesia, are created to supervise the cease-fire.
7. Laos and Cambodia have the right of neutrality and self-determination, and no foreign country may maintain military bases there.
8. The United States agrees to aid in the reconstruction of Indo-China.
9. All parties agree to implement the cease-fire agreement.

The terms of the cease-fire raise doubts about the probability of sustained peace in Indo-China. Although President Nixon stated, "The people of South Vietnam have been guaranteed the right to determine their own future without outside interference," there are serious doubts about North Vietnam's intentions to continue to recognize South Vietnam. The 145,000 North Vietnamese troops control nearly half the south and form "leopard-spot" bases from which guerrilla warfare could be conducted. Hanoi recognized the existence of South Vietnam as a separate entity, but it also demanded and won the organization of a *National* Council for *National* Reconciliation in South Vietnam, to consist of equal representation from the Viet Cong, the Saigon government, and South Vietnamese neutralists. Because all decisions of the National Council must be unanimous, any one of the three groups can use its veto and delay decisions.

President Thieu has certain advantages in his favor: more than one million well-equipped troops; the fourth largest air force in the world; and a vast amount of military hardware rushed into his country by the United States in November and December 1972 during the break-down in negotiations. The summit meetings between the United States and Peking and Moscow may work to Thieu's advantage by reducing military supplies to Hanoi. Thieu has the capability to fight, but a serious question is whether the determination and support of the South Vietnamese people are strong enough to succeed against future aggression by Hanoi. Furthermore, Thieu's recent repressive measures to maintain himself in power may encourage support for the Viet Cong.

Le Duc Tho, who was the chief negotiator for Hanoi, interpreted the agreement as another step toward "the re-unification of the country" and in general as "the necessary advance of history" that "no force could prevent."

Hanoi can use the Ho Chi Minh Trail as a supply route to its guerrilla groups because Communists occupy half of Laos and appear to be ready to extend their control. If fighting should break out again in South Vietnam the United States has the power to intervene, with its air force in Thailand and the Seventh Fleet off the Vietnam coast. But future intervention in Indo-China by the United States is questionable, partly because of American public opinion, and partly because Indo-China is no longer regarded, as it was a decade ago, as one phase of a Communist thrust for world domination.

5. Laos, Cambodia, Thailand, Burma

Laos

A small country of 95,000 square miles, Laos formed part of Indo-China until it was granted independence at the Geneva Conference of 1954. Situated on the borders of North Vietnam and South Vietnam, it has been involved in the Vietnam War because the country had for years been divided between the "neutralist" part under Prince Souvanna Phouma and the pro-Communist section under Prince Souvanouphong, half-brother of Souvanna Phouma, and head of the Communist Pathet Lao, or Laos Fatherland, forces trained and armed in North Vietnam. In 1962 fourteen nations agreed to guarantee its independence and neutrality, but this has proved to be a paper agreement that is virtually impossible to enforce.

The Ho Chi Minh Trail through the part of Laos controlled by the Pathet Lao forces was a major supply route for personnel and war materials for the North Vietnam forces fighting in South Vietnam.

Laos is so strategically placed, with frontiers on China, Thailand, Burma, and the two Vietnams, that if it should be taken over completely by the Communists, then pressure could be exerted upon Thailand and Cambodia. Its future is decidedly uncertain, particularly since its recent active involvement in the Vietnam War.

Laos. Meo tribesmen report for duty as guerrilla fighters against the Communists.

Cambodia

During the 9th to 12th centuries Cambodia was the center of the highly civilized Khmer Empire that probably stretched from Burma to the South China Sea. The ruins of the great Khmer Empire, that dated back to at least 900 A.D., were discovered deep in the jungles at Angkor Thom, the capital city, and Angkor Wat, the temple; the city covers about five and a half square miles, and with the temple it rivals the grandeur of the great pyramids of Egypt. Cambodia became a French protectorate in 1863 and remained under French control until the Japanese invaded and undermined the French.

In March 1945, Prince Sihanouk, with Japanese approval, proclaimed Cambodia's independence. The French returned in 1945, and allowed the kingdom to continue with a parliamentary form of government but still under French control until 1953, when the French were forced by the situation in Vietnam to grant Cambodia its independence.

Sihanouk decided that he did not want his nation to continue the parliamentary system of government, with its rival parties; instead he organized the one party, the People's Socialist Community, with himself as its leader. He turned over the throne to his father so that he himself could have more political freedom, and became Prime Minister, still calling himself Prince Sihanouk. When his father died, Sihanouk arranged for new elections controlled by his party, which then named him Chief of State as well as Prime Minister. Technically, Cambodia was in 1968 a kingless monarchy.

Sihanouk has generally shown himself more friendly to the People's Republic of China than to the United States, probably because he feels Communist pressure from China, and because Cambodia and South Vietnam are traditionally antagonistic to each other, and because their common boundary is disputed by both countries. Cambodia has received aid from the United States, Japan, France, and Yugoslavia; it is skillful in the practice of playing one nation off against another.

Thailand

Thailand is one of the few nations on the continent of Asia that escaped becoming a colony of a European power. It has retained its independence and has enjoyed a century of peace and little internal dissension. It is one of the major rice-bowls of Asia, is able to export much of its crop, and has valuable national resources of tin, teak, and rubber. Unlike most of its neighbors it has a comparatively high standard of living, and thus it has been little troubled by the "revolution of rising expectations."

It was allowed to remain independent because it formed a buffer state between French and British colonies, and neither side wanted the other to get it. Recent disturbances inside the country are the result of dissatisfaction with a government which is in the hands of the aristocracy and the army, and is in effect a dictatorship, although it is officially a constitutional monarchy with a written constitution. One reason why Thailand and its neighbor Cambodia are on rather unfriendly terms is that Thailand is a staunch member and supporter of the Southeast Asia Treaty Organization, SEATO; it is in fact a practical ally of the United States, which has air bases within its borders. One of its problems is a minority of 2,000,000 Chinese, who are suspected of being sympathetic with the People's Republic of China.

The Union of Burma

One of the largest nations of Southeast Asia, Burma has a population of about 24,000,000 people, in a land the size of Texas. Another rice-bowl of Asia, it exports large quantities of that crop. Until 1937 Burma was administered by the British as a part of India. In that year Burma was granted limited self-government although it wanted dominion status as a self-governing and independent nation within the British Commonwealth. Japanese occupation during World War II only intensified Burma's desire for complete independence, which it finally received in 1948, a year after Great Britain granted independence to India. Unlike India and Pakistan, it did not choose to remain within the Commonwealth.

At first governed according to democratic principles, it was soon convulsed by political assassinations; it was then taken over in 1962 by the army, which nationalized domestic and foreign businesses, and made the country both socialistic and authoritarian.

Its foreign policy has been that of neutralism or non-alignment, because it is acutely aware of its exposed position in relation to China, the importance of its rice crop, and its strategic location in Southeast Asia. Burmese leaders have been careful not to provoke their neighbors, and have been able to make extremely useful barter deals with China and the Soviet Union, exchanging rice for consumer goods and much-needed equipment. Although Burma consistently voted in the United Nations Assembly for the admission of Communist China to the United Nations, this support was not necessarily through sympathy for China but for reasons of diplomacy.

6. The Federation of Malaysia

Malaya and Malaysia

Malaya and Malaysia are not two different words for the same area. Malaya is a peninsula of the Asian mainland, and Malaysia is a nation formed in 1963 from Malaya, Singapore, Sarawak, and Sabah.

The Malay Peninsula is a long tongue of land stretching southward from the Asian mainland down toward the Republic of Indonesia. Its strategic position athwart the trade routes of Asia made it the object of several colonial nations, and was the reason for invasions by Indians, Chinese, Portuguese, Indonesians, British, and Dutch. The Malay people, mainly Mongoloid in origin, make up 50 percent of the population, with 35 percent Chinese, about 10 percent Indians and Pakistanis, and the remainder a mixture of races. Rubber trees were introduced from Brazil in the 19th century and made Malaya the greatest rubber-producing region in the world. Today's production from Malaya is one-third of the world's supply. Another valuable resource is tin, of which Malaya produces more than any other nation.

The island of Singapore became the capital of the peninsula, which the British took over in the early 19th century and called the Straits Settlements colony. Singapore today has a Chinese population of at least 75 percent, who are not sympathetic with the predominantly non-Chinese population of Malaya.

The colony of Sarawak on the island of Borneo was once the possession of the Brooke family of "white rajahs," who ceded it as a Crown Colony to the British government in 1946. Almost 50,000 square miles in area, Sarawak is larger than Malaya but has a population of only 800,000 compared with Malaya's nearly 10,000,000 people.

Sabah, which was occupied by Great Britain in the early 19th century, and was known as British North Borneo, is a little more than half the size and population of Sarawak. Both these island areas have Chinese populations of about 25 percent, who are an increasing potential problem as China gains influence in Southeast Asia. Furthermore, the Chinese control a great deal of the business and trade throughout Malaysia, and they are therefore resented by the inhabitants.

The Federation of Malaya

The Japanese swept down through Malaya in early 1942 and easily captured the strategic and renowned British naval base of Singapore because its defenses were designed to repel only

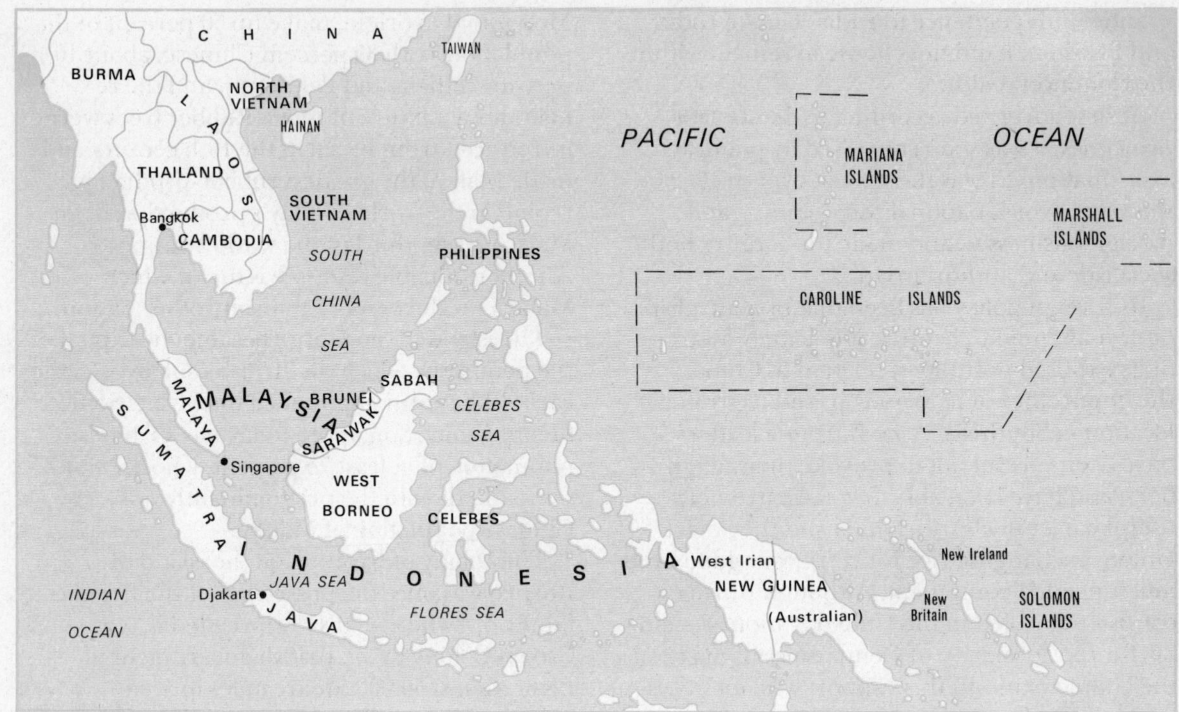

Southeast Asia

sea-borne invaders. This relatively easy success of the Japanese seriously undermined British prestige, and stimulated demands for independence when the war ended.

The British grant of independence to India and Burma was followed in 1948 by the creation of the Federation of Malaya of nine sultan-ruled states as a part of the British empire under a British High Commissioner. Complete independence for the Federation of Malaya was postponed because of a bitter civil war waged by Communist guerrillas. Most of the guerrillas were Chinese and readily distinguishable from the Malays, but it still took 500,000 British and Malay troops more than ten years to subdue the Communists.

In 1957 the British granted independence to the Federation of Malaya, which became a member of the British Commonwealth. Singapore, with its predominantly Chinese population, was not included in the Federation of Malaya, but remained a Crown Colony under the British.

Singapore was granted partial self-government in 1954, and three years later was given home rule or complete self-government in internal affairs, with Great Britain still controlling defense and foreign relations.

The Federation of Malaysia

The increasing threat of Communism in Laos and Vietnam, and the internal problem of their Chinese population, convinced the local rulers within the Federation of Malaya, together with Sarawak and Sabah, that a political union of all of them might better guarantee their safety. Singapore wished to join, but the sultan of the British protectorate of Brunei, between Sarawak and Sabah, chose not to join.

In 1963 the Federation of Malaysia came into existence when the fourteen states of Malaya, Singapore, Sarawak, and Sabah joined together under a federal government with a king elected from among their own number every five years by the Conference of Rulers of the fourteen states. The Federation of Malaysia operates politically very similarly to Great Britain, with a parliamentary system of two houses, and a prime minister chosen by the popularly-elected lower house, and responsible or answerable for all policy to it. The king performs the same functions as the sovereign in Great Britain.

Even before the Federation of Malaysia actually came into existence, Sukarno of Indonesia bitterly denounced it, claimed Sabah as Indonesian territory, and threatened to crush the new nation if it were created. This situation and an internal problem within the federation resulted in the "expulsion" of Singapore from the Federation.

The Republic of Singapore

In 1965 the Prime Minister of the Federation of Malaysia summoned Lee Yew, the Prime Minister of Singapore, to his office and stated that Singapore must secede from the Federation. The basic problem was that the 4,200,000 Chinese of the Federation were demanding equal rights with the 4,600,000 Malays. Because more than 1,250,000 Chinese live in Singapore, Prime Minister Lee Yew had been campaigning on their behalf.

Within two days Singapore seceded from the Federation and became an independent island-state of Singapore, officially the Republic of Singapore, a member of the British Commonwealth. One of its problems will certainly be its ability to survive economically, because it has been essentially a port town, the fifth largest in the world, handling 40,000 ships yearly. However, this is an uncertain base for economic stability, and Singapore will need to develop other resources. Strategically, Singapore has maintained close ties with Malaysia because their fate could be a common one.

7. Problems Facing Southeast Asia

Independence has brought its legacy of problems to the nations of Southeast Asia. These nations are collectively referred to as "developing" nations, but in most cases they are underdeveloped and are only slowly developing. One serious problem is that of extreme nationalism which can still create intense friction among nations who should be uniting in a common front against the threat of internal Communism and of expanding China.

The earlier antagonism of Indonesia and the example of Philippine opposition to the Federation of Malaysia are examples of nationalism which could seriously affect the future history of all Southeast Asia.

Other common problems are overpopulation which may result in the doubling of the present population of 245,000,000 to nearly 500,000,000 by the year 2000; a low level of education throughout the area; poverty which can only be relieved by the investment of a great deal of foreign capital in countries whose political stability is problematical and therefore a threat to foreign investment; very limited experience in self-government; and the continuing struggle for and against Communism.

Several of these new nations, especially

Southeast Asia. A mixture of the ancient and the modern.

Burma, Cambodia, and North Vietnam, and probably Indonesia, have accepted the Marxist belief in authoritarian rule. Leaders can argue, with some justification, that the people are not yet sufficiently politically mature or experienced to understand the democratic procedures, and that government control is necessary to organize backward societies for rapid economic and social progress. The Marxist doctrine has justified the seizure of economic power by leaders, who can claim, unlike Marx, that this kind of action supports nationalism as well as the interests of the people.

One reason for popular support of government socialism is opposition to Chinese settlers who had taken over so much of local business. Today all Southeast Asia nations bar Chinese immigrants, and some nations are gradually expelling their Chinese inhabitants.

One great economic difficulty, in some instances the major difficulty, is the dependence of these nations upon a competitive world market in which they must sell their raw materials, such as sugar, rice, copra, tobacco, tea, and rubber. While the prices of such raw materials tend to remain stationary at best, or sometimes move downward, the prices of finished products continue to rise. The nations of Southeast Asia, as well as developing nations in other parts of the world, must sell increasing quantities of raw materials in order to buy the same volume of finished products that they had previously bought from other more industrialized nations. Economically, they have to run faster in order to stay in the same place.

The future of Southeast Asia may depend to a great extent upon the outcome of the struggle going on in Vietnam and Laos. An end of the Vietnam War which prevents the Communists from taking over South Vietnam may mean a holding action against the domination of Communist China. Should the Viet Cong win, the great probability could be a Communist takeover in Laos as well as Vietnam, and increasing pressure upon neighboring Cambodia and Thailand.

Politically, these nations must finally work out their own problems. Because of their intense nationalism they suspect foreign influence of any sort as a new form of "imperialism." Often "white man's" so-called imperialism seems more dangerous than that of the Chinese Communists or of their own local Communists.

At present, the Southeast Asia nations seem to be unable or unwilling to work together even for their own economic well-being; eventually, however, their future, and perhaps their very survival, will depend upon the ability to cooperate and work for common ends.

Review Questions

Sections 1 and 2

1. Why are the Philippine people still dissatisfied, despite their years of independence since 1946?
2. How does the foreign policy of the Philippine Republic partly explain the unwillingness or inability of Southeast Asia nations to work together for common interests?
3. Why is the Republic of Indonesia, with its vast natural resources, in economic difficulties? Would not the investment of foreign capital help to solve the problem?

Sections 3 and 4

4. Why did the United States help Ho Chi Minh in 1945?
5. Did the United States commit itself under the Geneva Agreement to accept any responsibility in Vietnam? Did the Geneva Agreement oblige all the Vietnamese people to accept its terms?
6. Why did Ngo Dinh Diem, the South Vietnamese leader, refuse to permit the elections provided for in the Geneva Agreement of 1954?
7. Did any United States president, from 1965 to 1970, exceed his constitutional authority by sending troops to Vietnam?
8. Why did the Administration send United States troops into Cambodia in 1970 and become involved in Laos in 1971? Why did some critics oppose these actions?

Section 5

9. How is Laos an example of a country that wishes to remain neutral, but cannot do so?
10. How are Cambodia and Thailand examples of Southeast Asia nations which seem unable to co-operate against pressure from Red China?

Sections 6 and 7

11. What are the differences between the Federation of Malaya and the Federation of Malaysia? Why was Singapore subsequently requested to leave the Federation of Malaysia?
12. What are some of the basic problems facing Southeast Asia?
13. Why are some of the leaders of Southeast Asia apparently able to convince their people that socialism and autocratic rule are acceptable?

Glossary

Afrikaner. Member of the white race in the Republic of South Africa, descendant of the original Dutch settlers dating back to the 17th century. Language of Afrikaners is Afrikaans, and is not to be confused with Africans, which refers to natives of Africa.

Alliance for Progress (*Alianza para el Progreso*). A United States sponsored and assisted movement, supported originally by 20 Latin American nations, to co-ordinate and develop Latin American economies and to raise the standard of living. Sponsored by President Kennedy in the early 1960's.

Amnesty. A pardon for political prisoners. May sometimes be used for pardons for other reasons.

Apartheid. Literally "apart-ness." The policy of the whites in the Republic of South Africa of literal segregation of blacks from whites. Complete racial inequality.

Arab League. A loose confederation or association of Arab countries, particularly in the Middle East, who reflect Arab sentiments and are generally strongly anti-Israel. Not a very effective organization because there are many Arab rivalries.

Baghdad Pact, or CENTO. Central Treaty Organization of 1955, between Iraq, Turkey, Great Britain, Pakistan, and Iran for common purposes of security and defense. Originally called the Baghdad Pact, it was renamed the Central Treaty Organization in 1959 after the withdrawal of Iraq.

Balfour Declaration. A letter of November 1917, from British Foreign Secretary Balfour to Lord Rothschild, Chairman of the Zionist Federation, stating that the British Government favored "a national home for the Jewish people in Palestine." The beginning of action which led to the establishment of the nation of Israel in 1948.

Bangladesh. The new nation of Bengali people created when East Pakistan declared its independence from Pakistan in 1971.

Bantu. (1) A term applied to a member of any of several tribes of blacks in central and southern Africa, (2) languages spoken by several tribes.

Bantustan. A "reserve" established by the government of the Republic of South Africa as a "tribal homeland" for an African tribe. Regarded by Africans as a ghetto, outside which they may not travel without a pass. The Transkei is the pilot Bantustan, with seven more planned.

Bretton Woods Conference. A meeting of international financiers and bankers in 1944 in Bretton Woods, New Hampshire, to set up the International Monetary Fund and to stabilize national currencies by fixing exchange rates.

British Commonwealth. A free association of independent, sovereign nations which were formerly colonies in the British Empire, the title of which was changed to British Commonwealth and Empire. The Commonwealth is a purely voluntary association of members who choose to work together for common purposes. The Commonwealth has no common head, no common government, and no member has authority over any other. The non-sovereign colonies are included in the word "Empire." Members of the Commonwealth are: The United Kingdom, Canada, Australia, New Zealand, India, Pakistan, Ceylon, Ghana, Nigeria, Cyprus, Sierra Leone, Jamaica, Trinidad and Tobago, Uganda, Kenya, Malaysia, Tanzania, Malawi, Malta, Zambia, the Gambia, Singapore, Guyana, Botswana, Lesotho, Barbados, and Mauritius.

CENTO. *See* Baghdad Pact.

Collectivism. A general term that refers to all economic and political systems based on central planning and co-operation.

Colombo Plan. In 1950 the members of the British Commonwealth devised a plan for the co-operative development of South and Southeast Asia countries, totaling one fourth of the world's population. The British Commonwealth nations of the United Kingdom, Australia, Canada, and New Zealand co-operated to plan assistance in public administration, agriculture, industry, training of personnel, health services, scientific research. The Asian nations were Burma, Bhutan, Borneo, Cambodia, Ceylon, India, Indonesia, Japan, Laos, Malaya, Nepal, Pakistan, the Philippine Republic, South Korea, Thailand, Vietnam.

Communism. Basically this is communal or Society ownership of the means of production and distribution, as distinct from private ownership in a capitalist society. **Economically** Communism and Socialism do not differ. **Politically** Communism differs in that it does not allow the existence of opposition parties.

Condominium. Joint rule of two or more nations over a territory. An example is the early 20th-century rule by Great Britain and Egypt of the Sudan.

CONEFO, Conference of Newly Emerging Forces.

Coup d'État. A sudden change of government usually brought about by a group within the government, sometimes by a group outside the government, resulting in a change of government. Not the same as a revolution, in which a great part of the nation may be involved.

De Facto Recognition. A nation which receives *de facto* recognition from others is accepted by them as being an effective country with a government capable of carrying out its international responsibilities, even though it may have come into power by revolution. *De facto* recognition is tentative or provisional, and simply accepts the situation that a nation and government do *in fact* exist.

De Jure Recognition. This is full acceptance that a government exists *legally*, according to law. Usually such a government comes into existence through constitutional, not revolutionary, methods. Such recognition is usually accompanied by an exchange of diplomatic representatives.

Diaspora. (1) The historic dispersal of the Jews from Palestine, (2) the total of Jewish communities outside of Palestine.

Étatism. Participation by the national government in the economy of a country.

FLN. *See* National Liberation Front.

FRELIMO. *See* Front for the Liberation of Mozambique.

French Community. General de Gaulle in 1958 offered the African colonies of France the right to choose to become independent or to remain a community of independent nations associated with France in the French Community. The colony of Guinea voted to become completely independent; the others became members of the French Community, but by 1961 they had all chosen to break away from France and become independent, sovereign nations.

Front for the Liberation of Mozambique—FRELIMO. The anti-white group organized by Eduardo Mondlane to free Mozambique from Portuguese colonial rule.

GATT. General Agreement on Tariffs and Trade. In 1948 several nations agreed to negotiate on tariff reduction. The greater part of the world's trade is controlled by nations supporting GATT.

Geneva Agreement. The agreement signed in 1954 by a representative of the commander-in-chief of the French Forces in Indo-China and the representative of the commander-in-chief of the People's Army of (North) Vietnam, usually referred to as the Vietminh. Its provisions included (1) the division of North and South Vietnam by a demarcation line near the 17th parallel, with a demilitarized zone 5 kilometers each side of the line, (2) the right of citizens to transfer from one area to the other, (3) an election to be held in 1956 throughout both areas to determine reunification, (4) an International Commission of Canada, India, Poland to supervise the execution of the Agreement.

Good Neighbor Policy. The disavowal of the Roosevelt Corollary by President Franklin Roosevelt in the 1930's, based upon a treaty signed in Montevideo to the effect that "no state has the right to intervene in the internal or external affairs of another."

Great Trek. The mass migration of thousands of Boer farmers in the 1830's, who were escaping from British rule in South Africa to form new independent settlements.

GPRA. *See* Provisional Government of the Algerian Republic.

Kuomintang. The Chinese National Party, formed by Sun Yat-sen in 1891, dedicated to free China from foreign domination, to social reform, and to political democracy. Later, Kuomintang came under the leadership of Chiang Kai-shek.

Manchukuo. Formerly named Manchuria. In 1931 Japan invaded it, seized it from China, and renamed it Manchukuo under a puppet-emperor Henry Pu Yi, who had been deposed as a child in 1912, as the last Manchu emperor of China.

Marxism-Leninism. Marxism was the theoretical belief in the class struggle. Leninism was the actual organization of extremists to precipitate the class struggle that became the Bolshevik Revolution of 1917.

Monroe Doctrine. A doctrine proclaimed by President Monroe in 1823 stating (1) that the United States has no intention of intervening in European affairs, (2) that the United States would regard as "unfriendly" any attempt by European nations to intervene in the affairs of independent nations in the Western hemisphere, (3) that there should be no further colonization in the American continents and no extension of existing colonies. In brief, a "hands off the Western hemisphere" warning to European nations.

MPLA. *See* Popular Movement for the Liberation of Angola.

Nationalization. The process by which the state, that is the public, takes over some or all of the private means of production and distribution. In practice the government nationalizes by giving government bonds in exchange for shares of stock in a private company, thus securing public ownership of private businesses.

National Liberation Front. The FLN (*Front de Libération Nationale*) was the Algerian nationalist group which demanded and fought for independence from France in the 1950's and 1960's.

NEFOS. *See* Newly Emerging Forces.

Neutralism. The policy of not siding with any nation or

group of nations in peacetime. A form of isolationism. (cf. Neutrality.)

Neutrality. Non-participation in wartime with any of the belligerents. Taking no sides in wartime.

Newly Emerging Forces – NEFOS. In 1965 Sukarno of Indonesia, annoyed at the election of Malaysia as a temporary member of the United Nations Security Council, pulled Indonesia out of the United Nations and threatened to form a second United Nations consisting of new nations and the older nations with Communist governments.

OAS. *See* Organization of American States.

OAU. *See* Organization for African Unity.

Open Door Policy. The policy adopted in 1899 by the United States advocating and supporting equal economic opportunity for all nations in China. Later, the policy included United States support for the independence and political integrity of China.

Organization for African Unity – OAU. Organized in Addis Ababa in 1963 by thirty-two African nations, with a basic objective of freeing dependent African people. Its targets are particularly the racist Republic of South Africa, Rhodesia, and the Portuguese African colonies of Angola and Mozambique.

Organization of American States – OAS. In 1948 at the Ninth International Conference of American States in Colombia, the members set up OAS to co-ordinate the work of its members, to attempt to resolve disputes among members, and to protect its members against aggression. (Not to be confused with the OAS – the secret army organization of Algeria.)

Palestine Liberation Organization. This is the PLO, the large Arab group consisting of smaller groups, such as the PFLP, dedicated to the re-occupation by Arabs of Palestine, now part of the State of Israel. Under its leader, Yassir Arafat, it is less extremist than some of its constituent groups such as the PFLP.

Passive Resistance. Non-violent non-co-operation used by Mahatma Gandhi to force the British to give up their colonial control of India.

PFLP. *See* Popular Front for the Liberation of Palestine.

PLO. *See* Palestine Liberation Organization.

Popular Front for the Liberation of Palestine. Known as the PFLP, this organization is an extremist group of the Palestine Liberation Organization. It is dedicated to the elimination of the State of Israel. It was responsible for the skyjacking of four planes in 1970.

Popular Movement for the Liberation of Angola – MPLA. An anti-white organization dedicated to independence for Portuguese Angola.

Propaganda. Originally, it meant the spreading of information, from the word "propagate." But from the days of World War I it has acquired the special meaning of attempting to persuade people to believe whatever the propagandist wants them to believe. As used in this sense, propaganda means the withholding of vital information deliberately. If this vital information was given to the people, they might come to a quite different decision.

Provisional Government of the Algerian Republic. The GPRA or *Government Provisoire de la République Algérienne* was proclaimed by the Algerian rebels in defiance of the French. It acted as an independent government sending representatives to international gatherings and to friendly nations.

Roosevelt Corollary. The extension of the Monroe Doctrine by President Theodore Roosevelt in 1904, occasioned by the foreign debt situation of the Dominican Republic and the presence of foreign nations to enforce payment. "Chronic wrong-doing" by any nation in the Western hemisphere might oblige the United States to intervene in that nation's affairs in order to prevent intervention by European powers.

SCAP. Supreme Commander of the Allied Powers in Japan, after Japan's surrender in 1945.

Separatism. The desire or movement of a group of people to become independent. There has for years been a separatist group in Quebec province in Canada demanding separation from the Canadian government. Nigeria experienced such a movement when Biafra proclaimed itself independent.

UAR. *See* United Arab Republic.

United Arab Republic. In February 1958 the Republic was officially created by the union of Egypt and Syria. In September 1961 a *coup d'état* in Syria dissolved the union, but Egypt retained for itself the name of the United Arab Republic.

Viet Cong. Members and supporters of the National Liberation Front in Vietnam were known as Viet Cong, or VC, an abbreviation of Viet Nam Cong Sam, Vietnamese Communists.

Vietminh. The revolutionary Vietnamese army, the Vietnam Doc Lap Dong Minh Hoi, organized by Ho Chi Minh and committed to the creation of an independent Vietnam.

Vietnamization. The United States policy of turning over the defense of South Vietnam to the South Vietnamese government and troops. An essential part of the planned withdrawal of United States combat troops from Vietnam.

West Irian. Formerly the Netherlands New Guinea, the western end of the island. In 1963 it was officially recognized as a province of Indonesia.

Zionism. The belief of those who favor a separate home for the Jewish people. The movement was started by Theodor Herzl in the late 19th century, and supported later by the British who favored a Jewish homeland, as indicated in the Balfour Declaration of 1917.

General Index

Map Index

Picture Credits

Photographs were supplied by courtesy of the following: Australian News and Information Bureau: 208; Brown Brothers: 6, 8, 96, 154; Camera Press: 58; Eastfoto: 120, 160; Historical Pictures Service: 110, 113, 139, 140, 142, 143, 150, 151, 152, 157, 177, 178, 180, 184; Keystone: 37, 169; Mijon: 50, 54; Leo Thibault: 67 (bottom right); United Nations: 32, 119; United Press International: 17, 19, 20, 21, 22, 36, 41, 57, 60, 64, 84, 86, 89, 93, 117, 124, 125, 128, 159, 188, 191, 204, 206, 207, 210, 211, 215, 220; Varig Brazilian Airlines: 67 (top right); Wide World Photos: 25, 59, 66, 69, 90, 94, 158, 162, 186, 201, 203.